TOUGH GUY

TOUGH GUY

MY LIFE ON THE EDGE

BOB PROBERT

with KIRSTIE McLELLAN DAY

HarperCollins Publishers Ltd

HarperCollins books may be purchased for educational,
business, or sales promotional use through
our Special Markets Department.

HarperCollins Publishers Ltd
2 Bloor Street East, 20th Floor
Toronto, Ontario, Canada
M4W 1A8

www.harpercollins.ca

Library and Archives Canada Cataloguing in Publication
information is available upon request

ISBN 978-1-44340-461-7

Printed and bound in the United States

RRD 9 8 7 6 5

To Dani, the love of my life, and to my beautiful kids,
Brogan, Tierney, Jack and Declyn

CONTENTS

ACKNOWLEDGEMENTS

The Authors, Dani and her children wish to express their enormous gratitude to Dave Whinham for generously allowing them to access and make use of notes, other materials and interviews he conducted from 1993 to 1995 with a number of Bob Probert's friends and colleagues in contemplation of a book project. Although Bob and Dave decided to terminate the project, their work and these materials were valuable to this book.

Dani and Kirstie would also like to thank the following people for helping Bob fulfill his dream in making this book a reality: Leslie and Dan Parkinson; Norm Probert; Theresa Probert; Jim Wood; Penny Tayles; Sheldon Kennedy; Rick (Big Daddy) and Ricki Rogow; Darren Rogow; Ryan (Bushy) VandenBussche; Art Woofenden, Stacey Tayles; Stevie Yzerman; Paul Coffey; Chris Chelios; Troy Crowder; Colin Campbell; Maureen and Brad McCrimmon; Doug Gilmour; Marty McSorley; Don Cherry; Ron MacLean; General Rick Hillier;

Mark (Trees) LaForest; Eddie Mio; Tom Mullen; the gang at pyramidproductions.tv—Julie Sinclair, Carole Coutreau, Sonja Bloomfield, Shely Henry, Arana Lyle, Geordie Day and Vittoria Walter; Julie Folk at adrenalinereginasports.com; and Justine, Michelle and Carolyn at Salon Utopia in Lakeshore.

Kirstie McLellan Day would like to especially thank Dani, Brogan, Tierney, Jack and Declyn for their warm embrace and her husband and partner Larry Day for editing night and day. Special thanks to the gang at HarperCollins for accomplishing the impossible—Jim Gifford for giving up his weekends again, Iris Tupholme for believing, Lloyd Davis for his copyediting, as well as Noelle Zitzer, Neil Erickson, Allegra Robinson, Charidy Johnston, Cory Beatty, Rob Firing, Colleen Clarke, Jordan Whitehouse, Michael Guy-Haddock and cover designer Greg Tabor. Thanks to my parents, Joan and Bud McLellan, and kids and grandkids, Buddy, Kristin, Charlie, Lundy, Geordie, Paul, Téa, Jaxon and Griffin, for their unflagging love and support. A shout out to Theo Fleury for introducing me to Bob. Appreciation to Mitch Rogatz and Tom Bast at Triumph Books.

And most of all to you, Big Bob, thank you for sharing your story.

FOREWORD BY DANI PROBERT

It took Bob a long time to decide whether he wanted to write a book and tell the raw truth. But as our kids got older, they started hearing stuff about him that wasn't true. This really bugged Bob. He knew he was no angel, but he wanted the real story on record. He was hard at work on this book with his co-writer, Kirstie McLellan Day, when he died on July 5, 2010. I saw how much had been done, and the kids and I decided to see his dream fulfilled.

The following is Bob's story, the way he wanted it told.

I am so proud of you, Baby.

FOREWORD BY STEVE YZERMAN

I was born roughly four weeks before Bob, back in 1965. We played junior hockey against each other. He was in Brantford and I was in Peterborough. We were both drafted by the Red Wings in the summer of 1983, and became teammates with the Wings in the 1985–86 season. Probie began to make his mark in the National Hockey League in '86–87, the first season we were coached by Jacques Demers. It was quite a thrill to be part of the rebirth of the Red Wing organization, and Bob was a major part of that.

Over the next eight years, we enjoyed many great experiences together, both on and off the ice. Highlights included twice meeting the Edmonton Oilers, led by the great Wayne Gretzky, in the semifinals of the Stanley Cup playoffs. Probie played a huge role in those playoff runs. On the ice together, it felt good knowing Bob had my back.

Fans may remember him for his fighting ability and goal scoring, but he was much more than that. Bob knew how to play the game. He was an intelligent player with great hockey sense. For a player with fists of stone, he had incredibly soft hands. His passing, playmaking and scoring touch made him a rare commodity. He was highly respected among his peers. I recall walking into the locker room at the All-Star Game in 1988. All the greats, like Wayne Gretzky and Mark Messier, were there, and the first thing they wanted to do was meet Probie. I remember them coming over and asking me, "Can you introduce me to the big fella?" He was revered by players, and it wasn't just because he was a tough guy, it was because he was a great player.

Probie was a very popular teammate and a fan favourite. He was loved by all. He was an intelligent, streetwise guy with a quick wit. He was always putting people at ease with a good-hearted joke or friendly barb. He would light up the locker room when he walked in and said, "Hey, ya big dummy!" On top of his fine play, he made the game fun. Sometimes he'd stop in the middle of a fight to adjust his helmet, or he'd give Gerard Gallant and me a wink just to let us know everything was okay.

He left an incredible mark on all of us. It didn't matter who—a young hockey fan, a sick kid, an employee at the Joe Louis Arena, a member of your family—Bob would always take the time to say hello and engage in friendly conversation. People meeting him for the first time always walked away thinking, "Wow, what a nice guy." He endeared himself to everyone, and especially to me.

Hidden behind Bob's self-deprecating humour was a man who truly cared. He was grateful and loyal to people who treated him with respect. He was a rugged hockey player and an unselfish teammate willing to do anything for his team. He had a kind heart and a gentle soul.

Prologue

THE LAST CHAPTER

Each day, Bob Probert intended to be on the water by 10 A.M., but he never seemed to get there until about two-thirty. It took him forever to get ready and out the door. On the morning of July 5, 2010, he grabbed some Mini-Wheats and finished his ten-year-old daughter Declyn's Froot Loops. His in-laws, Leslie Parkinson and her husband, Dan, were there for a visit. Dan is chief of police in Cornwall, Ontario, a city eight hours northeast, on the St. Lawrence River. Leslie sat down beside him and quoted a passage from the Bible, then said, "You know, Bob, the Lord has big plans for you. You've just got to let go of the weights that are on you and yoke up with Him. His burden is light." Bob slurped down the rest of the cereal, nodded and said, "Yeah, I know. I am, I am." Then he downed his third Coke of the day and made it to his car by eleven o'clock.

He had to gas up the boat and go see his doctor because he was out of pills. Some mornings, it was tough to get out of bed. Seventeen years as the NHL's toughest enforcer will do that to a body. He'd been prescribed three OxyContin a day, but he took eight—two in the morning, two after lunch, two at dinner and two at bedtime. He'd dip the pills in Coke to dissolve the time-release coating, then chop up what was left into a line. It'd hit him quicker that way, and for a couple of hours his back wouldn't hurt, his hip flexor wouldn't bother him and he could walk without the feeling of knives jabbing at his knees. He'd fill a month's prescription, then hand them over to his wife, Dani, because if left up to him they'd disappear too quickly. Whenever she travelled, she hid them all over the house. He would call her each morning and she'd reveal where she'd hidden that day's stash. On Monday, she might say they were in the cigar box in the office; Tuesday's pills might be in a Baggie taped behind the painting in the family room. It was a good system. Finally, Bob wanted to control his alcohol and drug use. Dani felt his desire to straighten out had been brought on because the kids were now teenagers and they knew what was going on, so he felt accountable. Years of therapy in rehab also helped.

Probie smoked two packs of Parliaments a day, usually in his six-car garage. There was no room to park in there because it was filled with his Harleys, partly restored classic cars and various vehicle parts. The Proberts lived in their dream home on Lake St. Clair, right across the water from Detroit. Bob and Dani designed the house when they were flush, when he was with Chicago in 1999. He was receiving the biggest paycheque of his career at the time—$1.8 million per year. The home has a stately design—eight thousand square feet of grey stone, with a slate roof and limestone steps—and a beautiful yard that includes a huge swimming pool and resting areas under oak, maple and pear trees.

Bob hated to owe money. When he bought something, he paid cash. That included the house, which was worth around $3.5 million. He was an art connoisseur. He loved paintings. He hung an original Viktor Shvaiko in his family room. There's a photo of it in *Architectural Digest*. Somehow, he managed to convince the famous Russian painter to insert the number 24 on the front of the brasserie that dominates the left side of the Paris scene. The address matched his sweater number. But Bob never enjoyed anything unless he shared, so he bought the first limited-edition copy of the same painting, framed it and gave it to Dan and Leslie for Christmas.

Bob was the king of getting people to do what he wanted. When he ran out of Coca-Cola, he'd call his mother, Theresa, who lived in nearby Windsor, and ask her to meet him at the Yacht Club with a new supply. She kept several flats in her fridge for him just in case. He'd hop on his Sea-Doo 200 Speedster with its twin 155-horsepower jet drives and take off across the lake. The boat looked like something Batman might drive. It was twenty feet long, with a sleek, narrow front, aluminum rails, an extra-high wakeboard bar, and huge wings on the sides. It was so complicated, only he knew how to operate it. Although he wasn't a member of the private yacht club, he'd tie up, hop out, open the gate and let his mother through. If anyone hassled him, he'd laugh and tell them to relax. No one intimidated Bob Probert.

July 5 was a sizzler. The temperature was expected to reach 35 degrees Celsius. Bob complained about indigestion again.

He and Dani had just celebrated their seventeenth wedding anniversary. Dani Wood Probert is an incredibly beautiful woman, with or without makeup. She has intelligent green eyes, high cheekbones and a sculpted chin with strong, straight white teeth and thick, shiny, sun-kissed hair that brushes her shoulders. Dani had been bugging him for a couple of weeks to get a checkup. "You've got to stick around for our four kids," she'd say.

"Yeah, I know, Baby, I know," he'd reply.

"I'm serious, Bob," she'd say.

"I'm serious about you too, Wood," he'd laugh and pull her down on his knee for a kiss.

Then he went out by the pool and told the family to get ready. He said he'd be back in fifteen minutes to load up and head out.

Bob was sweating hard by the time he trailered the boat over to Pud's Place Marina, a public launch not far from the house. He'd been thinking about building his own dock—it would be so much easier to have his own hoist. Before he floated the boat into the water, he discovered it wouldn't start. The battery was dead.

He sped home to get his seventy-foot yellow power cord and battery charger. On the way, he made a detour to his buddy Donny Cadarian's house. Donny was having trouble with his boat too. Bob turned around and pulled in for a visit. While he was there, he mentioned he was feeling nauseous.

A couple of Cokes later, he was back home, hoisting his thirty-eight-pound battery charger into the back of Dani's 2002 Denali. Dani's aunt Penny, who lived with the family, and father, Dan, talked with Bob. Both noticed he wasn't his usual bouncy, goofy self. Bob took his daughter Tierney and her friend Sarah with him. Tierney was his buddy. She liked to do the same things he liked, including playing hockey. Tierney was turning thirteen at the end of July and already stood five feet, ten inches.

Bob headed back to the marina and worked on getting the engine to turn over. "Come on, baby, come on, let's go. Do it for me, baby, start up, c'mon . . ." Finally, it caught.

Penny stood by the breakwall at the end of Bob's property and waited for Bob and the kids to return. It was fun to watch for them. Bob would head across the lake, full speed, go wide around the big rock that jutted out just off shore to the north, then cut in fast on an angle. This time, he pulled near and shouted, "Is everybody ready?" They weren't quite, and because he didn't want to turn the boat off, he said, "I'll be right back!" and scooted around the lake. Sometimes, he would move out of the driver's seat and hand the wheel to one of the kids. Bob believed in all four of his kids, and he never said no. They could ask him for anything. "Can I go to my friend's house?" "Yeah, sure, go." "Can you drive me?" "Yeah, sure." It finally reached the point where Dani made a rule: they were not allowed to ask him for anything, because they already knew the answer would be yes.

Soon, Bob brought the boat back in to pick up Jack, his ten-year-old son, as well as Dani, Penny, Dan and Leslie. He jumped out and walked it back in to the breakwall so the group could climb down and step onto the platform. They counted the life jackets, making sure everyone had one, and decided to go east toward the pier at Belle River. There was a Greek restaurant there, and Dani wanted a salad. They rarely went that way, but the farther, the better. They loved being on the boat. Dani sat behind Bob as they flew across the water. They'd been married seventeen years, but she still liked checking him out. He had strong, wonderful shoulders, with huge traps and deltoids. When he held her, she felt protected. She squinted at the freckles on his back and thought, "He should have sunscreen on." There were a couple of moles she wanted him to get looked at too.

They were ten minutes out when Tierney noticed a rattling noise on the bow. She was sitting up at the front left. Bob called to her to open the storage compartment and make sure the anchor was secured. She looked and said everything was fine, but the knocking continued. Bob turned off the boat. They were in the middle of nowhere, but he was confident the battery had had enough time to recharge. He climbed up front and moved a few things around, then fired up the boat and they took off again. The noise was still there.

He looked over the side and saw that the black rubber bumper stripping that normally circled the boat had come away and was flapping around. He didn't want it to get caught in the jets, so he decided to tack it back on. He stopped the engines and Dani climbed out the back, onto the platform. She held the trim straight while Bob, with Dan's help, snapped it back in place. It was tough going, and required a lot of exertion. They really had to push hard with their fingertips to make it hold. While doing this, Bob was leaning right over the side of the boat, the top of his head almost in the water. Dani warned him not to fall in. Bob completed the front part, while Dan worked on the middle. Then Bob stepped behind his father-in-law and began tacking a piece closer to Dani.

Suddenly, he stood up very quickly and staggered. His arms were waving as if he were dizzy and trying to keep his balance. Leslie was on the back seat just behind him. She thought he was goofing around. Penny and Dan turned to face him. They grabbed him as he sank to his knees and fell back onto the driver's seat. His lips were turning blue.

"Oh my God, he doesn't look good—something's really wrong!" Penny shouted. She grabbed his wrist. "I can't find a pulse!" She turned to Dan, "Can you?" Dan was a cop, so he had to renew his CPR certification every year. He placed his fingers against Bob's carotid artery. Not wanting to upset the kids, who were now watching, he mouthed the word *no*. Dan pinched Bob's nose and blew. After a couple of breaths, Bob's lips began to pink up, but Dan knew that he needed chest compressions.

Dani, who'd been intent on making sure the bumper didn't pull away again, heard the commotion on the boat and saw movement from the corner of her eye. "What the heck?" she thought. She turned around and asked, "What's going on?"

Penny was just five foot five and weighed 115 pounds. Bob was six foot three and 240 pounds of dead weight. But somehow she found the strength to lift him under his arms while Dan took his feet and eased him down onto the bottom of the boat, which was behind the driver's seat and in front of the back bench. Penny knelt behind Bob with his head in her lap. Meanwhile, Dani was frantically dialling 911.

The kids were at the front of the boat, calling out for their dad. "Is he okay? Is he going to be okay?" Leslie was standing aft, watching her husband trying to save her son-in-law. She was praying.

Dan straddled Bob and started CPR. He tried for 100 pumps per minute. But they lost him again. There was no breath and his ears began to turn purple. Then the chest compressions seemed to kick-start his breathing. Dan was sure it would be like a drowning recovery—at any minute, Bob's eyes would fly open and he would just snap out of it.

Dani got hold of the emergency operator and told her they had just passed a small town outside Windsor called Puce, but she didn't know exactly where they were. She looked around, trying to keep from panicking, but all she could see were rows of small cottages in the distance. The operator told Dani it was okay because she had pinpointed Dani's cell phone, so Dani handed the phone to her mother while she started searching for the keys. They weren't in the ignition! What had Bob done with them? "Where are the keys?" she yelled. "I need the keys!"

Bob began to thrash around, frantically throwing his head back and from side to side while he struggled. Penny was not sure whether he was saying "I can't breathe" or reacting to Dani's voice, but garbled words were coming from his lips.

Dani found the keys stuck in the crack between the top and bottom cushions of the driver's seat, snatched them up and started the boat. She was unsure exactly what to do, but she got one engine going and slammed it into drive. Elated, she called to Bob, "I got it, Baby; I got the boat, Baby. It's okay, I got the boat!" Dani's love for her husband made Penny cry.

But Dani soon became frustrated when she discovered that only one engine had caught, meaning that the speed would not pick up. No one but Bob knew exactly how to operate the boat. They puttered toward shore.

Dan had recently been listening to a radio show where one of the medical guests had said blowing breath into someone is a waste of time. Instead, you should focus on pumping the heart, because there is enough oxygen in the blood, as long as you keep it moving, to keep the brain alive. Whether Bob was actually breathing or not didn't really matter to Dan. He just wanted to keep the blood moving to his brain until they reached emergency services. "Fight, Bob, fight," he said through gritted teeth.

Penny was using cool towels and splashing water on Bob's face. She was encouraging. "Omigod, Dan, you're doing it! Good job, Dan! You're doing great!"

Even though Dan's back was blocking their view, the kids were becoming hysterical. Leslie continued to pray aloud, at the same time trying to find out their location from the operator. She looked around and all she could see was water, no discernable landmarks. She had no clue where they were. "Please," she pleaded with the operator, "just tell me which direction the rescue crew will be coming from?"

Leslie was becoming desperate at the lack of action. She began waving a towel over her head to attract help and yelled at the operator, "Do you know who you're picking up here? This is Bob Probert!"

In the end, it took twenty minutes for emergency crews to

find them. All the while, Dan continued the chest compressions, forcing Bob's heart to beat.

Meanwhile, because it was so hot, a carpenter from Emeryville by the name of Pete Craig had quit work early and was sitting in the shade, monitoring his scanner. He heard Leslie mention Bob's name and picked up the phone. His neighbour had a Yamaha WaveRunner, a personal watercraft.

Leslie heard the sound of a water vehicle approaching and looked up. "Oh thank God, someone is here!" she said. A young man in a bright orange-and-red life vest, riding on a WaveRunner, pulled up beside them. "Oh thank God! Thank God!" Leslie said, "Are you a paramedic?"

"No," he said. "I'm Kai. I'm just a guy who lives in the area. My neighbour heard you on the scanner. How can I help?"

Dani said, "I can't get the boat going, and I'm not sure where we are!" Kai jumped in and took the controls while Dani scrambled onto the WaveRunner. Kai headed straight for his house in Emeryville and told Leslie to have the emergency medical services crew meet them there, but the boat still dragged along.

Leslie looked over at her husband. Dan was fifty-seven years old, stood six feet tall and weighed about two hundred pounds—strong and burly—but she was worried. He'd been working on Bob for at least fifteen minutes in the intense heat and she could see he was becoming exhausted.

As they neared shore, Dan gathered strength from the sound of the sirens and sight of the EMS crew waiting on the dock. But Bob was fading. His breathing was becoming shallow, and then, when they were five minutes off shore, it just stopped.

Penny began slapping Bob on the face. "I love you, Bob, we love you. You're gonna do this, look at me, Bob."

Tierney had her arm around Jack and Sarah. All of them were sobbing. They had been watching their dad, hoping he would come out of it. Now they turned away. A moment later, Tierney turned back toward Bob. "Daddy, I love you . . ." Her cry echoed across the water.

On shore, the rescue crew quickly boarded the boat, bringing with them an automated external defibrillator, which they used to shock Bob twice. There was such a crowd gathered around that Dan couldn't see exactly what was happening, except that the paramedics were working very diligently.

Bob's face was a pale greyish colour. Penny hated to leave him there, but she still held out hope. Someone had moved the kids over to a grassy patch in the shade. Penny found them and hugged them and said, "Just pray for your daddy. He's going to be okay." She left them to find Leslie and Dani, who remained near the scene. But on her way, Penny almost collapsed on the beach. She was shaking and panting so badly it took her a few minutes to regain control.

Dani paced the beach like a panther, often stopping to stand on her toes to get a better view of what was happening in the boat. She tried to remember the last time she and Bob had made love. It wasn't for lack of trying. She had been with the girls up at the cottage for a week, was back for one day, and then he left the next day for an appearance in Vancouver. When he came home, she had gone back to the cottage again. There had just been no time. They hadn't made enough time.

Dani waded into the water, wanting to circle the boat. She needed to see something, or at least hear what was going on. Then, suddenly, everything went black. When she came to, she was underwater and a firefighter was pulling her to shore. She found her feet and he helped her toward Leslie, who grabbed a towel and began drying her hair the way she had done when Dani was a little girl. Dani looked up at her mother. "He's going to be okay, isn't he, Mom?"

Dan stood in the water at the bow, waiting. The intense rescue effort lasted more than half an hour before Bob was rushed by ambulance to the hospital. The family was advised to make their way there too. Bob's face was covered by an oxygen mask and there were tubes everywhere. Dani reached to touch him as they loaded him into the vehicle.

Dan and Penny took the kids home, while Leslie and Dani caught a ride to the emergency room with the good Samaritan carpenter, Pete Craig. As Dani sat in the private waiting area, she made plans. She hoped this scare might do Bob some good. Maybe he would clean up his diet, work out more. One thing was for certain, she was going to make sure he got regular checkups. Recently, he told her he'd had blood work done, but who knew if that was true? She was going to sit down with him and read him the riot act. When it came to his health, things were going to be different.

Not long after they arrived, a nurse and a social worker joined them in the waiting area. Leslie's heart sank. She recalled being joined by a similar poker-faced duo in her father's hospital room when he died. She wrapped her arms around Dani and pulled her into a chair. She knew the next person to come through the door would be a doctor.

Penny thought it seemed like an eternity getting the kids home and picking up the car before she and Dan were finally headed to the hospital. When they were about five minutes away, Dan's cell phone rang. It was Leslie. "He's gone," she said.

TOUGH GUY

1

LIKE DON CHERRY SAYS

Tie Domi was a little fucker, and I figured, "Why not?" You know? I didn't have to fight him, but I said, "Aw fuck, let's go. Give him a chance for the hell of it, eh?"

He was saying to me, "Come on, Bob, Macho Man wants a shot at the title." He called himself Macho Man, like the big-time wrestler. I said, "Ah, you little fucker, okay, come on!" He got lucky when he grazed me and I got cut just above the eye. He didn't really hit me, just wandered through with a left. It didn't even hurt or anything. Whole thing only lasted about thirty seconds because the refs jumped in before the fight really got going. So he skates to the box and he pretends like he's putting on the heavyweight championship belt, a hot-dog move.

Later, the coach, Bryan Murray, asked me, "What the fuck are you wasting your time with that little goofball Domi for? You've got nothing to prove."

"Aw fuck," I said, "I gave him a shot."

Murray said, "Bob, you should know better."

Yeah, I fought. I think that helped me make it into the league, because they saw that I could play and also fight—do both. It's kind of a rarity in today's game. Guys who can do both now sign big contracts. I wish I was playing today. Not just as far as money—I was happy.

A lot of people are down on fighting in the NHL. They say it doesn't belong in the game. But like Don Cherry says, "When Probert was fighting, did you ever see anyone get out of their seat and go for coffee?"

2

GO EASY, AL

I've got this big red mark on my foot. I burned it on the exhaust pipe of my bike last week. I keep saying to my kids, "Watch the pipes, watch the pipes," and the other day I got on the bike real quick and forgot. I've been riding bikes for years and I still forget occasionally. I got my first bike in 1990, a Kawasaki Vulcan 750, and then in '91 I bought a really fast dirt bike. I got my first Harley in '92, and I've been riding those ever since. My father had one when I was a kid. He was on the Windsor police force and drove Harleys for them. He'd come home and take us for rides. My dad got me into hockey. His name was Al. Al Probert.

I don't know how he met my mom. I do know that they met at an older age. He was thirty-six or so when I was born. Her name is Theresa Brannagan. Dad's parents were from England. My grandfather's name was Jack. He was awesome. We used to spend a lot of time over at his house—sleepovers and stuff like that. My older brother, Norm, and I played lacrosse. Papa Jack always went to our games. We lost a big game one time, and my dad came up to me after. He was pissed and really giving it to me. Papa Jack pulled him aside and said, "Go easy, Al. Bob tried hard and had a really good game." Papa Jack was a big supporter. He was a happy guy—very happy, and a lot of fun to be around.

My dad had drive. He was tough. I was always told to toughen up, be strong, strong like a bull, not to show weakness. My dad was in the army reserves for three years and then transferred to Germany. When he got out of the army, he went right into the police force. He was born in 1929 and became a cop in 1954. He was big—my size, six foot three, around 220, 225. My grandfather was a smaller guy. Grandma was small too—real small. And yet they had this big son.

My Papa Jack died in 1973, when I was eight. I remember that funeral. You know how kids are. It hadn't really dawned on us that he was dead, so we were acting up in the back of the car and my mother said, "Guys, keep it down back there. Your grandfather just died." We just didn't get it. It was the first death I had experienced. I remember seeing him laid out and I was trying to be strong. I went up to my dad after and said, "Did you see me, Dad? I didn't cry. Everybody else did, but I didn't." But I cried that night. I didn't want people to think I was a big wimp. As I get older I find that's not the case at all. Crying's okay.

There was some kind of family stuff going on at my grandfather's funeral—something between my mother and my dad's brother's wife—and that was it. We never hung around with our cousins anymore after that.

I think I'm like Papa Jack. I like to have fun. I look like my dad, though. People say I look more like my mother, but I think I look like my dad.

I grew up in south Windsor on a quiet street, in a small brick house. Virginia Park Avenue. I played street hockey with all my buddies. It was a dead end, so we'd set up in the middle of the street and play all day.

I was not very good in school, but I could figure things out. I liked tools and stuff. When I was in Grade 2, the teacher turned on an electric fan and held up a piece of paper. He asked, "How many think the fan is gonna blow this paper across my desk?" Everybody raised their hand except me. Then he said, "So who thinks the fan is gonna suck the paper in?" And I was the only one who knew it would. But I did not like to sit in classrooms and I couldn't remember one damn thing I read. When I was in rehab, I was diagnosed with ADHD—attention-deficit hyperactivity disorder, which is now pretty common among kids. At Northwood Elementary I would sit at my desk and not hear a word the teacher was saying. I'd be watching a movie in my head—a movie about what I was gonna do when the bell rang. Sitting there drove me crazy—I had to do something. I was already a nail biter, but being in school all day made it worse. I bit them till there was almost nothing left, and later, when I lost my front teeth, I learned to use the teeth on the sides. Adapt, you know?

I started playing hockey when I was four and got into an organized league when I was five. My dad took me down to Adie Knox Herman, the local rink. I loved it. I started as a forward—a left winger—and played left wing my whole career.

Yeah, sometimes I'd switch and play right wing, even though I was a left-hand shot, but never centre, never defence. The kids on the street would get out and go to the end of the street and play on the pond. There was a picture in *The Windsor Star* of my father lacing up my brother's skates. That's what he used to do. He'd put my leg on him and he'd tie my skates.

I liked my dad. He didn't smoke, but he liked to have his beers after work. He wasn't a big boozer, but it was acceptable to go to the Legion and have a few pints. He'd have his gin and tonics, but I very rarely saw him drunk—a couple of times, maybe, but he was for the most part in control. His hair was grey, like mine. It was good and thick, but more straight than curly. He wasn't all macho. He'd pat us on the back and say things like "Good job." He didn't say a lot, but when he did talk, you'd listen. Otherwise, you'd get cuffed across the head. I remember mouthing off and all of a sudden, *whack!* I learned real quick not to push him to that point, so it didn't happen often. I could count on one hand how many times he did that. I'd stagger around a bit and my ears would ring—not a pleasant experience.

My mother had a paddle, and she'd say, "If you don't behave, you're going to get this!" I was ten and kind of like a shit disturber, so one day I got it on the butt. That night they went out and I sawed that thing in half with this little saw that I had in a tool kit I got for Christmas. The paddle was a threat, and I wanted to get rid of it.

I remember when she went to go use it the next time, she picked it up and started yelling. I ran to my room and she locked me in. My dad wasn't home, so I turned on the tears.

She felt so bad she said, "Okay, come on out," and gave me a cookie. I learned to put on a pretty good show. I was a pretty good actor and I learned how to manipulate her at a young age.

My dad was an old-school cop. He applied street justice with his nightstick. He had a reputation. I remember him coming home from work after having been in fights. One time, he had to go break up this big bar brawl and one of his elbows was all cut up from rolling around in the street. I thought that was so cool. You know, if I hadn't gone into hockey, I think I might've been a cop. As it is, I have managed to interact with police officers many times anyway.

When I was in Grade 8, my buddies Tony DiCocco and Dave Cantagallo and I snuck into school at lunch and got spotted by the lunchroom monitor, so we took off down the hall. I got out first, with Tony right behind me, but by the time Dave reached the door, it whacked him in the forehead, and split it wide open. There was blood everywhere. That's how wrestlers bleed so badly. They cut the forehead, where the blood vessels are very close to the surface. Tony and I couldn't just leave him there, so we ran back and some teachers showed up and Dave ended up in the hospital for stitches. Tony and I were sent to the office, and I thought my dad was going to be mad, but he never said a word.

My dad used to take us through the police station and give us the tour, show us the jail cells, lock us in. We'd go out to one of his buddies' and get to shoot his guns. Dad had quite a few guns of his own, probably twenty or so. After he died, my mother had one of his partners come over and sell them all for $2,500, which I'm still pissed off about. I mean, it might have

been a wise move—I was seventeen and Norm was eighteen—
but he had some cool things, like a Luger that his uncle took
off a German during World War II, and four Lee-Enfield
rifles, with the pump action. He had a Model 57 magnum and
a couple of .45s. He had a couple of little snub-nosed Detective Specials with the short barrels—Colt police issue. Just a
real cool collection.

My dad used to take me to Red Wings games. He had a
buddy, Pat D'Amore, who owned a construction company,
and he would go and check on this guy's property after hours.
To thank my dad for watching his place, he would give us tickets. It was pretty dangerous over at the Olympia in the '70s. In
1976 a businessman was killed over there after a tennis match,
just walking to his car. The security guards had gone home and
turned out the parking lot lights—even they didn't want to be
around the Olympia late at night. When my dad took Norm
and me to games, he'd bring his little snub-nosed .38. He'd
drive across the border with it in his belt. He'd whip open his
coat, show his badge and say, "I'm going to the game." When
we walked to the car after the game, he'd have it in his hand,
dangling at his side. It made Norm and me feel pretty safe.
Our old man wasn't going to let anyone screw around with us.

3

A BIG GUY WITH GOOD HANDS

I like to think I'm a good passer. That was my problem—a lot of times I'd pass instead of shooting. I just enjoyed making something happen for someone else. There's nothing like watching a teammate score on a play you set up.

I had some good years, and some good coaches who knew that I could play. A lot of guys never got that chance. You're only as good as your coach wants you to be—I believe that, and I think I also had the drive. That's what helped me make it into the NHL. I see a lot of guys who have the talent, but they don't have that push, that eye of the tiger.

Rick Cranker was my midget coach. Just a great guy. I still run into him today around the city. Between the ages of ten and thirteen, I was always one of the better guys on my team. I was fortunate, because I was always a foot taller than most guys. Not many caught up to me heightwise, which seemed to help me stay among the top two or three players all the way up. I liked it. The only thing I didn't like was my big feet.

I was always embarrassed about having size 13 clompers. I'd always buy shoes that were a size smaller and stuff 'em in there. Nowadays, I don't care.

My brother, Norm, is a year older. He played hockey with me all the way up and was drafted by the Windsor Spitfires, the local major junior team, and that was pretty much the end of his hockey career. It was just one of those things—bad timing. The Spitfires were a very good team at the time. They went to the Ontario Hockey League finals. He didn't get the playing time he would have gotten any other year. He tried to hang in there by playing a year at St. Clair College in Windsor. I think it was tough on him when he didn't make it. He kind of struggled with booze and drugs.

I have been drinking for a long time. The first time I drank, I was fourteen. The family went to a party at my aunt's in Michigan, and my dad brought a cooler of beer home with us— American beer in cans, all different kinds. Schlitz, Budweiser, Pabst Blue Ribbon. I was putting them away in the fridge, thinking, "I wonder what that tastes like?" So I opened one and knocked it down. Nothing was happening. I had another, and another. After drinking about five of them I started getting a buzz, then it really kicked in. I was like, "Wow, this is pretty neat," but I knew I had better get to my bedroom before someone saw me staggering and falling down.

I guess I threw up all over myself during the night, because when my mother came to wake me in the morning, she said,

"What's going on? What's wrong with you?" To this day, when I eat fish I sometimes have an allergic reaction, so I blamed it on tuna. I told her that when I had dinner at my buddy's the night before, they'd put tuna in the Kraft Dinner. I was a quick thinker. My mother bought it, and after that she was always worried about me eating tuna.

I was lucky, because I could easily have choked on my own vomit. Having a couple of beers became a regular thing. I had a high tolerance. My dad would be downstairs watching TV and my mother would be sleeping, and I'd sneak up to the living room or into the back yard and drink by myself. I liked to have between four and half a dozen. I'd hide the cans and get rid of them the next day. I liked the buzz. I really liked it.

I started hanging out, finding guys who liked to drink. At first, we'd get blasted at a weekend party, then I wouldn't do it again for probably three weeks. And then the time between started to get shorter and shorter until it was every weekend. Then twice a week. At that time, it didn't affect my hockey. We made sure not to drink before a game. After? Yeah, sure. Possibly even the night before. But when you're young like that, you sweat it out the next day. I remember my dad was pissed about it when he found out, but he took it easier than he might have because Norm had paved the way. In his final year of midget, Norm totalled his car after partying. Anything I did after that didn't seem so bad.

One night, I was about sixteen and walking home from a party when a black-and-white drove by, going the opposite way. So I just took off through the nearest yard. They pulled a U-ey and starting chasing me, trying to cut me off. I hopped a couple of fences and headed for the school, hoping to make it across the playground because I figured the car wouldn't tear through the grass. But they had called for help. So the next thing I knew, they had me surrounded.

They took me in, questioned me and had to let me go. It was pretty funny, actually—what were they going to charge me with? Running down the street? I don't know why I did it. I must have felt a resentment against authority. If I did that today, they'd probably Taser me. I have been Tasered by the cops, and let me tell you, I can think of better things to do.

I just didn't give a shit about much. I failed half my classes in Grade 9, and my marks went downhill from there. But hockey was going great, I was a winger on my midget team, Club 240, and was getting a little attention. I was six foot two and two hundred pounds and still growing, and I had some ability. I could gain possession by moving my opponent off the puck, and I had hands, so I put up a few points.

For me, the best thing about hockey was the team, the guys. I wasn't as serious as I could have been. I never worked on my skating or bothered with off-ice training. But then we went to a tournament in Vancouver when I was sixteen. It was an eventful trip. I broke the law, lost my virginity to an older girl, and managed to make some scouts look my way.

I had made fake IDs for all the boys, so we were able to buy as much booze as we wanted. It was pretty clever, considering there were no computers back then. I found this rub-on lettering in a craft store. I scratched each buddy's name onto the cards, drew in a line for a signature, attached a school picture, rubbed on the word ALBERTA across the top and coloured it in red, then added the guy's weight and height. Finally, I'd laminate it. It looked like a real student ID card. We were never questioned, not once. It was awesome.

I was pretty good with my hands—not really artistic, but I could think up stuff that required a little skill if it had to be done. The cards made it possible for us to buy booze and go to all the bars. We met some girls who were staying around the corner from our hotel. I think they were kind of like runaways. One of them was a pretty blonde. She was a rough talker, but I found her interesting.

She was the first girl I ever saw naked. She just slipped her pants off and handed me a condom. I'd seen pictures of naked girls, because my dad used to have a stash. But this time it was in the flesh. I came out and gave my roomies the thumbs-up, but it was awkward. I didn't have to pay her—I didn't have money. She wasn't a working girl anyway, just well prepared.

There were some really good teams at that tournament, and the beer and sex must have helped because I was named the left winger on the All-Tournament First Team. The scouts sat up. The next year, 1982, I was drafted by the Brantford Alexanders major junior team. At the Alexanders' orientation camp, I was a little nervous. The guys were all so clean-cut, kind of like altar boys, so I started to get worried. But after the parents disappeared, we had this huge bonfire and downed several cases of beer. It was a relief.

My dad had a stroke in the spring of '81. I was at home with my mom when he came in from work. A blood clot had travelled up his leg and he was having trouble talking. My mom was yelling for me, "Bobby! Bobby! There's something wrong with Daddy!"

His whole left side went numb, and he never completely regained his strength there. I kind of avoided him after that, and I always felt guilty about it. It was embarrassing to bring our friends around because we didn't want them to see him like that. He just wasn't the guy he'd been. He was weak and had trouble walking and talking. He just sat there in front of the TV, a shadow of who he had been. He was bitter too, really angry with himself, and I think that's why he snapped at all of us so much. He had always taught me that weakness was a terrible thing.

A year later, he had another stroke. At the hospital, lying in bed, my dad looked so frail. His face was grey and his lips were white. He talked about Brantford and told me to get my skates sharpened and to get a haircut. A couple of hours later, he slipped into a coma and died. I didn't cry.

The day after his funeral, I reported to camp.

I've read a million times that all the problems I had were due to my dad dying when I was seventeen. People were always looking for some kind of reason. It would be easy if there was some type of abuse there, but there wasn't. I never really came to a conclusion. I was told I had a Marilyn Monroe–type syndrome—a fear of success. Or maybe I couldn't handle the popularity. But that's just a bullshit diagnosis, because I had been drinking long before I was successful and long before my dad died. It just happened that when things were good, I would celebrate, and I just got a little addicted to the fun. I always seemed to take it to the next level, you know what I mean? Why do things half-assed? Do it big. Right?

That first year, I lived with a family. Our goalie, Allan Bester, who eventually played for the Toronto Maple Leafs, was billeted with them too. The lady of the house was around twenty-nine and her husband was probably about forty-two. The first year was kind of brutal because I was seventeen and already boozing. I just liked to always be stoned or drunk. I was kind of a shy kid, and the booze turned me into someone who wasn't that shy. I could talk to girls, for one thing, and then it just became a physical addiction. I could not have just one or two beers. If I did, I'd have twelve. The thing you've got to remember is it's not like we had a normal nine-to-five job. We'd put in two hours at the rink, be done by noon, then go for lunch somewhere and have pops.

At the season wrap-up party, I got in a fight at a bar, got split open, went to the hospital and got stitched up, went to another bar, and brought the waitress home. I snuck her into the basement of my billet's house, into this crawl space area, and we ended up passed out. Early the next morning, I woke up, and there was my landlady doing the wash, and I was like "Shit!" The waitress and I were hiding under an old mattress. I was thinking, "If my landlady sees us, we're screwed."

She walked upstairs to go put the clean laundry away, and I snuck the waitress out the back door. This girl was probably like twenty-one or something—a few years older than me, blonde, tall, nice-looking. Why did she come home with me? Maybe she felt sorry for me. I was covered in Band-Aids and stitches. Who knows? I wasn't one of those guys who turned on the charm— "I love you baby, your eyes are like . . ." whatever. I never really had a line—seriously. I can't figure it out. I had naturally curly hair—maybe that was it.

As I said, I snuck her out and thought I'd gotten away with it, but the landlady must have heard the sliding glass door. She looked out her window and saw this girl walking away. She stomped downstairs and confronted me, and I said, "What are you talking about? What girl?"

She called her husband, and when he got home, they called the team, and the team called me in and told me the season was over anyway, so they sent me home. My mother got a letter from my landlord, saying he was a recovering alcoholic and he thought I had a drinking problem and needed help.

I guess I would say I was an alcoholic by then. When we first started buying beer, we would split a case between four of us. And then they came out with the eighteen-packs, so we'd split that between two of us. Then we'd split a two-four between two of us. So by the time I was eighteen, I was drinking twelve beers a night, but I could go to sixteen without passing out. There was usually a competition to see who could drink more than anyone else. I'd always win. I was big—at seventeen I was already six foot three and over two hundred pounds—a big guy who could drink more than anyone else. It was cool.

That first year in junior, I was suspended from a game. My coach was Dave Draper—his nickname was Zippy. He heard about our extracurricular activities with booze, and another forward, Terry Maki, and I were sent home. Terry and I had been hanging out with this group of girls who actually were nice girls, but the coach got a call saying that they liked to smoke weed. I was never a big weed smoker, and I had done plenty of other things to get suspended, but not this. But Coach wouldn't listen. He said he'd had enough.

I headed back to Windsor, partied hard and was back on the ice with Brantford a week later. By this time, I only showed up at school to meet girls or hang out with my friends. I was failing almost every subject—never cracked a book. I barely went to class. Zippy gave me a choice—go to school or get my ass out of bed and come down to the rink. I dropped out of school and showed up at the rink at 9 A.M. every day. I didn't graduate from high school.

I had my first really successful fight that year. I got into it with this tough guy from Kingston, and I happened to get a lucky one in and knocked him down. Word spread around the league that I was pretty tough. Now, I'm not an angry guy. It takes a lot to piss me off. But when you *do* piss me off, look out, because now I'm pissed off, and if I reach my boiling point, then you have a problem. I noticed guys starting to give me a wide berth, so I took it upon myself to learn how to fight to protect my teammates, and that role just kind of happened for me.

I was pretty lucky. I was one of the taller guys in the league, so I had a long reach. I used that to my advantage as I developed my technique. The thing I liked to do was just grab a guy by the sweater or shoulder pads and hold him straight out. Then I'd pull my head back so he couldn't hit me. Next, I'd throw a punch.

He couldn't reach me because he was too far away—the full length of my outstretched arm, plus another few inches because my head was way back—but I could connect. Lots of times, this approach flew out the window. I'd say to myself, "Okay, I'm going to do this, this, and this," and then when it came down to it, I forgot and did whatever came naturally.

Scrapping was part of the game for me. There were a lot of guys who could skate way better than I could. They weren't as big, but they were faster and more agile, so fighting was one way I could make it to the big leagues—something extra that I could use to get ice time.

I lost my front teeth after my first year in junior, but not in a fight. I was home for two days and playing pickup hockey, when the guy who lives right down the street from me now, Ron Sanko, went to pass the puck and I poke-checked it. The butt end of my stick came up and caught me in the mouth. One tooth was just hanging there. The other was cracked right in half. It was brutal, because I had just gotten back into town and I had been looking forward to going to school the next day to see all my friends. It was embarrassing.

My first season in junior ended with 12 goals, 16 assists and 133 penalty minutes in 51 games. We finished fourth in the Emms Division—named after the former GM of the Boston Bruins, who owned junior teams in Barrie and Niagara Falls and signed Bobby Orr—and made the playoffs. In eight play-off games, I had two goals and two assists and 23 penalty minutes. We lost in the division semis to the Soo Greyhounds.

That June, in the NHL entry draft, Detroit's general manager, Jimmy Devellano, chose me for the Red Wings—in the third round, forty-sixth overall. He said that what clinched it for him was a fight where he saw me punch out a guy's upper bridge. Philadelphia had also shown some interest, but Detroit got me. I couldn't believe it. I hadn't been picked in the OHL draft until the *seventh* round! Jimmy D was calling me a Clark Gillies type of player—a big guy with good hands. He was the one who really pushed to get me. I think he felt kind of bad for me because my father had died. But I think another reason he wanted me was because Detroit was building a team for the future to give the fans hope. In the '60s they'd made it to the Stanley Cup final four times, but in the '70s people called them the "Dead Things." They were lucky to get six thousand out for a game. In seventeen seasons between 1966–67 and 1982–83, they'd only been to the playoffs twice.

But by 1983, the Wings had a new owner, Mike Ilitch, and they had an amazing draft that spring. With the fourth-overall pick, they took Stevie Yzerman; in the second round, right winger Lane Lambert; in the third round, me; in the fifth, left wing Petr Klima and defenceman Joey Kocur; and in the tenth, Stu "The Grim Reaper" Grimson.

Jimmy D brought most of the guys who were drafted to Detroit to meet the press. The Wings really needed publicity. When Stevie and Joey and Klima and I first started, most the guys on the team couldn't use their free tickets because half the time they couldn't find a taker. I stood behind Stevie Y. He was almost half a foot shorter and fifty pounds lighter. He was fairly serious. You know right away that certain guys are never going to be sitting next to you in a jail cell, laughing off a hangover. But there was something about Stevie Y that I liked.

I can't put my finger on it, but he had that quality only a few guys have—one that would make you step up for him. Maybe it's called leadership.

4

A LOT OF GUYS WERE DOING IT

Just because you are drafted doesn't mean you ever play in the NHL. I went back to junior the next season. I didn't think I was going to live with the couple I had roomed with my first year, but the coach had me call and apologize, and they took me back. It didn't last long. I came in pretty drunk after the rookie party and they called the team. So I moved in with the owner of the Alexanders, Jack Robillard. Actually, two of us did, Bob Pierson and me. Jack had a really beautiful house—an indoor/outdoor pool, just a huge place on a huge lot. He had all the toys, snowmobiles and cars we could drive around. It was awesome. And he and his wife were hardly ever there. They had a live-in nanny, so we had the run of the place.

No, I didn't sleep with the nanny, but at one point I did sleep with a landlady. She kind of hit on me. Her husband never found out. As far as looks go, she was about a six. She had nice big eyes, but she was a little heavy—the sand-had-settled-to-the-bottom type. She kept throwing comments at me like, "Come on, big boy, why don't you take care of me?" Finally, one day I just said, "Okay." She called me into her bedroom, where she was lying on the bed. We started making out, and then one thing led to another and we had sex in her bed.

Afterward, I was like, "Oh shit! Why the frig did I do that?" because I was worried about the husband. I knew him and he was an okay guy. It got worse. She was becoming a pain in the ass, nudging me and trying to arrange it so we would be home alone together, so I kind of passed her off to my buddy, another big boozer. He started being nice to her and complimenting her, and they had an affair. I was so happy because I wanted out of that situation.

Another good buddy was having sex with a different landlady. So many guys in junior were doing it—banging landladies. It's still happening today. A couple I know took in two players, and the wife started having sex with one of them—and the guy was okay with it! I told my wife, Dani, this story and she said, "Can we billet a couple of Spitfires next year?"

We had a tough team. Todd Francis was a fighter. Shayne Corson was tough. Then there was me and a couple of other guys too. A very physical, strong team.

Shayne was the number one draft pick for Brantford in 1983. That fall, he showed up at camp driving a brand new Camaro Z28. He was cocky as shit, so after practice, Todd went out and shit on the hood of his car to show him, "You know what?

You're an asshole. You need to walk the line here." Shit on his brand new car, right on the hood. Shayne didn't know who did it. It didn't straighten him out, of course. Shayne was pissed, but he just laughed it off. He had to clean up the hood himself with a couple of paper towels, still full of attitude. "Ha ha, you fuckers! You just wait until I find out who did it!" That's typical Shayne. We got along good, though.

Hockey was pretty good that year. We usually played in front of crowds of two thousand or so. The fans were good to me, but Coach Draper was always on my ass to shoot and stop passing all the time. In our fifth game, on October 1, 1983, I tied the score with a goal against the Oshawa Generals in the last five minutes. The year before, the Generals had gone to the Memorial Cup final against Portland. They had Dave Gans, who ended up only having a cup of coffee with the Los Angeles Kings, but in '83–84 he had 132 points. They also had Dan Gratton, who was drafted in the first round by L.A. in 1985, but barely made it out before he was back. He played only seven games in The Show. John MacLean played part of the season with the New Jersey Devils. He went on to score more than 400 goals in the NHL. Their goalie, Kirk McLean, was awesome. He played fifteen years and was with the Canucks when they went to the Stanley Cup final in 1994. And they had Mike Stern. He and I were the same size, and our stats were similar. He'd wind up that year with 76 points and 118 penalty minutes. I had 73 points and 189 minutes.

I was on a line with Shayne and Todd, and we had good chemistry. Three big forecheckers—Shayne was six foot two and 180, and Francis was six-one and 210. We kept teams in their own end. By October 28, when we met the Belleville Bulls, I already had seven goals and had been in a couple of good fights. We had a solid rivalry going with Belleville, but we embarrassed them 4–2 that night, so they came back on Halloween really pissed.

I remember one guy, I think it was Ali Butorac, a defenceman. He wasn't that tall, but he was husky. He skated over to our bench and started mouthing off, which took a lot of balls because we had an intimidating team. But Belleville had a tough team too, so if any club was going to do it, it was going to be them. And two of our guys—Rob Moffat, a big defenceman, but not a fighter, and Doug Stewart, a winger—grabbed him and pulled him into the bench and put him on the merry-go-round. In fact, Rob spat in Ali's face. And that's when their bench cleared. Todd turned to me and said, "Screw this, let's go!" and he went over the boards, with Shayne and me right behind him. We were handling ourselves pretty well, and lots of guys stepped up. Even our goalie, Chris Pusey, left his net to take on their goalie, Craig Billington. But we were outnumbered, and three Belleville players went after Todd all at once. They took him on mafia style—two held him while one used him as a punching bag—and he ended up in emergency with an eye injury. Eight of us got ejected and suspended, which left eleven guys to play thirty minutes. We won the game, though. I think that fight kind of made us jell as a team.

I came back for the next game with my adrenalin really going. I wanted to make an impact, I guess. It helped that it was in Windsor, and I scored a pair of unassisted goals against the Spitfires. But with only a one-goal lead, I figured I better help make sure they didn't come back. So on the next faceoff I got into a little tussle, and that guy was carried off. My jersey was off, so I skated to the box bare-chested, and my whole family and all my friends went crazy.

A couple of nights later, against the Sudbury Wolves, I scored my first hat trick. I wasn't bad in front, although Zippy was always giving me shit for playing with the puck. He said I tried to get in too close. But I had been working on my slapper, and on December 9, when we played the Kitchener Rangers, I whipped in a twenty-five-footer in OT. We were within a point of first place in the Emms Division. Besides Corson, Stewart and me, there was Mike Millar, who got fifty goals that year and showed up for a while in Hartford, Washington, Boston and Toronto before ending up in Europe. There was also Bruce Bell, a kind of all-purpose defenceman who played a few years in the NHL, mainly with Quebec and St. Louis. When my confidence was up and I was feeling good, I'd celebrate. We were always being offered free drinks and female company.

Thirty-five-goals is pretty good for a fighter, so I was picked to play for the Emms Division in the OHL All-Star Game in Guelph. So were our goalies, Bester and Pusey, as well as Bell. Our coach, Dave Draper, was the coach of the Emms team. I was pumped, and when I get that way, I get antsy. The night before the game, we went out to this bar on the University of Guelph campus—everybody who was playing was there—and a couple of us got a little carried away. Bell and I were room-mates, and for some reason we either didn't get the wake-up call or didn't hear it, but we were late for the skate. We made practice, but missed the photo session. I think Coach Draper was really embarrassed by that. He came to our room and told us he was thinking of sitting us.

Zippy was a nice guy, an honest guy. He didn't lose it very often. He told us to go home for a week and figure out life, really think about what we wanted to do, because we had both been drafted by NHL teams. He said we needed to contem-plate how badly we'd screwed up. He added, "When you come back, it's a fresh start. I just want you to play and stay out of trouble." Then he left—he had a few calls to make.

I knew this wasn't good. Jimmy D from the Wings was going to be there, and so were the scouts from Quebec, to see Bruce. My family was on the way, too. One of Zippy's calls was to Shayne Corson, and the other to another guy from our team, John Meulenbroeks. They replaced Bruce and me. He also suspended Jim Mayne, a player from Guelph, and replaced him with his teammate Trevor Stienburg.

Jimmy D was crazy mad. He said he drafted me because he saw potential even after a pretty mediocre first year in junior. He said he couldn't believe I was blowing my opportunity with the Wings and making him look stupid. Zippy decided I needed a bigger lesson and sent me home for another week suspension.

We ended the season in second place, twenty-five points behind Kitchener. We faced the Soo Greyhounds again in the playoffs, and lost to them again. I finished third on the team with 35 goals and 38 assists for 73 points in 65 games, behind Millar (50–45–95) and rookie Jason Lafreniere (24–57–81). Even though I was suspended, I was invited to the Wings' training camp in the summer of '84. I was still eligible to play junior for another year, so they sent me back down.

Over the summer, the Alexanders had moved to Hamilton, changing their name to the Steelhawks. Draper was still the coach. He was quite knowledgeable about the game, a good teacher for future pros. He was also a guy you could go and talk to, and he didn't seem to hold a grudge. We had some good heart-to-hearts. He told me he needed me to change because I was leading some of the other guys down the garden path. He said he was going to tighten the reins. He'd heard about the shit on Shayne's car, and said that was uncalled for and he didn't want to see anything like that again. He also banned hazing. Sometimes, rookies would get stuffed—naked—into the shitter on a bus, or they might have to play tug of war with a skate lace around their dicks, stupid things like that. But there were some great traditions too. Everybody gets the hair shaved off their entire body when they make it to junior—I did, even Gretzky did—and now Zippy wanted to get rid of tradition. I argued against it, but he said there was no way we could shave the rookies, and he hoped that missing the All-Star Game had taught me a good lesson and that I had matured.

I played the first four games in a bit of a slump. I was trying hard to buckle down, not to go out at night. But then we had a rookie party, and everyone got fucked up and we decided to honour the shaving tradition. I ended up taking all the heat from the coach. He sent me home.

I didn't mind that so much, but I didn't like him bad-mouthing me in the media. He told Ted Beare, the sports editor of the Brantford *Expositor*, that he was going to try to find another team for me. "We've taken an awful lot from him over the years . . . enough is enough." I look at those old articles and I think, "Here is a coach talking shit about his own nineteen-year-old player to a reporter." Zippy also told Jimmy Devellano that I was disruptive and that he didn't give a shit what I did, but I wouldn't be invited back to Hamilton no matter what. Jimmy D didn't want me floating around, getting out of shape and into trouble. He decided to sign me to a pro contract while I waited for a trade to a new junior team. I hired Donnie Meehan as my lawyer, and on October 1, 1984, I signed a three-year two-way contract with an option for a fourth year. If I played in the NHL, my salary would be $65,000, then $70,000, $80,000 and $85,000. In the minor leagues, my salary would be reduced to $25,000. If a deal could be worked out with another team in the Ontario Hockey League first, I would be paid $5,000.

I went to Detroit and began practising under the Wings' coach, Nick Polano. I was brutal—certainly not ready to join The Show yet. I couldn't take a pass, I tripped over pylons, and my skating wasn't there, either. I was so nervous—you should have seen my fingernails. Being shitty was embarrassing, but the guys put up with me. I put in extra time on the ice and learned to do dry-land training—speed bag, weights, resistance training, all that stuff that takes you to a new level.

Up until this point, I hadn't figured on really making it. Most of guys I played with in junior ended up being drafted, but they became minor-league lifers. And I am talking about really good players. But after practising with the Wings and talking to Jimmy D, the light bulb turned on. Playing in the NHL began to look like a very real possibility for me.

5

CRISPY

While I practised with the Wings, the coach of the Sault Ste. Marie Greyhounds, Terry Crisp, and his general manager, Sam McMaster, heard I was available and thought I might be the missing piece of the puzzle for their run at the Memorial Cup. They polled the team and no one objected to my joining them. One of the guys, Graeme Bonar, who had also played for the Spitfires, said that having me on the team sure beat playing against me.

Crispy was tough. He'd played for the Philadelphia Flyers for seven years in the days of Dave Schultz and the Broad Street Bullies, and he was building a similar team with the Greyhounds. Crispy ran his team like boot camp—work hard, play harder. Jimmy D tried to scare me before I went, telling me I'd put him and my mother through all this shit and that this was my last chance, and that Crispy would put my ass on a slow boat to China if I fucked up. When I got up there, Crispy called me in and said his team played "old-time hockey" and he felt I was a good fit for that. He told me they were going for all the marbles that year, and as far as he was concerned my slate was clean, but he wouldn't put up with any more screwing around.

It sounded good to me.

Meanwhile, I got a girl pregnant, and I got the call. I had just settled into the Soo, but I wanted to do the right thing. She wanted an abortion. I thought about going to Crispy and telling him, "Hey Coach, I'm sorry I can't play, but this girl needs an abortion so I have to go be with her," but I didn't think that would fly. I called one of my best buddies to handle it for me. He said he would drive her to the doctor and be with her. That was pretty much it for us. We talked after that, but it just wasn't the same.

Crispy put me on the first line with Bonar and centre Wayne Groulx. Again, we had good chemistry. Groulx scored 59 goals and had 85 assists for 144 points. Only Dave MacLean of Belleville (64–90–154) had more points. Bonar tied for the league lead in goals, with 66, and was fourth with 137 points. I appeared in 44 games, and had 20 goals and 52 assists for 72 points. Crispy's strategy was simple: "Just play hockey." Guys were running me right and left, but Terry didn't want me answering the phone. I did what he said. Then we arrived in Hamilton for a game that was being televised on Global TV as the OHL game of the week. The Soo against my old team. They always had a good rivalry, going back to when the Steelhawks were in Brantford. Hamilton's coach was Bill LaForge. He had a reputation for building teams of fighters. The OHL commissioner, David Branch, came in to talk to us ahead of time about keeping things clean and not making hockey look bad. As he spoke to us, he kept looking at me—he seemed worried.

During the first period, there was a lot of yapping back and forth on the ice, and I was getting more and more pissed off. Things heated up and everybody started shoving, and suddenly we had a scrap. Everybody squared off—even the goalies were going at it. The fight went on forever—like, twenty minutes. Ten guys were thrown out, including me. LaForge was suspended for the rest of the season, including the playoffs.

Brad Dalgarno, the guy who replaced me in Hamilton, was my size and not afraid to mix it up, but he was only sixteen, so it wasn't too tough to put him down. I moved on and found three of my guys who needed support. I remember looking at Crispy, he nodded, and I tagged all three Steelhawks—*bam, bam, bam.* It was fun, really fun.

The fans everywhere in junior were really supportive. I liked going to Ottawa, where my mother's sister, Aunt Pat, and her husband, Uncle Mike, lived. One time, we were scheduled to play there and I gave them a call. I told them they could meet me after the game if they wanted to. I came out a bit later than expected, and they were a little worried because everybody was on the bus already. Uncle Mike was a teacher. He said, "Bob, there's a bus out there with twenty-some players. The coach's ears are probably blowing out smoke!" So we headed out, but there was still a huge crowd waiting for autographs and stuff. Aunt Pat had a big shopping bag full of food for me, and I told her to hold onto it tight. Then I opened the exit door and said, "Sorry, everybody, but we have a woman here with a baby!" Everyone moved aside and we made it to the bus.

People always tell me, "Bob, you have no sense of time," and I think they may have something there. I've heard some complaints about it, but I like to line up a lot of activities. Anyway, why say no? Crispy once told me he would have the players tag-team me when I played for him. Like, "Wayne, take Probie with you today, and when you are done, hand him off to Scotty." He said he knew I accepted a lot of invitations because they always sounded like so much fun, so he'd call up guys he called "great character kids" and tell them to keep me busy *the right way.* One time, a buddy told me that the guys used to complain that, after twelve hours of hanging out, going to eat and watching a movie, they were tired, while I was still ready to go. Crispy's plan worked most of the time, but sometimes it worked the other way around, and *I* planned the activities.

Joel Brown, a defenceman, was a tough guy who scrapped a lot. He'd been traded from the Ottawa 67's to the Kitchener Rangers and was playing with Shawn Burr, who would become my teammate in Adirondack and Detroit. I've heard announcers say that, as the fight went on, it seemed like I got stronger. For me, during a fight, instead of getting tired, something inside would take over. I wanted to win so badly that I overcame the fatigue. I guess it's the adrenalin and everything. It was embarrassing not to win, and if you lose a fight, and then you lose the next fight, and then you lose the *next* one, the team could get rid of you or send you down. All of a sudden it's like, "This guy is not helping us win games, and he's not changing the momentum. He's actually hurting us, so let's trade him or get someone else who's tougher." There's a lot of pressure to stay in the league, and part of staying in the league is being able to win your fights.

In one game, Joel threw out a big haymaker and got me square in the forehead. I just looked at him and started laughing. It was a situation where the look on his face dropped, and it was over after that.

Crispy gave me a lot of credit. I have to say, I owe him. He gave me a chance when I needed it. He would tell me things to prop me up, like, "From the blue line in to the other guys' net, there aren't many guys better than you." He said I had soft hands, and could see the ice and make moves. He had a theory that guys were a little scared, so when I'd get the puck, he told me to take the little cushion and use the room to snap it in the net. My confidence was at an all time high in 1984–85.

The Greyhounds dominated the OHL that year. We led the Emms Division by twenty-two points and won all thirty-three of our home games, finishing with a record of 54–11–1. Nine players on our roster went on to appear in at least one game in the NHL: Wayne Groulx, Wayne Presley, Rob Zettler, Chris Felix, Derek King, Tyler Larter, Kenny Sabourin, Jeff Beukeboom and me. Crispy went on to coach the Calgary Flames to their only Stanley Cup championship, in 1989. Groulx won the

Red Tilson Trophy, awarded to the most outstanding player in the league; Crispy won the coach-of-the-year award; our goalies, Scott Mosey and Marty Abrams, won the award for best goals-against average; and King was the rookie of the year.

In the playoffs, we beat Kitchener, Hamilton and Peterborough to win the J. Ross Robertson Cup for the league championship. That meant we were headed for the Memorial Cup, the national junior championship. Three other teams made it: the Prince Albert Raiders (the Western Hockey League champions), the Verdun Junior Canadiens (the Quebec champs) and the Shawinigan Cataractes (the host team). In the semifinal game against Prince Albert, I had a big fight with Ken Baumgartner. The Raiders were leading when he crosschecked me into his own net. He managed to get my sweater up over my head, keeping my arms tied up, and then he pulled me down. For me, it was a big embarrassment. Nobody likes to lose, right? I had my dad's words in my head—"You've got to be strong. If you lose a fight, you look like a loser or a wimp."

So I was pretty mad. We were mouthing off to each other in the penalty box. "Yeah, when I get out of here, we're fucking gonna go!" Usually, I didn't like to say a lot, but sometimes I would if I was really pissed. And this time I was seriously close to my boiling point. "You motherfucker, as soon as we get out, we are gonna go, right here! Right here, buddy, right here."

Our penalties ended, we got out, and we fought. The thing is, when I left my penalty box, I didn't shut the door—I just jumped out and met him along the boards. We were wrestling and pushing, and he ricocheted off the glass to the doorway in front of my penalty box and fell in under me.

I was on top of him, and his head was under the bench. I'm throwing down punches, but he's got his helmet on, and he's throwing up punches that are connecting to the side of my head. One of the linesmen was sitting on my back with two hands on my shoulder pads, but I wasn't going anywhere. He had to climb over the boards to get between us. Then he tried to get his arms underneath mine to pull me off, but I was still not letting go. The other linesman was bending over Baumgartner, trying to drag him away from me underneath the bench. Finally, they managed to break it up. It's funny— Ken got up, and the back of his jersey was all shit-brown from the dirty floor of the penalty box. Nobody got hurt, though. I fought him a couple of times in the pros after that. He was always pretty tough.

I was escorted off, and that was it for my junior career, we lost 8–3 to the Raiders, who went on to beat Shawinigan 6–1 in the final. It was disappointing. I really thought we had a shot at winning the Memorial Cup that year.

6

SOMEBODY DO SOMETHING

In the summer of '85, I was having a pretty good camp with the Detroit Red Wings. I led the team in scoring in the intrasquad tournament and was the team's top scorer in the preseason. This was my third NHL camp, and by now I was starting to feel like I belonged at the pro level. Crispy had built me up, so I was trying harder. The first two times, I figured, "What the hell?" If I didn't make the Wings, I'd just go back to junior. This year, that was no longer an option.

Harry Neale was the coach in Detroit at that time. I don't think he and Jimmy D were all that concerned that I was a "troublemaker," but I worried I might get sent down to the American Hockey League because the Wings had three good left wingers ahead of me: John Ogrodnick, a fifty-goal scorer in 1984–85; Warren Young, a free agent they'd signed to a big-money contract after a breakout year in Pittsburgh; and Petr Klima, who had defected from Czechoslovakia that summer. I did get sent to Adirondack that fall, and my ego was sore. I was kind of crushed.

The Adirondack Red Wings played in Glens Falls, New York, about fifty miles north of Albany, in the eastern part of the state. I lived with our goalie, Chris Pusey (my Brantford teammate), and a defenceman, Dave Korol, in the upstairs of a house. I converted the dining room into my bedroom, and they always complained that it stunk like a cat box. Even though I was disappointed that I wasn't in The Show, I liked the minors. The bars were open until 4 A.M. and there was no pressure. Bill Dineen, our coach, played for Detroit in the '50s. He was a good guy.

We were in the North Division with Moncton, Fredericton, Halifax, Sherbrooke, and Portland, Maine, which meant there was lots of time for bar bonding on our road trips— we used to go up to the Maritimes and play Moncton twice, Halifax twice, Fredericton twice and then go home. We had a system: win a game, then go out and drink. The next day, we'd practise for a half an hour to forty-five minutes, and have a couple more that night. When I broke into the league, everybody was doing the liquid lunches. It was almost mandatory, like a team activity. On non-game days, we would go somewhere and have some beers. It was good for morale. It brought the team closer together. Now, everybody goes their separate ways.

I ended up splitting the 1985–86 season between Adirondack and Detroit. My first call-up was in the first week of November. The Wings hadn't turned it around yet—after twelve games, they only had one win. I guess they figured I couldn't hurt them any worse.

A lot of times, Mark LaForest (Trees) was called up with me. In his first week, some guys on the team grabbed him in the shower at Joe Louis Arena. They blindfolded him, stripped him down and tied him spread-eagle to a hotel luggage trolley. Oh yeah, naked, the whole nine yards. The other rookies couldn't do anything about this—they had to just sit there and watch. The guys shaved him head to toe and painted his toes with black paint. Then they kept going all the way up his leg so it looked like a barbershop pole. Trees just started singing "Jumpin' Jack Flash" at the top of his lungs, like nothing's bothering him at all.

Then they rolled him out to centre ice. All the cleaning ladies who were cleaning up the aisles and the rows between seats were making funny comments like, "You poor honey. It looks like you might be cold." Trees was still singing away and the vets were yelling, "We knew you'd like it, you freak!" The idea was to scare and intimidate the rookies, and here he was, singing the Stones the whole time, enjoying himself. I was so proud of him.

Finally, the veterans told us, "Okay, go get him." I came running onto the ice. "Trees! Way to go!" I untied his arms and legs and brought him back to the room, and we laughed about it. Because Trees was a goalie, the guy in charge of his hazing was veteran goalie Eddie Mio. So I got the idea we should shave Eddie. I said, "This is what we're going to do. I'll grab him and wrestle him down. There is no way he's going to get away from me."

Trees said, "I don't know, Bob. They are going to kill us."

I said, "Should we tie his legs up?"

Trees said, "I don't think so."

I said, "I'm serious."

"No, Bob, there is no way that this is going to happen."

Five minutes later, in the middle of the dressing room, I jumped on Eddie and put him down. I yelled, "Trees! I got him!" Trees was horrified. He said, "For God's sake, Bob, let him go!"

A couple of days later, Danny Gare and Dwight Foster went to Mio and said, "We're going to shave Bob Probert." And Eddie said, "Yeah, well, I'm not going to have anything to do with that." And they said, "C'mon you know him, he's from your hometown. Anyway, he tried to get you. Go in there and hold him down. We're not really going to shave him." So Eddie said, "I'll do that."

Eddie came up to me and said, "Bobby come over here, I need to talk to you." I walked over and we're talking when all of a sudden Eddie lunged at me and about five guys grabbed me from behind. I started to fight them off, but Eddie whispered, "Bobby, don't fight! And don't hit me, please! The guys are just trying to scare ya." So I settled down a bit, and they put me on the table and tied me up.

Then Dwight Foster took the razor and shaved me, and the boys gave me the same treatment with the paint that they gave Trees, except I didn't leave the locker room. When they were done, they all got the hell out of there. The trainer and the equipment manager ended up releasing me.

The next day we all had a laugh about it. It was water under the bridge. I was officially part of the team.

That season, I played 32 games in the AHL, scoring 12 goals and adding 15 assists; in Detroit, I got into 44 games, scoring 8 goals and assisting on 13.

And I had 152 penalty minutes in Adirondack and 186 with Detroit. I knew that if I wanted to stay in The Show, I would have to fight all the tough guys, and that is what I did. My third scrap in the NHL came in the first period of a game against the Flyers on December 14. I took on Dave Richter. He was a big southpaw—six foot five, 215. He was just there to fight. I did all right. Obviously, you try the best you can to ask the guy to acknowledge that you're going to fight him so that you don't jump him. For me, I just wanted an honest fight. You grab my arm, I grab yours, and we'll see who wins. That kind of thing. Some guys got dirty. They would pull hair or gouge your eyes. But in general, most of the heavyweights in the NHL were pretty good. Some of them would get into just tying up your arms and trying not to get hit and throwing a few punches to seem like they were in a fight. But most of them would stand back and throw punches. In the big scheme of things, I think the fans want to see two guys try and take each other out, not just dance around a little.

Then I had quite the battle with Rick Tocchet, who had twenty-three scraps that season. John Barrett, one of our big defencemen, hit Rich Sutter and put him right into the bench, and Rich's twin brother, Ron, took exception. It started a melee, and Tocchet and I went at it right in front of the penalty box. I was fighting fair, but Tocchet gave me a couple of headbutts. I returned the favour, so in the end it turned out to be a pretty fair fight. My brother, Norm, was up in the stands with his buddies. When he saw Tocchet give me the dirty shot, he ran all the way down, toward the penalty box. When he got there, he thought, "Well, what the hell am I going to do now?"

The team in Adirondack was a mix of career minor-leaguers (guys like Geordie Robertson and Ted Speers), guys near the end of their pro careers (Eddie Johnstone, Barry Melrose, Brett Callighen) and guys just starting out (me, Shawn Burr, Joey Kocur and Adam Oates). We finished first in our division, beating out the Maine Mariners by a point, and faced the Fredericton Express in the first round of the Calder Cup playoffs. In game one, their tough guy, Richard Zemlak, who put up 280 penalty minutes that year, was sent out to stir things up. I gave him a shot, but because the fight was over pretty quick, I didn't think he'd be back. In the second game, he came out and bumped into me, and then he decided he didn't want to go. But it was too late—I couldn't let him come at me and then let it go. It wouldn't have been good for my health in the future. This time, I didn't give him any room, so it was pretty one-sided. Afterward, he said he knew he looked bad and that people were calling him a gutless chicken. That's the pressure you deal with when you're a fighter.

We split the first two games in Glens Falls, then the Wings took game three in Freddy Beach. Two nights later, Fredericton was beating the heck out of us. Midway through the second period, we were down 5–1 when the coach pulled Trees. Pusey went in, and he played okay for a while, but in the third, Fredericton started pouring it on again. After scoring a goal, they skated by our bench, pumping their fists. I just hated that kind of cockiness. Less than a minute later, they popped in another one. So now it's 7–1, and here they come again, pumping their fists and taunting us. They were winning—why do that? Trees was standing on the back of our bench, going nuts. "Somebody do something! This can't happen! These sons-a-bitches. Somebody do something!"

I looked at their goalie, Frank Caprice. He was standing on his head. No way were we going to get anything past him. But somebody had to do something. I was coming off the bench and I saw their defenceman, Neil Belland, who actually played a bit with the Vancouver Canucks, with the puck. I chased him into the Fredericton end, and as he went around the net I cut close into Caprice. He went up against the crossbar. His gloves went one way, his stick went the other, his mask dropped, the net went flying, and he ended up on his back, spinning around on the ice. Belland turned around and came at me. I grabbed his head and put him under my arm. I had my back against the boards, waiting for somebody else to come. But nobody did. So I let Neil go and skated right over to the box. Not one of their guys touched me.

Caprice was carried out on a stretcher and I was suspended for the rest of the series by AHL president Jack Butterfield. Fredericton's coach, Andre Savard, complained about the cheap shot and goon tactics and all that. But to me, the problem was who they were. Not one guy on their team stuck up for Caprice.

So now the series was tied 2–2. We went back to Glens Falls and beat them 9–3. Caprice was pretty shaky that night. I don't think he could really see the puck yet, because he had been knocked out pretty good. And then we beat them 5–4 in their building in double overtime.

I didn't play in the semifinals against Moncton. I'd gotten a DUI back home in Windsor. I'd been celebrating when the cops pulled me over and threw me in jail for the night because they said my eyes were bloodshot, I smelled like alcohol and I was staggering. So I had to deal with that. Moncton was not a physical team, so I don't think Dineen was sweating it. He wanted me for the final against the Hershey Bears. They had a lot of tough guys.

We beat Moncton in five games, while the other semifinal, between Hershey and St. Catharines, went the full seven. That gave us six days off between games. Our coaches had a playoff rule—nobody was supposed to go to the bars. But during the layoff, Trees and I went drinking in a bar in Glens Falls, and guess who walked in? Coach.

The next day, Trees went up to Dineen to apologize. "Listen, I'm sorry. Bobby and I were out having a couple of drinks in the afternoon. It was beautiful out."

The coach said, "Okay, well, I caught seventeen guys yesterday."

The Hershey Bears kind of intimidated our team. They were Philadelphia's farm team. They hit more than us, there were some big guys there, and they had a lot of talent. For the first game in Hershey, they had something like eight thousand people in the arena. On the second shift, I went into the corner and Mike Stothers, who was a big defenceman, challenged me. I took him on. Their captain, Don Nachbaur, took exception, so on my next shift he challenged me in front of the Hershey bench.

The next day, a writer for the Glens Falls *Post-Star*, Gordon Woodworth, wrote that my "demolition" of Nachbaur gave our team "quite a bit of room to maneuver" in game two. They stopped hitting us. There were no more shenanigans after the whistle. And because our talent was better than their talent, we won the Calder Cup.

The night we won the Calder Cup, there was a huge celebration. People were handing us Champagne bottles on the ice. We all ended up at this bar called the Trading Post. Trees had to piss, but when he got to the washroom, there was somebody in there. He started banging on the door. After a while, this big guy came out and gave him a look. About an hour later, when Trees was headed out, this big guy he interrupted in the bathroom was standing by the door. So Trees came up to me and said, "Probie, see that guy over there? The one who looks like a fridge, with muscles everywhere?"

I said, "Yeah."

"He's going to kill me."

I said, "Oh really?"

So I said to the guy, "You got a problem with Trees?"

He said, "Yeah, I do. What's your problem?"

I took out my teeth and put them in my pocket. And I go, "Okay, let's go, Hulk Hogan."

A bunch of us went out into the street. I didn't want to get suspended, so I let him give me five or six good ones in the face. Then I grabbed him, strung him out and said, "Everybody see he hit me first?" I ended up submitting him into the ground. My buddy and teammate, Shawn Burr, said it was scary. I found my jacket and went back inside for another beer. Later, I stopped by the hospital for a couple of stitches. Taking care of my teammates was my job, on and off the ice.

The first time I ever did cocaine was that night we were celebrating the Calder Cup championship. I had always been scared of it. I'd heard what it could do to your brain, so I had stayed away. But while we were out, one of the players said, "Come in the bathroom, I want you to try something."

I was like, "Nah, I don't do that."

He kept it up. "Come on, you'll love it. It'll sober you up and make you feel good!"

"No, no. I'm good."

Later on, at the end of the night, we went to another guy's place and he said, "Bob, come with me." We went upstairs. By this time I've got a buzz, so I'm not as scared of it. We went into his bedroom and a bunch of lines were all set up on his dresser. He handed me a rolled-up bill and I did some lines. It was an instant love. Oh yeah. I had been kind of slurring a little bit from drinking, but all of a sudden, I wasn't as messed up. And it gave me this energy. I felt like Superman. It was just like, "Wow! This is awesome!" I went back an hour later and asked him for more. "Have you got any more of that stuff?" But no, he was out.

I was staying at the Queensbury Hotel in Glens Falls. (I had given up my apartment with Pusey and Korol.) I got back to the hotel and went over to the lady at the front desk—she was a little older than me—and I said, "Hey, do you know where I can get any cocaine around here?" It was just as if I was asking her where to buy a toothbrush. She gave me this look and shook her head. "Uh no, I don't know anybody." But that's how it was, after the first time. I wanted more.

The next day, I was getting a ride back to Detroit with an older player. One of the younger guys was following us to the highway. We were going west and he was headed north. We got to the junction and pulled over to the shoulder. The older guy pulled out a package and split the Baggie in half with the younger guy. We had a full day's drive ahead of us, so the older guy wanted to do a line before we hit the interstate. He looked at me. "Hey Bob, do you want some?" I had been thinking all morning about how good it had felt the night before, so I said, "Sure." When you do coke sober, you notice this weird taste in your mouth. I started spitting, but the older guy told me, "No! Don't spit. Let it drain down, get in your system." I did what he said, but I remember wanting to spit in the worst way.

We won the final game of the Calder Cup series on May 21, 1986. By the twenty-eighth, the Red Wings organization had heard about my DUI and set it up for me to go into rehab. And they were putting it on my bill. I didn't think I had a problem. I just knew if I didn't go, there would be consequences. The date was delayed when it turned out that I had mononucleosis and strep throat.

I went home for the summer. I was living at my mother's, so

there wasn't much opportunity there to do drugs. My friends in Windsor were not into coke by any means, but we did all like to party. On July 2, I was drinking with my hockey buddy, J.D. Urbanic—he was playing for the Spitfires and had been drafted by Boston—at Tune-Ups Tavern. It was closing time, 1:25 A.M., and the waitress asked us to leave. We ignored her and kept drinking, and security called the cops. I was arrested for assaulting a cop. J.D. was charged with obstructing police.

On July 22, I felt better and finally tested negative for mono. They sent me to the Hazelden Foundation in Center City, Minnesota, a facility that was used a lot by other professional sports teams and athletes. I met a girl at the airport who was going there too. She was young, in her twenties, blonde, good-looking. They picked us up in a van and I got to know her a bit during the trip. It's funny—when you first go there, they separate you immediately for orientation, but for the first five days, you're all together, so I hung around with this female.

There was a nice walking path in the forest there. One day, we came up to this big, black ash that had been struck by lightning, and we decided to lie down on it and start making out. One thing led to another, and we did it right on the trunk. And then the second time was, like, stupid. We decided to do it by the side of the walking path. It was crazy, because all of a sudden we heard people coming, and we had to dive into the bushes. We didn't get caught, but she told this chick, who said she was going to tell on us if my girl didn't get honest. So she got honest. A couple of the staff came to my building and said, "We have reason to believe you had sex with one of our female clients." So they moved me to another place in Minnesota. I didn't think it was fair. I didn't have a chance to get honest. All of a sudden, they just showed up.

I remember leaving in the van, and there was that blonde, watching me go, while she got to stay. I'm like, "Bitch." She was pretty hot. She'd had a big diamond ring on, and said she was married to a guy whose parents were rich in the sports world. I read about their divorce in the paper the next year. It was a big scandal in the States. They had a terrible custody battle, and she "got honest" about his cocaine abuse and received a ton of money.

I spent another month at Abbott-Northwestern Hospital in Minneapolis. They didn't credit me with the week I'd done at Hazelden, which I thought was brutal. The spin in the media about my moving was that Hazelden didn't have a good enough gym. We were up at six-thirty, and then there was a lecture from nine until nine-thirty, group therapy from ten till eleven-thirty, and then lunch. Group again from one to two in the afternoon, then family sessions. The papers were all over it. The team was talking about how I had turned things around, and how I had to take it one day at a time and all that bullshit. I went along with it. No way was I going to sabotage my chance to go to training camp in September.

Hazelden wasn't so bad because I had started a thing with a good-looking staff member there. She was hot and blonde. When I got released, she flew home with me. I brought her to my mother's place to stay for a week. My mom really liked her. I didn't make out with her until we got back home. We dated for a little while, but it didn't last long.

The Wings continued to arrange press interviews for me

where I'd talk to these guys and say things like, "I was really close to throwing it all away. I am just lucky Detroit stuck by me." I thought having this kind of stuff on the record would be helpful in my future court dates. I was also worried about getting my driver's licence suspended for a year. That would mean I wouldn't be able to drive the new Monte Carlo SS I had bought for $22,000 with my signing bonus.

7

LET'S DO IT AGAIN

In October 1986, I was sentenced to two years' probation for assaulting a Windsor police officer the night I refused to leave Tune-Ups Tavern. But there was a provision that, if I didn't drink in that time, my record would be erased. But those two arrests became a huge headache. In November, after losing 2–0 to the Leafs, my teammate Petr Klima and I were stopped at the airport by some uptight customs officials. Klima had defected from Czechoslovakia the year before, and he didn't have his travel visa with him. And because I was on probation, I was on a temporary visa, which I didn't have with me, so I had to wait to get it sent up. Pricks.

That whole year was fun, but I got into a lot of trouble. I was red-flagged at customs, red-flagged with the Windsor police, and red-flagged with the Wings. Starting with training camp. I injured a knee and then had arthroscopic surgery after I'd gone out for a shift and the thing just locked on me. They operated on it and trimmed out the cartilage. Two weeks later, I was back playing. It was good for about ten years and then they had to do it again.

One night in December of '85, Trees and I were in Quebec City for a game. Neither of us had been there before. Trees said, "Listen, Bobby, I'm not playing tomorrow. But you know, they've got a real good team with Peter and Anton Stastny and Michel Goulet. So let's take it easy tonight. No more than six or seven beers with dinner."

We went to this great restaurant. We had some beers and we were out of there by nine-thirty. The snow was falling, so we went for a walk. We heard a band playing Led Zeppelin music and went into the club to check it out. I went up to the bar to grab us a couple of Jack and Cokes each, and Trees ordered four beers from the waitress. One thing led to another and we ended up getting back to our rooms at 4:30 A.M. There was a note on the door: CALL THE COACH.

I crumpled it up, but there were more. One on the light switch, the pillows on the beds, the phone and the night stands.

Trees said, "Oh God."

The next morning, we went down to breakfast not feeling so hot. We probably had a stench on us. Harry Neale was our coach and Colin Campbell, who we called Soupy, the assistant. Neale said, "You two, come here."

Trees said, "Bobby, let me do the talking."

Neale looked at Trees and said, "Where were you last night?"

Trees said, "Out."

Neale looked at me, "Where were *you* last night, Bobby?"

Trees said, "Out."

Neale said, "What time did you get home?"

Trees said, "Late."

Neale said, "Well, you weren't in your rooms at one-thirty."

Trees said, "Well, it was later than that."

Neale said, "Okay, that's $300 each, and by the way, Trees, you're playing today."

We won 5–4. Trees was the first or second star, and I got a goal and an assist and did all right in a fight. The next night, we got on a plane to go to Hartford and ordered two beers. As we were cracking them, I said to Trees, "Let's do it again."

I was twenty and I thought I was invincible. In December 1986, very close to Christmas, a hockey buddy and I went drinking at a place called Peachy's in Windsor. We left there and started hitting all the Windsor bars—at least five different ones. We were doing shooters and schnapps and got completely wasted. We made it to my car and I drove my buddy home to Detroit. Then I headed back through the tunnel to Windsor, although I don't remember coming across.

I stopped at a light at the intersection of Ouellette and Wyandotte, and there was a car beside me. The police report said the driver claimed I definitely looked intoxicated. I guess I was slumped forward with my head bowed and my eyes half-open. This fucking other driver squealed his tires and took off at the green. I floored it and it was like I was in a dream. I was floating along, watching him go, and then all of a sudden hitting the brakes, *eaarrrrrk!!* The other driver said I swerved around a parked cab on the side of the road, cut it hard and went across the road into the other lane. He said I overcorrected, and that's how I ended up on the curb and *boom!*—straight into a concrete utility pole on the driver's side. The pole broke and landed right on top of the car. You should have seen my Monte Carlo. It was completely wrecked.

Apparently, a couple of guys pulled me out and laid me down on the sidewalk. I remember being loaded into the ambulance on one of those flat boards. The paramedics were tickling my feet to see if I was paralyzed. I asked the ambulance driver, "What did I hit? Was anybody hurt?" He told me, "Nah, you hit a pole."

They took me to the hospital and left me sitting on one of those doctors' benches in emergency. I remember thinking, "I only have one shoe on." The doctor came in and patched me up. I had separated some cartilage in my rib cage and had cuts on my face. When he finished stitching my face, I said to him, "Can I go now?" He said, "Yeah, go ahead, but don't tell anybody I said okay." There had been cops stationed outside the door, so I got up and opened it a crack. They were gone. I swung it wide and looked down the hall. Not there either. I beat it out of there, hobbling as fast as I could go, and I almost made it. I grabbed the big door, opened it and I heard, "Hey, where do you think you're going?" The two cops caught up to me and took me downtown, where they tried to get me to blow. I was still pretty pissed and hurting pretty good. In their report, they said I kept telling them to fuck off before I finally agreed to take a Breathalyzer test. The legal limit was .08 and I blew .17.

I spent the night in the cooler. They let me out at 8 A.M. Meanwhile, Jim Lites, a lawyer who worked in the Wings' front office, had heard about the incident. I was supposed to see him as soon as they let me out. I walked into his office and he told me to sit down. I did, and he started ripping me a new one—for an hour. Just yelling at me, telling me how much of an asshole I was, that I was an embarrassment, and I made the Wings look bad, which was all true. But it wasn't like, "Hey Bob, glad you're alive." It's was like, fucking, *boom!* "Now get the hell out of here."

Good to see you too, Jimmy.

The Wings suspended me indefinitely because of the DUI charge. Stevie Y was a pretty straight shooter, and when I would do something that got in the news like this, he'd give me this look like, "What the fuck are you doing, Probie?" But he would step up for me over and over again. He told the papers that whenever we went out, he never saw me drink anything stronger than club soda and that the team was not going to bail out on me, because I was his friend.

So now I had two trials in January—one for this latest incident and one for the DUI in April, just before the Calder Cup. Donnie Meehan was my lawyer and my agent for my first contract. He was good, but I needed a trial lawyer.

My dad had had a good buddy, Don Wiley. He was a detective on the Windsor police force. They'd ridden Harleys together in the traffic division. Don kind of kept an eye on Norm and me after Dad died. Jim Lites and Colin Campbell called Don, and he said there was one guy who could get me off, and that was Pat Ducharme. Don said Pat was one of those lawyers everybody in the police department hated because he had so much skill. So I hired him to help me out.

Wings coach Jacques Demers lifted my suspension on Christmas Eve after a face-to-face. He was touchy about the subject. He had just done a commercial against drunk drivers, and five years before he'd lost his best friend to drunk driving. I felt bad, so I promised him I would never drink again.

In the middle of January, I was fined a grand and had my driver's licence suspended after pleading guilty to the utility-pole incident where I refused the Breathalyzer. I testified in that case. I got on the stand, and the prosecutor was pretty good. His cross-examination went something like, "Mr. Probert, you are known in the NHL as a real tough person, aren't you?"

I said, "Yes, I am."

He said, "As a matter of fact, I have read articles that have said you are the heavyweight champ of the NHL, if there can be such a term."

I said, "Yeah, I've heard that too."

He said, "If guys on the hockey rink try to take you on, it's not likely that there is anybody in the NHL that is ever going to seriously give you a run for your money because you are so tough."

I said, "Oh, there are some tough guys there, but I do all right."

He said, "And similarly, when the police officers come at you, if you don't want to go in a room and they want you to go in a room, and if you don't want to blow in a hose when they tell you to blow in a hose, there is no police officer alive that is going to physically make you do that, is there?"

I said, "You're probably right."

He said, "In this case, we understand, there were six officers who couldn't make you even go into the room to take the test. Would you agree with that?"

I said, "I'd say so, yeah."

When I left court, I turned to Pat Ducharme and said, "I wasn't very good, was I?"

Ducharme said, "As a witness in a criminal trial? No, not especially good—that is, unless you were auditioning for *Saturday Night Live*."

I was convicted for that one. At the end of the case, the judge said, "If telling the police officers collectively to fuck off nineteen times is not a refusal, what on earth is?"

At the end of January, I was acquitted of the impaired-driving charge from the previous spring, but I had to pay two grand and my licence was suspended for a year for failing to take a Breathalyzer. The prosecution wanted to send me to jail, but Ducharme hired a forensic science specialist from Toronto named Rita Charlebois. In the incident from April, I had knocked back maybe five Molson Lights at the bar in about two hours. She testified that because I was six foot three and weighed 210, that wouldn't be enough to make me impaired. The judge understood, and I stayed out of prison— for the time being.

8

THE PIZZA'S GONE,
AND SO ARE YOU

On January 25, 1987, we were starting a stretch of four days
between games, and the New York Giants were playing the
Denver Broncos in the Super Bowl. I started watching the
game at home, but it sucked being alone. The Super Bowl was
a big deal to me. There were three times I always got to get
drunk. My birthday, Christmas and the Super Bowl. I just had
to. Those were my requirements. So I met some friends at a
bar. I decided to take it easy and not drink. It was stupid to go
to bars, because someone would always say, "Come on, Bob,
have a shot," and I would be like, "No, no, I'm not drinking."
And they'd say, "Just one beer," and I'd say, "Okay," and then
I'd have to hide it from the team. It was just a whole, big circle.

I don't think it affected my hockey. A lot of people thought
I played better when I was boozing. In the times when I'd get
straight, I'd hear, "He doesn't seem as mean, he's on too even
a keel."

This particular Super Bowl Sunday, I only had a couple of rum and Cokes. I really behaved myself. But my life was under a microscope. Somebody recognized me and blew the whistle.

Jacques Demers had been good to me. I got lots of ice time. He played me on the first or second line. He was a very verbal coach. Some of us thought that his "Hurrah, hurrah, go get 'em, guys!" chant, day after day, got kind of old. But I liked that he didn't use a lot of videos. He was old-school. His dad had been an alcoholic, and he was always telling me about that. He really wanted to connect with me, so at one point, right after we had won a big game where I had done all right, Jacques and I had a couple of beers.

Pat Ducharme called Jacques up and said, "Why did you do that? Now he feels that even you think it's okay."

Jacques told him, "I don't know, Patty, I don't think he's an alcoholic. I mean, he was fine. He had a couple of beers and he was fine."

After the Super Bowl thing ended up in the paper, Jacques called me in and told me I had to go to rehab—this would be my third time. I told him that if I wanted a beer, it was my fucking business, but he said if I didn't go, I didn't play, and to top it all off, my rehab bill was going to come to three grand. Fuck!

On February 11, 1987, I entered Brentwood Recovery Home for alcoholics in Windsor, which was run by a hard-nosed priest named Reverend Paul Charbonneau. Father Paul, he didn't powder anyone's ass. The Wings had arranged for me to enter the program on a work release, so I could play. I lived at the centre, but they let me out for games and practices.

About a month later, during a game with the Minnesota North Stars, Joey Kocur scored for us in the first minute. A couple of minutes later, I picked up the puck and headed in. Frank Musil hauled me down, and the ref gave me a penalty shot on their goalie, Kari Takko. I was so nervous, it was brutal.

I started a few steps away from centre ice, took five strides and played with it a bit while bringing it in over the blue line on my backhand and crossing over to my left. There were two places I was going to shoot—either up on his glove hand, or his five-hole. I picked the five-hole, moved it to my forehand and fired a wrist shot. Takko slammed his pads together, but was too late. The puck bounced off one pad, and I got lucky—it squeaked through on the left. Let me tell you, it was a rush.

I ended up getting kicked out of Brentwood for breaking the rules. Sometimes I got special treatment in rehab. Counsellors would hit me up for tickets. I'd come back late, but that would be okay as long as I gave them an autograph for some kid who was going to come by at noon or something.

But Father Paul did not like my attitude, and it didn't help that I stopped by a strip joint in Windsor. You really shouldn't do that when you are in rehab. I met a couple of French sisters who were dancers. We got to talking, and one gave me her number and said to call her. So I did. I took her out for dinner at this place downtown. She ordered vodka and orange juice and said, "Aren't you going to drink?" I said, "You know what? I've got to drive tonight. Maybe I will later." I didn't want her to know why I wasn't drinking, right? She might not think it was cool if I said, "I'm sorry, I'm an alcoholic," you know? So I played it like I was driving and I didn't want to get a ticket. We went to a bar, and she ordered a pitcher of beer. She poured hers and then she poured one for me. It was just sitting there, getting warm, and I'm thinking, "Okay, I'll just pretend." But before you knew it, there was another pitcher and I had a pretty good buzz on.

The last straw came one night a couple of us were kind of hungry, so I ordered a pizza. Someone knocked on the door to my room. It was Father Paul, holding this pizza up on his shoulder. He chucked it back over his shoulder, onto the floor, and said, "The pizza's gone, and so are you."

I couldn't believe it when I was picked to play in the NHL All-Star Game on January 20, 1988. The headline in *The Windsor Star* said, ALL-STAR SELECTION PUTS PROBERT ON CLOUD NINE, and for once they got it right.

Right after it was announced, I was in Windsor one night, and I went to cross the border for practice in the morning. One guy wouldn't let me through, so I called Pat Ducharme, who came down but still had a tough time convincing them that all charges in the U.S. had been taken care of and that everything was fine. Pat got me cleared and we arrived at practice late. I got dressed, took out my front teeth and skated on. But I stopped to tell Pat to talk to the coach and explain why I was late. Everyone was all sweaty, but I was still dry, and Soupy skated by and said, "Come on, Probie! Geez, you missed the whole practice and you're standing there like an idiot. Get to work." I looked at him and I said, "I'm thaving mythelf for the All-Thtar Game."

That game was one of the career highlights for me. It was in St. Louis. I couldn't believe some of the people on the ice—Mario Lemieux, who had six points, Mats Naslund, five assists; Denis Savard, a goal and two assists; Dale Hawerchuk, two assists and a goal; and Wayne Gretzky, who scored at 18:46 of the first, a goal I assisted on. A year earlier, if you had told me that was a possibility, I would have laughed in your face. What a rush.

At the end of March, I got a letter from Jimmy D that said, "I am very pleased to tell you that you have reached the third plateau of your 'Special Incentives' bonuses for the 1987–88 season. When you reached 60 points your salary was increased to $150,000 for the season." (This was a bonus of $65,000 on top of my regular salary of $85,000.)

His letter added, "Bob, I can't begin to tell you how happy we all are with the season you are having. Making the NHL all-star team was an honour I am sure you will never forget."

I think I just happened to be in the NHL at the perfect time for my style of play. I didn't like to instigate, but I did like protecting my teammates.

It helps if you like the guys. My role was simple: "Nothing happens to Stevie." I didn't necessarily hang around with the guys on the team. I kind of went my own way, and I got into trouble. Maybe at that time, I should have been hanging with the players a little more. But Stevie and I were friends. He was a nice guy. Really nice, classy guy. He genuinely cared about his teammates.

I think playing with Stevie was like playing with Joe Sakic, only Stevie was a lot more outgoing and more business-minded than Joe. Joe is just a good guy and doesn't care about anything other than playing the game and his family.

Stevie was pissed at times when I'd get in trouble, because I played on his line. But I always thought that was understandable. I was amazed at the talent Stevie had. For his size, as opposed to a Lemieux, he was unparalleled. Stevie would do anything for the team. That's why he was such a great leader. He'd go down and block shots, so it was easy for the coach to say to a guy on the fourth line, "How come you're not blocking shots, when our best player is lying on the ice in front of pucks that are coming at a hundred miles an hour?" He'd go into the corners. He'd do what ever it took to win. When Scotty Bowman took over, he asked Yzerman to forget about scoring and play more defence. People thought Stevie was gonna ruffle some feathers and demand to be traded. But no. He figured Scotty Bowman's got maybe ten Stanley Cup rings. He must be doing something right. And they ended up winning. That's amazing when you are a fifty-goal scorer and you are told to go on the checking line—and you do it.

I played with a guy who was always in my ear. "Hey Probie, did you see that guy go after Stevie? You should go out there." And this guy was a fairly big guy. One time, I turned to him and I said, "Your gloves glued on?" I never liked players who would go and stir the pot, and then run away when it came time to face the music.

The fights I did best in were the ones I was truly mad and upset. I didn't like going out and instigating. I didn't enjoy the idea of having to go out and fight this or that guy tonight because he had a rep. It was a lot of pressure.

I used to get pissed off when the fights weren't clean, like fighting with Brian Curran, who everybody called The Colonel. We had five scraps—1986, 1987 and three in 1988. First of all, he'd wear a mask, so I would cut the shit out of my hands, and then when the fight was over and he was down, I'd go to skate away and he'd grab for my ankles. I mean, what are you trying to prove? The fight is over, you lost, take it like a man. There's no need for that. If you are a professional hockey player, you're supposed to have a little bit of pride, not do something stupid like that.

I had a philosophy when a guy took a dive on me. Next time, you won't need to be diving, because it's really going to hurt.

In October of 1987, Dave Semenko jumped me in a game in Toronto. Earlier in the game, I had scrapped with Wendel Clark, and it was a little one-sided. Wendel had to grab the ref's jersey as he was skating off. He had a lot of pride—no way was he gonna be carried off.

It was Semenko's job to take care of things, but he didn't do it the proper way. I moved in front of the net on a play, and he came from behind. He suckered me, then tied up my sweater. I was trying to get out of it when Mike Cvik, the tallest linesman in the league, moved in. Semenko was still throwing them, but Cvik was holding me and I couldn't get an arm loose. I was yelling at him, "Let me go! Let me go!" Everybody got into it—Gallant jumped in, Yzerman tried to help out, lots of guys were there. After the fight, I remember Demers yelling at the ref and tugging on the back of his collar, which was a signal

With my mom and older brother, Norm, in Windsor, August 1965.

My dad, Al Probert (right, in helmet), was the family's original tough guy.

My grandfather, Papa Jack, was always there for us. He took my brother Norm (left) and me to our lacrosse games.

I was always
a left winger,
even as a kid.

One of my first media
interviews, with my
teammate Marc West
(centre), with interview-
er Arnold Anderson at
the Civic Centre
Auditorium in
Brantford, Ontario.

At the draft in Montreal in 1983 just after the Detroit Red Wings called my name.

Goofing around with Petr Klima. We had a lot of fun together.

Courtesy Dani Probert

I was always honoured to wear the A on my sweater. Here I am getting patched up as our captain, Stevie Yzerman, looks on.

Courtesy Mary Schroeder/Detroit Free Press

With Shawn Burr (left), Joe Murphy and Steve Chiasson. Most of the Red Wings got red-and-white "rally cuts" just before the 1988 playoffs.

Courtesy Dani Probert

My Monte Carlo
in an accident
in 1985. I made
it out with only
a few scratches,
bruised ribs and
a black eye.

Shane Churla
and I got into
three scraps over
the years.

Courtesy Richard A. Margittay

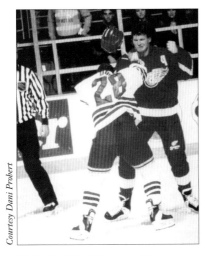

Fighting Tie Domi on December 2, 1992. Domi was tough to fight, but his big head made a good target.

Fighting Tony Twist of the Quebec Nordiques on October 30, 1993. Tony packed a good right punch and could take one, too.

My technique was to get a hold of a guy's sweater and then string him out. Here I am up against Stu Grimson on October 8, 1993.

Getting ready to go with a couple of Leafs, including their goalie, Ken Wregget.

It looks like I had reached my boiling point with Jay Caufield of the Penguins, November 13, 1992.

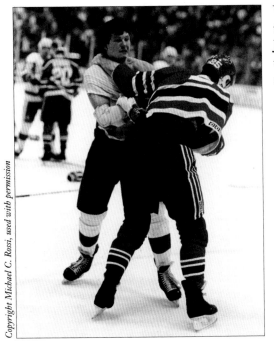

Versus Troy Crowder of the New Jersey Devils, January 28, 1991. Troy was a good fighter and an honest guy.

Up against Jeff Chychrun, January 15, 1989. He was a good fighter and had the intimidation factor with his size and reach.

Sometimes the refs came in too early.

that meant "dirty move." I wasn't worried—Semenko was still playing. I looked forward to meeting him again.

There wasn't a buildup for the next time, like there would be with Domi, but when Semenko came back to Detroit in January, I'm sure a lot of people knew what was going to happen. The play was in Toronto's end, and was going to our end. Semenko was the last man to leave his own zone, so I hung around. I was ready to return the favour from the last game. He tried to get my shirt off, but I got one arm out and tagged him a couple of times. I knew it was over and stood back, and as the ref came in, Semenko was on one knee. He went to get up, but he was hurt, or stunned, and that was pretty much it for him. He didn't play too many more after that.

9

PROBERT . . . YOU IDIOT

I had a little trouble staying current with my probation requirements, so the Wings cut a deal with a judge that I would spend one night in jail. They didn't tell me, because they were afraid I would disappear. Assistant coach Colin Campbell phoned me up and said, "I'll pick you up at 8 A.M. Have a suit and tie on."

I said, "Where are we going?"

Soupy said, "I'm not telling you. Just have a suit and tie on and be ready."

So the next morning, I got into his car and he said, "Okay, look. We're going to see a judge. We've cut a deal. You're going to spend one night in jail."

I said, "Oh, that's just fucking bullshit!"

He said, "We've cut a quiet deal. The media doesn't know. The judge is going to clear out the courtroom and all you are going to do is spend one night in jail. I brought some stuff for you. Sweats and a toothbrush."

So we appeared in front of the judge, and he says, "Mr. Probert, I don't agree with this, I feel your punishment should be much harsher, but we're going to have you spend one night in jail for breaching your probation. What do you have to say for yourself, Mr. Probert?"

And I said, "Well, I think it's a joke, Your Honour!"

Soupy looked really choked and he whispered, "Probert . . . you idiot."

The judge looked up from his binder and said, "You think it's a joke, Mr. Probert?"

I was trying to step away from Soupy because he was kicking me, and I said, "Well, I don't think it's right. They didn't tell me about this."

The judge said something like, "Mr. Probert, I'm allowing this deal against my better wishes. But I know you will be back here. You'll screw up again. So for now, you'll spend one night in jail. Now get out of here."

It turned out okay. I ended up playing cards with the guys in the jail. They were all really cool.

Soupy was assigned to work with me full time. He was helping me stay in shape. He was always riding me. We would practise skating in the morning, and I didn't have a washing machine, so sometimes I didn't have underwear. So I'd get Soupy to give me a pair of his. One morning, Soupy came in, and I was sitting there eating a burger from Wendy's. He got upset and said, "Probe, I've had it with you. You don't wash your underwear. You're eating a burger, you're not taking this serious, and I've just had it!"

And this buddy who was kind of a fan happened to come up and he said, "Probie! How are you doing?"

I said, "I'm pretty good."

And this buddy said, "You're the greatest."

Soupy said, "Why are you saying stuff like that to Probe? He's a mess."

My buddy said, "God gave him gifts. He's the man!"

Soupy said, "You're right. God did make him, because no man could create such a piece of shit like this."

I thought that was harsh, so I got a little upset. I said, "Hey Soupy, you could always take me?"

Soupy said, "Sure, I'll box you." Soupy had played for the Penguins, Oilers, Canucks and Wings and had done a little bit of boxing back then. But he was about ten years older than me. So we went down to the dressing room, moved the benches, put the gloves on and had three one-minute rounds. At the start of each round, I'd drill him in the head and he'd try to paste his forehead on my chest.

The next day at the game, Soupy had two black eyes and Gerard Gallant looked at him and said, "Geez, Collie, did you not sleep last night?"

We always had a lot of free time at the airport, so I'd do my dollar-bill trick—you know, tie it onto a thread and throw it out there. Somebody would walk by and notice—usually a little kid or an older person—and I'd reel them in. Then you'd give them the bill so there were no hard feelings. We always had a lot of fun.

In 1988, I had the best playoffs of my life, with 21 points, enough to break the team record that Gordie Howe set back in 1955—ten years before I was born. Yzerman's knee was hurt, so I got to play on the top line with a few different guys, including John Chabot and Petr Klima. Every night before the games, our line would go out and have a couple of beers. We beat Toronto and St. Louis, and then in round three, the conference finals, we were up against Edmonton. We were playing awesome, but the Oilers were a powerhouse, with Wayne Gretzky, Mark Messier, Jari Kurri, Glenn Anderson, Grant Fuhr—all five in the Hall of Fame—plus Esa Tikkanen, Craig Simpson, Steve Smith, Marty McSorley, Jeff Beukeboom, Kevin Lowe, Bill Ranford and Craig McTavish. Just a killer lineup. They ended up winning the Cup that year and the next. We were down 3–1 in the series and facing elimination. But the night of game five, a few of us did the typical thing—went out for some beers. Someone suggested a popular club called Goose Loonies.

The front office was positive I was not drinking. Three players on the team, including me, were on a drug called disulfiram or Antabuse. It's for alcoholics—it makes you throw up if you drink. But what I would do was go into Colin Campbell's office and switch the pills with Bayer Aspirin that I took from our trainer's room. I'd open up the bottle of Aspirin and dump them into the Antabuse container. Come to think of it, any poor bastard feeling sore who popped an Aspirin from the trainer's room must have wondered why he puked when he went home and had a beer with the family that night.

Every morning, I'd go in to see Colin and he'd say, "Okay, open up!" and throw a pill in my mouth. I'd go *ahhh* and I'd swallow it. When Demers asked Soupy, "Are you sure Probie's not drinking? Come on, he smells like booze today," Soupy would say, "There's no way he can be drinking. I watched him take his Antabuse."

The night before the Edmonton game, the coaches checked for curfew and found there were a bunch of guys still out. Neil Smith, our assistant general manager, and Soupy asked the guy at the front desk the same question we asked him— "What's the happening bar in town?" Next thing you know, they showed up at Goose Loonies. Soupy looked at us and said, "You guys need to get back to the hotel now!" I had a buzz on, but I walked outside with them and said, "Okay, guys, we'll be back at the hotel in just a minute. Here, I got your cab," and like an asshole, I threw some money in the cab. We stayed for another couple of drinks and then went back to the hotel.

The problem started the next morning at breakfast. We had a centre by the name of Brent Ashton who went off on Petr Klima in the restaurant. He started yelling, "What the fuck is wrong with you, taking Probie out? He's got enough shit going on, and you're taking him out and getting him drunk! Come on, what the hell are you thinking?"

Keith Gave was this asshole who wrote a column for the *Detroit Free Press.* We never got along because he was always one of those reporters that was just waiting for something, so he could report the shit, you know? The negative stuff. He was sitting in there having breakfast, but now he's got wind of this story. He goes to Jacques Demers, our coach, and says, "Hey, I heard some of the boys were out drinking last night." And Jacques, who was probably worried about his own ass, should have shut the hell up and said, "There's no truth to that." But no—he threw us under the bus. That way, if we lose, it's not his fault, because the guys were out drinking, right? He called a meeting and he says, "Guys, if you win tonight's playoff game, going out might be on the back page. But if you lose, it'll be front page."

Sure enough, we lost, and it was front-page news. And Jacques was all over it. Of course, I was the ringleader, right? Jacques said we cheated our fans, and he told *The Windsor Star,* "They made Bob Probert a hero in Detroit. I hope the next time he steps on the ice he doesn't get an ovation, because he doesn't deserve it." He went on and on. One of our defence-men, Lee Norwood, piped up as usual. He said, "It's going to be up to Petr Klima and Bob Probert to get geared to the rules or they won't be with the Detroit Red Wings." Norwood wound up ending his career with a plate and eight screws in his ankle when his Harley fell on him. Karma is a bitch.

The papers were calling, and everybody was acting all freaked out. "Fuck it," I thought, and I packed a bag and took off in my 'Vette to Daytona Beach with my buddy.

After the Goose Loonies incident, the team was telling me I had to go into rehab again. I told them, "No way. I just got a boat and a new car and I've been in rehab three summers in a row!"

The Monte Carlo was living in some guy's wrecking yard, so I went out and bought a Corvette convertible, triple-black— you know, roof, body, interior. I was twenty-three and it was the cat's ass. I loved that 'Vette, but it attracted a little too much attention, especially from the cops. I'd make a left turn and I'd get a ticket.

That same summer, I bought a thirty-one-foot Formula 311—an offshore racer. It looked like something out of *Miami Vice* because it had what they called a Palm Springs paint job— white with hot pink and turquoise and black. We'd take 'er out on Lake Erie and go freighter-wake jumping. Out there, you can get a good ten-to-twelve-foot wave off a freighter. What you want to do is catch the top of the wave in the middle of the boat, because that's when you run. The whole boat would launch, just grabbing air. Lake Erie is such a large lake that it has big, big waves. The troughs open up, so when you come off one you are flying. We could get that whole thirty-one-footer up out of the water with both the props spinning in midair. It's a rush—a natural high.

I started running into people who did cocaine. Once you are on the train, you see the stuff everywhere. Most parties I would go to, most bars, people were in the can, doing it. Lots of guys had it on them. It was amazing. Not on the team, though. Cocaine was magic. You could drink more and still stay pretty straight. I liked not getting stupid, but still getting a buzz from the alcohol.

I was making about eighty grand a year, but my expenditures were high. I'd spent $80,000 on the boat, $33,000 on the 'Vette, and I started buying cocaine by the ounce—twenty-eight grams for $800 a week, which is forty-two grand a year. I spent all of my savings.

In September 1988, Petr Klima, who was a pretty good buddy, and I got suspended. I'd been sent down to Adirondack and fined $200 a couple of days before because we had missed a team bus and a flight from Chicago to Detroit for a game. Petr and I were at my house the night before, and we were supposed to report the next day by 11 A.M. We stayed up late, so we called up and postponed our first flight. It was time to leave for the second one, but we postponed it again. We headed out to catch the next one, but got held up at the titty bar near the airport. We finally got on the last plane, but didn't get in until about 12:30 A.M., so the team left us a message on our phones, saying, "Don't bother staying. You're suspended. Go back home."

I think they were stricter about being late in the minors than they were in The Show. One time, Trees was sent down at the same time I was. We were flying out of Detroit on the red-eye. He met me at my mom's house in Windsor because he didn't have a car. I was packing, and he kept saying, "Bobby, we can't be late."

I said, "No problem. No problem."

But he was sweating it and I still had stuff to do. So I said, "Listen, my brother, Norm, will give you a ride. I'll meet you at the airport."

He said, "You're not going to be late?"

I said, "No, no, I'll be on time."

Trees and Norm took off. They got to the Windsor–Detroit border, but Norm-bo had forgotten to bring his ID.

Finally, Trees convinced immigration to let Norm drive him to the airport. But they had taken so long to get through that I was already on the plane, ready to go. When the pilot announced we were leaving, I got out of my seat, ran down the jet bridge, and up to the gate. The agent at the gate was shutting the door, so I stuck my arm through the crack at the last minute. This made her pretty mad. She was yelling, "Sir! You must remove your arm! We cannot take off until I close the gate."

I said, "I know, but we gotta wait for Trees!"

We went back and forth for a few minutes. And then I heard Trees running up the ramp. "Bobby, I'm here!" I can't imagine doing that now. Holding up the door when the flight is ready to go. I'd get thrown into jail. But the Red Wings were a tight team. No one was out to get someone else's job. We looked out for each other on and off the ice.

Once, Petr Klima and I stopped by my buddy Tom Mullen's to look at a couple of cars. Tom was ten years older and a good guy. He owned TNT EDM, which was a tooling company in Plymouth, Michigan, that did work for Ford. Tom was always good to me. I did a few endorsement deals with him, and we'd golf and stuff. He lived clean. Petr and I had had a few beers after practice and we had brought a few along. We were supposed to take a bus to go over to Adirondack "for some extra training," and we were both pissed about that. We were a little juiced up, and Petr says, "I ain't going to play there. Screw them." And I said, "Yeah, screw them, we don't need any more training." So we missed the bus. Then we decided to use Tom's phone to try to call a radio station to do a live interview, but Tom stopped us. He said, "You two idiots! Don't do it! You'll regret it."

I always liked Petr. He was a good guy and a great hockey player. It seemed to me the Red Wings sort of gave up on him. Maybe they thought he didn't give a fuck, I don't know. We got in trouble together a few times.

10

A GAZILLION GIRLS

I started having serious problems with management, and they told me to enter the Betty Ford Clinic in Rancho Mirage, California, or else. I did, but I only lasted a week. Then I stopped at a bar and hopped a plane back to Detroit.

The American government had pulled my work permit because the Wings had suspended me. So I was stuck in Windsor—I couldn't come across. At the end of October 1988, I moved into the Relax Plaza and stayed there until the first week of December.

It wasn't so bad because it was full of beautiful girls, especially the blonde at the front desk named Dani. I kept looking at her. She was incredibly hot—drop-dead gorgeous, actually. She likes to say that I asked everyone else out except her, but she's full of crap. I called up my buddy, Dino Rossi, and said, "I've fallen in love and found the girl I'm going to marry," and it turned out to be true.

I asked the other girl at the desk if Dani had a boyfriend. She said yes, but they were having some problems. So I said, "Do you think Dani would go out with me?" And she said she'd ask.

Dani thought I was an arrogant asshole because there were "a gazillion girls" calling and coming to visit. It didn't help that the manager went up to my room when I wasn't there and took pictures because a few things got tossed around during a couple of parties I had. So I'm not sure if she would ever have given me her number, but thanks to her mother, she agreed. It just so happened her parents, Leslie and Dan Parkinson, were in town and had come by to see Dani when I was in the lobby. Dani nodded her head toward me and whispered, "Mom, you know who that is? That's Bob Probert, the hockey player." Leslie turned to have a look. My hair was longer and I was in a leather jacket, waiting for my ride. Leslie turned back to Dani and said, "I don't care who it is. Stay away from him." So when her girlfriend asked if I could call, Dani said, "Sure, give him my number."

I called her up and said, "Domino's Pizza, did you order a pizza?" and she said, "What do you want, Bob?"

We went out a couple of times. On our first date, we went to a Chinese restaurant called the House of Lee in downtown Windsor. She was only twenty, and a little shy and quiet. I had been seeing girls who were used to partying. I wasn't used to a nice girl like Dani, but I really liked her. We went swimming the next night, and when we got to the Relax Plaza, she went to work and I went up to my room. I kept calling down, asking for extra pillows. After the third time we went out, we really hit it off, but we didn't want the hotel to know, so we started sneaking around. She'd sneak up to my room from the back stairwell. Those were the good old days.

My lawyer, Pat Ducharme, showed up at my room for a meeting. I was a little messed up on something, flaked out and having trouble focusing. He looked at me and said he couldn't represent me anymore. He said, "You're just too much trouble and too much heartache, man. I hate to do this—I'm probably going to regret it—but I don't want you to bother me anymore and I don't want you to call me." Then he headed for the door.

I was a little surprised and said, "You're not serious."

He said, "I *am* serious, Bob. Go do whatever you're going to do. If you're just trying to commit suicide on the instalment plan, do it and get it over with. You're driving us all nuts."

I felt bad. "Don't leave," I said.

"Okay," he said, "are we going to really talk?"

I said, "Do I have to?"

He had tears in his eyes and said, "If you don't let me help you, it's too frustrating for me. I can't bear it. I can't stand it."

So we had a really good talk that night. He told me that I didn't realize how much I was hurting people. He said, "You know, Bob, what I feel pales in comparison to what your mom feels, pales in comparison to what your grandma feels. I'm torn up, but what you're doing to me is nothing compared to what you are doing to them."

I was a little shocked at that. I mean, I was providing for my family, taking care of them, you know? "Really?" I said.

"Aw, Bob. Your mom cries herself to sleep every night." I felt just awful, horrible. We talked for a couple of hours. Afterward, he was kind of like, "I don't give a shit. I'll hang in there with you." And that was kind of a turning point between us.

By November 22, I was back on the roster. Pat Ducharme found a clause in the NHL collective bargaining agreement that said if you are physically fit to play, you have to be paid. The Wings had argued that because I was breaking team rules by coming late and showing up with the smell of alcohol on my breath, I wasn't fit. But under the CBA, there were only certain conditions that qualified you as physically unable to play. So Pat sent me to a whole series of doctors, like an orthopedic surgeon, an internist and a sports specialist. We gathered a bunch of medical reports talking about what great shape I was in. The Wings had fourteen days to reinstate me or it was a breach of my contract and I would become a free agent. The Wings were pissed and told the papers that I forced them to take me back. When I was asked about it, I said, "I exercised my rights."

All kinds of rumours were circulating about me. I know the Wings got wind of them. Everything I did got blown out of proportion. I was living under a microscope. I was at a party at a hotel in Detroit just before Christmas. It was one of those "Let's get a room because the bar is closing" parties. At about 3 A.M., a girl at the party fell on the floor and went into convulsions. She had epilepsy. Another girl got on the phone and called the ambulance. The girl who had the seizure came around, but when help got there, that's when I decided, "See ya, time to go." As the paramedics were walking in, I was walking out and someone leaked a story. It got better and better until it was just like the scene where Uma Thurman overdoses in *Pulp Fiction.*

I couldn't get a speeding ticket without it being news, and it was always screwed up. If I was 100-percent sober driving to practice at 9 A.M. and got pulled over, instead of the facts, it would be, "Bob was drunk, going a hundred miles an hour, with no licence."

Dani and I weren't exclusive. There were a few others at that time—Teri, Jackie, Michelle, Drita. I would start by calling Dani, but if she wasn't home, I'd just go down the list. One night, a buddy came with me in the 'Vette to pick up Jackie. I was living in downtown Detroit and she lived out in the suburbs, about half an hour away. Maybe it was from playing hockey, but I was always aware of what was going on around me. I noticed that when I moved over a lane, there was a car way back behind me that would move over too. I'd take an exit, he'd take the exit. I said to my buddy, "I think there's somebody tailing us."

"Nah," he said. So I got off at the next exit and sure enough, he got off. I said to my buddy, "Yeah, there is definitely somebody following me back there." I pulled into Jackie's driveway, and five minutes later, this car turns into her street, drives past us, pulls into a driveway, pulls out of the driveway and parks on the road, but nobody gets out. I threw the 'Vette into reverse, gunned it down the street and pulled up right next to this guy. He was an old fucker, and he looked scared. He slammed it into drive and took off. I think he thought he was going to get away from me, but I was in a 'Vette, right? Good luck, buddy. Anyway, I started chasing him, and we were running red lights, going through stop signs, all over the east side of Detroit. The guy got so scared, he pulled up on the front lawn of the Rosedale police station. Drove right up and called them from his car phone, saying, "This maniac is chasing me!" I got out of my car, walked up to his window, and at the same time, two policemen were coming out of the station. I told the cops, "This asshole's been following me." And they said, "Okay, wait over by your car. We'll check it out."

They talked to him, then came over to me and said, "Hey Bob, there's nothing we can do. He's a private investigator. He's hired to follow you. We can't charge him, we can't do anything." And they told me not to move while they let this asshole go, because they knew I wanted to break his windows and pull him out of the car.

But, when they said someone hired him, right away I thought it had to be the Red Wings—in particular, Jim Devellano. I called Pat Ducharme and asked him to find out who hired this asshole. He called me back and said, "When I confronted them about the investigator, they denied it." Pat told them, "The guy admitted it right to the police, right there when he pulled up on the police lawn." Pat said, "It's ridiculous, Bob. I mean, they are denying the obvious."

Pat said it wasn't illegal because it wasn't harassment. The guy was just keeping his distance and watching a public figure in a public place.

I found out later what had happened. It all started the summer of 1988, when Jimmy D brought me into his office and made me an offer. It was just between him and me, nobody else. If I would come and see him everyday at twelve noon, he would give me an Antabuse pill and a crisp hundred-dollar bill. Every day, all summer long. Jimmy showed me his stockpile. Eight grand in hundreds, locked up in his desk.

I told him no way, forget it. The summer was for me, not a time to worry about the hockey club. So they hired a detective agency—two full-time detectives. Ten years later, Jimmy D finally admitted it in the paper, and Soupy told me the truth to my face. The Wings wanted to know what I was up to because there were rumours I was doing drugs. So they hired the detectives. These guys worked the entire month of July. Jimmy wanted a report of where I was, twenty-four hours a day. They rented an apartment directly across from mine and they had cameras on me. Jimmy D got pages and pages of stuff on me. The detectives kept track of who came in and out of my apartment and followed me to clubs. But the main thing Jimmy D worried about was how fast I drove. The detectives reported that one night I came home and drove up to the sixth floor of the parking garage and did pinwheels in the 'Vette. They said they watched me in my boat going super-fast up and down the Detroit River. They also said they couldn't keep up with me on the freeway, because I'd be doing 125 miles per hour. But after I confronted one of them at the police station, the detectives told Jimmy the job was too dangerous and quit.

At that time, there was a doctor of some kind working with our team. His theory was that I was taking drugs because I was self-medicating. He would give me these capsules full of amino acid. He said they produced dopamine and that if I took them, I wouldn't crave cocaine. I started meeting with him weekly. But he was always trying to be around me. He'd want to go shopping and stuff. I'd call Ducharme and complain, "Listen, you got to get this guy away from me. He's driving me crazy. He wants to hang out with me. He wants to be buddies now." Then, one day, I slept in and missed practice. We were playing in St. Louis the next day. I missed the first flight, but caught the next one. When I arrived, there was a message for me to go to his room. He told me, "Well, the coach is telling management right now that you're doing drugs. I'm here to help you, so if you have anything with you, you better give it to me." I said, "Yeah, I do," and I gave him what I had. Right after that, I was suspended indefinitely with pay, and told to stay away from the team because I was a bad influence.

The Wings were making big changes in 1989. They traded Miroslav Frycer, sent Joe Murphy to the minors and cut Tim Higgins and Doug Halward. On February 5, the team was talking to the Oilers about trading me, Klima (who was having problems of his own, with alcohol) and Adam Graves for Jimmy Carson and Kevin McClelland. The Wings put the word out that they were trying to trade me. One newspaper called it a "rummage sale for Bob Probert." Jimmy D told the papers he was actively trying to make a trade. He said he was talking to the Los Angeles Kings and the Winnipeg Jets. Article after article was written on my personal life, and I was pissed off about it. It was tough sitting out through that. I loved Detroit.

11

BUSTED

The coke was becoming a problem. I was doing it four or five days a week, an 8-ball each time (depending on how good it was), and then I'd take a couple of days off and go back at it. I did it one time before a game and it was brutal. I just didn't have any energy. I remember sitting on the bench, one hand over the boards, looking around and thinking, "They know. Twenty thousand people know what I was doing before coming into this game." I was totally paranoid.

Dani's dad, Jim, made me an offer. He said, "Listen, kick the habit. This shit you're getting now is shit. I did this way back when. I don't do it anymore. You want the good stuff? I'll make you a deal. Stop doing the drugs right now. You and I will go down to Bolivia for three weeks, we will go down and do the best of the best, and that's it for the year. We come back and you are straight for the rest of the year."

I think he meant it, but I never took him up on it.

Windsor and Detroit are five miles from each other—fifteen

minutes if you take the Detroit–Windsor Tunnel. The border wasn't really like a border to me, especially before 9/11. I used to cross with a library card. I have even crossed with no identification. That's how easy it was back then. Now, you've got to have a passport. They are so frigging strict that, even if they know you, even if you cross and come back five minutes later, they hassle you. They are such assholes over there.

I was having a few problems coming and going across at the tunnel, but nothing major. Customs would take a good look at my papers, but usually they left me alone because I played for the Wings. I did notice they were starting to get kind of pissed at me because of my drunk-driving problems.

I grew up with a buddy named Jeff Clark. His parents owned a tool-and-die shop in the States, so he had a green card. He was dating a girl named Ann, who was an American. She was a dancer. On March 1, they went to the home game in Detroit to watch me play. I had just bought an ounce of coke. I chucked it in the glove compartment, and then the three of us drove across the border back into Windsor to party at this bar called Penrod's.

Dani was living with her grandmother in Essex County, southeast of Windsor. I picked her up at about 2 A.M. because she had been working the late shift at the Relax Plaza. I pulled up in my truck, a Blazer. Dani called it a pigsty because I had been living in it. I had been staying with Laurie Graham, a friend of Petr Klima's wife's. She had an extra room, but we were incompatible. I couldn't have girls over, and I couldn't drink because she'd mark the bottles. I wasn't much of a reader, and I remember telling Dani that my relationship with Laurie was strictly "plutonic."

Sometimes I'd stay with friends like Jeff, and sometimes I'd crash in the truck. Dani drove us back to the bar because I was a little juiced. We got there and joined the party that was still going on. We played darts and I did some drinking. Then Ann and Jeff wanted to leave. Jeff had left his car in downtown Detroit, and Ann had a kid she wanted to get back to. I told them, "Listen, I'll pay for a cab." They didn't want to do that. So I said, "Well, I'll pay for a room. You guys can stay here," but they didn't want that either. Finally, I said, "Oh screw it, I'll give you a ride back." First, I went into the bathroom to do a little coke to sober me up. Then I split the coke I had left into four Baggies and gave two to my buddy to hold. I put the rest in my pocket. We hopped into my Blazer. I was driving, Dani was beside me, and the other two fell asleep in the back. I was pretty leery about crossing the border, but I was thinking, "They're not going to pull me in. They know I'm a Red Wing player."

I was wrong.

It was about 5:30 A.M. when we were going down Goyeau Street in Windsor, which is right before the Detroit–Windsor Tunnel. I asked Dani to hold the wheel while I scrambled a little bit. I had to stash the Baggies of coke. The bigger one had a rock that weighed about twelve grams, and the smaller one had a rock that was about two grams. I also had a Deering coke grinder with me. It was about two inches high and about as big around as a Skoal can. I needed to hide it too. I stuffed the coke into my underwear, but the grinder was too big. I tried my pants, under my shirt—everywhere. I should have thrown that son of a bitch out the fucking window in the tunnel. It wasn't worth much, probably about thirty bucks. The thing was, they had stopped making them because they were finding them as part of the paraphernalia in drug busts. Finally, I managed to fit it in my inside suit-jacket pocket. I had it wrapped in a plastic bag with an elastic around it.

I remember Dani looking at me with these big eyes. She didn't know what was going on. She was a good girl who never got into all this. I don't think she had ever even seen a grinder.

We pulled up to the last booth on the far right and the guards asked for our paperwork. Keep in mind, it was kind of a screwed-up situation because Ann was American, while Dani, Jeff and I were Canadian. I had a work permit and Jeff had a green card, so there were a lot of different documents.

They'd probably read rumours about me partying in the paper, because the guy looked at my passport and said, "Pull it in," so we parked. They took us inside to the customs and immigration office, where they looked at my visa and checked all our birth certificates. They asked how much money we had on us, where we worked, how long we were staying, all that. Then they said, "Okay, you can go." We thought we were out the door. It was like, "Whew!"

It's possible that they were buying time, because as soon as we were walking back to our truck, one of them says, "Just a minute! You guys! Back in here, now!"

I still thought everything was hunky-dory. But while they had been checking our papers, others had ripped my truck apart. On the ground underneath my seat, they found one of those amino-acid capsules that the Red Wings were trying out. They assumed it was something illegal. They also found a six-pack of

beer in the back seat, which was unopened, and a bottle of pep-
permint schnapps that had been there for about a month.

We sat in this little room, the four of us, while they finished
going through the truck. The officials were very hush-hush.
They seemed very serious. We were all pretty calm, not saying
a whole lot. I was worried about Dani.

One of the guards looked at Jeff and said, "You! Take your
coat off and put in on the table." They went through it, then
took him away for a strip search. Jeff came back and he looked
cooked—like, done. I was next.

They told me to stand up and take off my coat. I took it off,
put it on the desk. Two guys went through it and found the
grinder. When they took it out of the plastic bag, I knew I was
fucked because there was powder residue in it. And with zero
tolerance, it was good as having a Baggie full.

They said, "Come into the back room." I did, and they
told me to take off my shirt. Then they said, "All right, now
your pants." I dropped my pants to my ankles. "Okay, now
your underwear." I was wearing boxers. I usually wear boxers,
but these were the stretchy ones, so they were a little tighter
around the leg. I pulled my underwear straight down and the
Baggies went down with them. I was standing there with my
arms at my sides, trying not to look at the corner of one of
the Baggies, because it was sticking out a little. They told me,
"Okay, turn around—turn back, okay, pull 'em up." I leaned
over, and as I was pulling up the underwear, the guy spotted
a glint off the Baggie and said, "Hang on a minute, what's . . .
Hand me that." So close. I handed him the bigger Baggie, but
the smaller Baggie stayed in my shorts.

They put me back in the waiting room and I asked to go to the bathroom.

They said, "No, sit back down." A few minutes later, they said, "Okay, you can go to the bathroom." So I went in there while a guy stood by the door. He was watching me as I started to take a piss. Then he let the door close and stood outside. As I was pissing, I took out the Baggie, dropped it in the toilet and pissed on it. Then I thought, "What the hell?" I was already damned. I picked it up and ran it under the tap, pulled out the rock, cut it up a little and used it. Then I put the rest of the rock into the Baggie and shoved it into my shirt pocket.

They took me to a holding cell and left. I still had my wallet, with all my money and a couple of credit cards, in my pocket. I was sitting in there on this stool with no one around, so I crushed up more of the rock, rolled up a dollar bill and did a couple of lines. Five minutes later, three of them came back for a secondary search, "Get away from the door! Up against the wall!" Just like in the movies.

They patted me down again, and the Baggie fell to the floor. They were pissed because they had already written me up for a certain amount—11.4 grams—and finding the rest made them look bad. I'm thinking they tore it up and flushed that report, because the papers they gave my lawyer said 14.2 grams. Whatever.

At this point, I still kind of had a feeling that maybe they were going to cover the whole thing up—let it slide. But about 7 A.M., when they escorted me over to the Federal Building and fingerprinted me, I knew I was in pretty serious trouble. As they were getting ready to move me down to the jail, the *federale* who was with me said, "There's a lot of press out there." Someone had obviously blown the whistle. Seems everybody is always on the take, right?

Pat Ducharme had introduced me to this big-time law-yer, Harold Fried, who represented a lot of famous people in Detroit. Right away, I started calling him Hairball. It was a good nickname for a guy whose hairline was moving back. Harold was good. He had done some immigration stuff for me before. He was driving to the office, and he heard the news about my arrest on the radio. He came down right away because I had to make an appearance in court. It was packed with reporters. Harold did all the talking.

Dani, Jeff and Ann weren't charged with anything. They were just sent home. I felt relieved about that.

I know I fucked up, but do you wanna know what really pissed me off about the whole situation? Two things: first, they confiscated my truck and tore it all apart. After I had been to prison, I found out that my parole officer Rick Loos-eveldt's son, who went to high school in Detroit, had some kid ask him if he wanted to buy some speakers and amps. Apparently, this kid had relatives who worked at the Federal Building. The kid claimed he was allowed to go through my truck and take my big boom box and my amps. He said to Rick's son, "Yeah, I got Bob Probert's stereo. Wanna buy it?" Then I got my phone bill, and somebody had made a couple of calls on my car phone. And my sunglasses were gone. I had a few good pairs too. Thankfully, I had registered the truck in my buddy's name, so they had to give the truck back. It was all torn to shit though.

The second thing I didn't like was what a couple of my teammates said. Most of them thought I was gone for good. Stevie Yzerman stepped up for me. He made the comment, "I don't think we've seen the last of Bob Probert yet." But some of the others, they were brutal. I was protecting these guys, and then they go bad-mouthing me like that? I remember that Gilbert Delorme said I'd had enough chances and should be thrown out of the league forever. The next year, he went to Quebec, and I ran the fucker. He was a defenceman, so I waited for him to go behind the net with the puck, and then I just went full blast at him and checked him hard into the boards. It ended up splitting his whole elbow. He couldn't play the rest of the game, and I didn't care. I wanted to hurt him because of those fucking comments. You don't say that about your teammate, no matter what. You might *think* it, but you don't say it to the press.

And Lee Norwood couldn't keep his mouth shut again. He said if I had gone to him, he could have led the way and kept me out of trouble, like he was Superman or God or something. Not cool.

Meanwhile, the U.S. Immigration and Naturalization Service wanted me in jail before my trial. We all went to the courthouse so that Harold could do some high legal manoeuvring. In 1989, aliens did not have the same right to due process that full American citizens had. But I had an awesome legal team, and the court found that statute unconstitutional. I was free until the trial, and everyone was ecstatic that it all worked out the way we wanted. We left the building through the staircase to get away from the media.

We were patting everybody on the back and saying, "Yay!!" and all that stuff, and then Harold got serious and turned to me and said, "Probie, just stop right there. Do you understand how serious this is and what we've just been through?" It was like sitting out in the sun and somebody throws cold water on you. I lit up a smoke and said, "Hairball, lighten up! Hey! We're free. I just got released. We won. We won!"

After the trial and sentencing, and after I'd served my time, I was able to continue playing in the States until my immigration status was cleared up. My case helped change the legislation for aliens, which meant regular guys who might be in the same boat could earn a living while they waited on immigration to decide if they could stay in the country. I'm glad something good came out of it.

I didn't want to cross the border back to Canada, in case they wouldn't let me back into the States, so the next night after work I asked Dani to come over to the American side and meet me. We hung out together. I didn't have a car, so we'd walk to get groceries. A couple of nights later, we went to the Meijers supermarket and bought all this food, so we called a cab. There were tons of people standing in this little lobby area, kind of looking at us, and a teenage girl came up to me and asked, "Are you Bob Probert?"

I smiled at her and said, "Well, yes I am."

She looked at me and said, "I want you to know you're just a disgrace." She just ripped me apart in front of the whole crowd. I started thinking about what she said, and I got pretty bummed about it.

A couple of nights later, Dani and I stopped in at the Anchor

Bar. We were playing pool, and I was having a beer. Unfortunately, it was right across from the *Detroit Free Press* building, and Keith Gave ratted me out in the paper the next day. U.S. immigration stepped in and said I had to get to rehab because it looked like they were dragging their feet on the whole cocaine bust. They sentenced me to attend this facility called the Holly Gardens Treatment Center, near Flint.

Harold was all for me going to rehab. He figured the court would go lighter on me if I showed I was trying to get straight. But Dani had a pretty tough time with me going there. For me, it wasn't that big a deal. I mean, I wasn't looking forward to it, but she cried when she drove me up there.

Mike Ilitch, the owner of the Red Wings, came up to see me in his limo and took me out for lunch. Mr. I said he wanted to see how I was doing. He told me the team was behind me, and they would try to help me out as much as possible. John Ziegler, the president of the National Hockey League, had just given me a lifetime ban—"for now." And Mr. I stepped up on my behalf when they had a big, formal hearing about it. I had the utmost respect for him. He stood by my side.

Dani came to see me on weekends. She'd bring me pecan pie and she baked chocolate chip cookies for everybody. At first it was great, but I started seeing this little blonde nurse there named Katie. It's weird. I'm not saying I'm a stud by any means, but I think what happens is these girls get into the caregiving business because they want to help people. Maybe it's like a codependency kind of thing, you know? Anyway, Dani and I broke up. She seemed fine with it, because she was still kind of seeing this other guy, Kevin, who she had gone out with before she met me. Katie ended up in a bit of trouble when she helped me get a car to leave the grounds to have a few drinks with a couple of guys I met in there. We found a bar and got blasted. I found out later they were underage, like, sixteen and seventeen.

On September 26, 1989, at 2 P.M. I was sentenced to six months in jail by U.S. District Judge Patrick J. Duggan. I was thinking, "That doesn't seem that bad." I mean, I thought there was a chance of getting probation, because Harold had argued that the law was written to stop people from bringing drugs over to sell, and everyone agreed the drugs I had on me were for personal use. The argument didn't fly, but he gave it a good shot, and I think it helped the judge go lighter.

I looked over at Harold. He had tears in his eyes.

On October 17, 1989, the details of my sentence came down: three months at the Federal Medical Center in Rochester, Minnesota, three months in halfway house, three years' probation, a $2,000 fine, plus costs of $3,680. And the kicker, an incarceration cost of $1,210 per month. I would be paying rent in jail.

On November 7, Mr. Ilitch chartered a jet for just Harold and me, and I went to jail. It was like a dorm. My room had a window and a thick, heavy door, which was open until 11 P.M. We would be locked up until 6 A.M. It could have been worse. It could have had bars.

I was federal prisoner number 12211–309, and I wore prison garb or whatever you call it—I think it was brown. I was in there with Jimmy Bakker, the evangelist, and Billy Giacalone, who was a mob boss in Michigan. At that time, Jimmy Bakker was getting his picture taken with inmates—he'd charge five dollars for a Polaroid picture. But then some big, black guy sent one home to his family, and they sold it to the *National Enquirer* and the headline said they were lovers in prison. Jimmy stopped posing after that. He was kind of wimpy. He was always complaining about how he twisted his back getting out of the top bunk. Then, one day, we had to get immunization shots, and he started crying. I turned to him and said, "C'mon buddy, it's not that bad. It's not Jessica Hahn."

Billy Giacalone is the guy they say was behind the Hoffa disappearance. But he was really cool. He was a Wings fan. He said, "Hey Bob, if you get in trouble and someone is bugging you, just pick up a chair and crack it over their head."

On day two, I was in the food line when all of a sudden this guy cut in front of me to get his pop. I said, "Why don't you go to the fucking back of the line like everyone else?" He turned around and made a comment like, "When you get out, you'd better watch your back. I know people in the NHL." I actually thought we were going to go right at it there in the cafeteria, but that's all he said and he went on his way.

I was a little angry. Nobody wants to be in a place like that. It turned out jail was brutal for a guy who doesn't like to be cooped up. I'd look out the window every day, knowing that I couldn't go anywhere. It would really hit home when I'd see the double fences and see the cars patrolling around. By the time I got out, I didn't have any fingernails left.

I really hated being stuck in the kitchen. Two days before Christmas, I was in the kitchen doing pots and pans. I was fucking bored. My job was to put these pots and pans on a conveyor belt, and then one guy sprayed them and another guy dried them. So I walked over and sat down at this little table right next to the kitchen for a smoke break. I lit up, and the guy in charge came over and said, "Hey, it's not break time. Get back to work."

I said, "All right."

He left, and I just stayed there and kept smoking. He came back and said, "You're still here. I told you it's not break time yet. Get back to work."

I said, "For eleven cents an hour, you can take this fucking job and stick it up your ass."

He said, "Is that right? So that means you're not going to work?"

"I guess so." I said.

So he left and came back with this female guard and said, "Against the wall, please." I went up against the wall. They pulled my arms behind my back, cuffed me and took me to fucking solitary for refusing to work. What they do is they put you in solitary, and then they have a hearing. And the days that you have spent in there are used against the time you are sentenced. So if you are in there, like I was, for three days, and you're working off a week, then you only have four days left. So I was in there two days and then it was Christmas. My mother was on her way up to see me, so the associate warden, an older lady, said I could come out until the hearing a week later.

When my mother was there, I went outside for a cigarette and she came with me. And there was this big guy out there with his wife, and they were leaning up against the wall under the cameras. They were facing each other. All of a sudden, she hiked up her skirt and he stood there, banging her. I was like, "Fuck!" It was gross, like two dogs humping. My mother and I did a quick U-turn and headed back inside.

At the hearing, I walked into this room and there were three broads. They were just so effing cocky, thinking they were God. One of them asked for my side of the story, and I told her what happened. I said, "I was working in the kitchen and I made a comment." She read it out to me. She said, "For eleven cents an hour, you can take this job and shove it." I corrected her. I said, "No. I said, 'For eleven cents an hour, you can take this *fucking* job and stick it up your ass.'" They didn't like that, those three power-tripping broads. They ended up sentencing me to a week.

It was an experience, though. You are no longer in general population. You are locked in with a roommate. The first roommate I had was in there for murder. He and his partner were at their house with a bunch of dope, and someone broke in. My roommate was sitting on his couch with two girls, and his buddy got up to go to the bathroom. Then these two guys came in with guns drawn to rob him.

His buddy peeked around the corner from the bathroom and fired one shot, hitting the one robber and killing him instantly. Then he stepped out and started shooting. The other robber ran out of the house and wasn't hurt. That was the story he told me. That roommate got transferred, and then they stuck me with this Indian kid who was eighteen years old. He told me Indians get stupid when they drink. Apparently, he got into a fight with his best friend and pulled out a knife and killed him.

He got a fourteen-year sentence. While I was in there, I was sleeping with one eye open.

We got one hour a day in the yard. It was separate from the main yard. They'd cuff you to move you, so you were led out, and then they'd take the cuffs off. You could have a couple of cigarettes and play basketball for an hour, but that was it. I was going nuts.

I wasn't allowed to smoke for the first three days, and neither was my roommate. So what we'd do is take a card from our mail and take a dab of the toothpaste we got every morning, open up the card, put toothpaste inside, close it and make it stick together. Then we'd punch a little hole in the corner of the card and start unraveling our white prison-issue socks. We'd tie the threads together, loop that through the hole and then shoot the card under the door and across to one of the other cells. They'd pull it in and tie cigarettes to the string and shoot the card back.

Every once in a while, when we went to shoot the card across, a guard would come by and step on it, breaking the string and grabbing the smokes. Then it was like, "Oh fuck!" You want a cigarette so bad, and there goes your line, there goes your card, you're fucked. It was funny at night—you'd look out the little window and see all these things flying back and forth. People getting smokes.

People get really inventive in there. There were guys who made their own hooch. The guys that worked in the kitchen would steal some bread dough, get a bucket and add raisins—

or any kind of fruit they could find—and water to make wine. It would sit for about thirty days, so they started in November. Some of the guys told me the guards would look the other way around Christmas.

People smuggled in drugs all the time. One guy offered me a joint. It was about a week before I was supposed to go home. He said, "Hey Bob, do you want to smoke a joint?" I said, "Aw, no. I'll pass." And it's a good thing I did, because the next day I had to do a urine test. They do them randomly. One test, and if they find drugs in your system, you're fucked.

Jail was tough, but I mean, it wasn't anything like Alcatraz.

Stevie Y, Soupy and Demers visited me in January. Of course it made the papers. Stevie was awesome. He never said anything really bad. He wished me the best. Whenever I got in trouble, he'd tell the papers, "Well, we hope Bob can get a handle on this and be a better person." Whereas Demers called me a cancer after I got busted. After I was busted, he said, "the cancer is gone." Funny how I wasn't a horrible disease when I was out there scrapping for that team. I think he was worrying about his own ass.

Jim Lites, the Wings' executive vice-president, came to see me in Rochester. He called it the Big Wall. He had never been inside a prison before. At that time, the security clearance procedure was kind of like what happens at the airport today. You clear your pockets for the metal detectors, and they X-ray your shit and pat you down. Jim Lites told me it was the scariest thing.

Jimmy D came too. Jimmy was a bachelor. His whole life was the hockey team—right or wrong, it was. I think he felt that guys like me were like his kids. He was kind of consumed with straightening me around. Later, he would tell me he was relieved to see me in jail, because after he read that detective report he thought I was going to kill myself in a car accident—or die in a bar scrap over drugs or get shot over a chick. And if that didn't happen, he thought for sure I was going to crash my boat. Anyway, he hoped the law was going to do a better job of rehabilitating me than the team or the treatment centres had.

The one thing that I really, really missed while I was in there was a woman. A piece of ass. Female ass. Dani sent pictures, but they weren't, you know, Polaroids, so I had to use my imagination. Polaroids weren't allowed.

I got my GED while I was in jail. I actually took a college course, Written Communications, but I didn't finish it. I went to one class, and it was a four-hour lecture with a fifteen-minute break halfway through, and I was a smoker, so that was a problem. And then we had an essay to do—four pages, so many hundred words, due the next day. I said, "Screw this," and I never went back.

On January 2, 1990, I was ordered deported as soon as I finished my time in the halfway house. Harold got U.S. immigration to agree to let me stay in the States on a work permit while we appealed. But I couldn't get a voluntary departure order—in other words, if I left the States, I could never come back.

I lived in a halfway house from February to mid-April, but first they sent me to this psych ward in Bethesda, Maryland, for assessment. There were a lot of crazy people at this facility. They attached wires all over me and then injected me with this stuff called procaine, an anaesthetic. I had to sit in a chair, and I was getting this great buzz and I wanted more. So I pretended it wasn't having an effect on me. Turns out the computer was tracking my reaction, which told them that I had attention-deficit hyperactivity disorder, or ADHD. Pat Ducharme thought that was bullshit. He said some professionals get so hung up on a particular diagnosis that they look for it under every rock and around every curve, and they find it because they look for it so hard.

The papers were tipped off, and I remember reading a column where one of the reporters called it "a tension deficit disorder."

They were trying all these different medications on me, like Depakote and Ritalin, to help me focus. While I was there, I started a thing with one of the nurses, and she ended up coming back to Michigan with me for a week. She was different than all the others. She had dark hair.

I had been assigned a probation officer named Rick Looseveldt and placed in Eastwood, which is a drug treatment centre in Pontiac, near Detroit. It was kind of a ghetto. I did the drill there—ninety AA meetings in ninety days and lots of piss testing.

Rick was told that I would be able to practise with the team. The Wings were ready to get me back into training so I could play the next season, but that caused some problems right away. I had gone through lots of treatment in prison, but the director wanted to take me back to square one. He believed you had to take yourself all the way down—get rid of all your defences, all your personality, and then build back up from that point, which meant I could not go out at all. I thought the director was a prick. We had a conference about whether I could go to practice, and he refused to let me.

I called Rick and told him I was ready to walk out of the halfway house. Rick told me, "Don't go anywhere until I come and talk to you. If you walk out of there, it's a violation of your probation and I'll be forced to take you back to court. Bob, the publicity will sink you." So he came over, and we talked for an hour or so, and we worked it out that I could skate if I worked on a "journal." So I would write a few thoughts down on a piece of paper each day. Things like, "My goal is to be sober, one day at a time, to be happy and free, to be successful in my work, to have my own business someday."

I started skating alone for the first three weeks, with Soupy helping out. There were four games left in the season, and it didn't look like the team was going to make the playoffs. The Wings thought I could give them a hand, but we had to talk to Ziegler about lifting my lifetime suspension. When he banned me, he came down hard.

There was an NHL bylaw that allowed the president to ban a person for life without a hearing, without evidence, without any kind of input from the player. My lawyers wrote a letter saying this wasn't right. They pointed out that that bylaw had been passed when the former executive director of the Players' Association, Alan Eagleson, was in bed with the president. Eagleson hadn't properly represented the players' interests. The players didn't have protection, and so we were going to sue.

Over the eight months since the bust, Ziegler had softened

a little bit. He wrote back and said he never intended it to mean I wouldn't have a hearing, so we got one.

In early March, my mother, Jimmy D, Mr. Ilitch, my lawyers—Ducharme and Fried—and I met with Ziegler at the Ritz-Carlton in Southfield. There was no publicity about it at all. It was very quiet. Ziegler made the arrangements, and the NHL even paid for a suite, which was like a big boardroom. He told us we could say whatever we wanted. Mr. I was very low-key. He just said, "We want our Bob back. We miss him in our club and his teammates miss him. He is a person that we know has worked hard at his rehabilitation." I don't remember him saying much else, but it was pretty effective.

Jimmy D said I had a drinking problem and that he was shocked because the Wings had no idea I was on drugs. But the team wanted me back really badly and I had worked very hard on my rehabilitation.

Harold talked about how much I had paid out of my own pocket to get rehabilitated and how much I had already lost from being in jail. He said that I didn't need more punishment. Ducharme said there were a lot of other guys who had been suspended for drugs, but nobody else had been banned for life.

I told Ziegler that I wanted to straighten around and that hockey was really important to me. I said that if I could come back, I'd talk to kids so that I might be an example of how, when you have troubles, you can work your way back.

Ziegler let me back in. He told the press, "Based on the drug tests and probation reports, I am satisfied the conditions have been met." And he said he felt that losing one year and $200,000 was enough punishment.

I was not drinking and not using, but I was white-knuckling it and not really happy about it. I was so tired of treatment. The truth was, I honestly didn't know why I couldn't drink.

Rick Looseveldt thought it would be more therapeutic for me to play than to go through the whole summer wondering how the fans felt and whether I could still play. He went to see Judge Duggan to talk about the difficulties we were having, and the judge backed us. That gave Rick a little more power with the director. So there was this big meeting—Rick, Jimmy D, Soupy, Jacques Demers and Jimmy Lites. Everybody was saying, "I think Bob's ready, I think Bob's ready!" and they looked at Rick, who knew it was all up to him to get permission. Rick knew the Wings were fighting for the last playoff spot, and from a business aspect, making the playoffs is big money. He weighed that pressure on the team with how I was doing in treatment and said, "Aw shit," and called the director.

The director said, "Oh no, he's not ready, he should not be allowed to play."

Rick asked, "Why not?"

"Because he hasn't completed his journal. He has four more pages to go."

"Is that the best you can give me?" Rick said. "You are saying Bob can't play because of three or four pages of a journal?" And he overruled the director. I was going to be allowed to play the next night against Minnesota. It was a Thursday-night game, and then there were back-to-back games against Chicago—on Saturday night at the Joe Louis Arena, and Chicago Stadium on Sunday. I could play at home, but not in the Sunday game, because I wasn't allowed to travel out of state.

Rick came back to give me the news. I was pretty happy about it. Rick said, "I pick up any negative vibes, and you're not going to play. Understand?"

I nodded. I understood.

We got to the rink and talked to Demers about an hour and a half before the game. He wanted me to play. The team was in danger of finishing in last place in the Norris Division, but I was uptight about going back. Being off that long, I wasn't sure how the team and the fans would accept me.

I skated out for the warmup on March 22, 1990, and the fans were just awesome. The newspaper said the crowd was chanting, "Probie! Probie! Probie!" It was good. People were happy to see me back. I just wanted to prove that I belonged there. Minnesota scored a couple of quick goals, which took the crowd out of it, and then I got a goal and they took it away. Disallowed. That made me kind of mad, so I tried to spark things up. But I don't think anyone wanted a year's worth of pent-up frustration taken out on them. I ended up getting another goal in the third. The fans appreciated that. I felt the apple in my throat when they cheered.

Detroit fans were a lot more forgiving than most people claimed. I heard people say that they were fed up with me and were not going to put up with my crap, but that was bullshit. The fans were the most understanding of all. They wrote me letters telling me they were praying and pulling for me to come through. The Detroit fans were great people, great fans. They loved the game. Prima donnas were not their style.

Even though we lost 5–1, everybody in the room seemed pretty happy that I was back. The next day, the newspaper said I was wiping a tear from my eye when the fans welcomed me back. I don't really remember that. I mean, I didn't have tears running down my face, but I'm sure I was a little choked up.

I was tired, but I felt good. I remember thinking that the players weren't playing for Jacques. There wasn't much spark on the team. Even with the chance of making the playoffs and how important the game was, I just didn't feel drive on the team.

Rick had made the decision to let me play Saturday, but no way was I supposed to fly to Chicago for Sunday. The program director was absolutely against it—absolutely against me playing, period. And Rick thought I was pushing it too hard. A lot of people with substance-abuse issues fight it by working ten hours a day, seven days a week, so they don't think about drugs or alcohol. But Harold got on the phone and told Rick that Jacques was short of players. Rick talked to his chief, who said, "Well, I'll leave it up to you, but if Bob were an accountant in the halfway house and it was tax season, and he needed to work overtime on Sunday, would you say no?" And Rick said, "Probably not."

He called me at the halfway house Sunday morning and said, "Bob, nobody knows about this, but how are you feeling?"

I said, "I'm a little tired."

He said, "Listen, if you're really tired and feel emotionally drained, just tell me, and I'll tell the team and the press that you wanted to play, but I said no. Nobody will ever know about this."

And I said, "I want to play, I should be with my team."

Rick said, "Okay, you will be."

And then I got lucky and scored the game-winner on Saturday and a goal that tied it in the third period on Sunday, although we lost the game 3–2. My life was back on track.

Harold Fried wanted me to stay out of trouble, so he hooked me up with a guy from Detroit who was kind of like a sponsor. His name was Ricky Rogow, but everybody called him Big Daddy. He owned a restaurant in West Bloomfield, Michigan, called Big Daddy's Parthenon, which had amazing Greek food. Big Daddy, Harold and I had lunch in Harold's office, and Big Daddy gave me his business card and said, "You call me. I am not going to call you." And then I ran into him four weeks later and he said, "Ah. You didn't use the phone number I gave you." I said, "I will." Then, about two weeks later, I called him. I didn't have too many clean friends, but Big Daddy was always up for something fun.

We both liked to eat. One night, there were five of us guys on my boat. We went to a restaurant on the east side of Detroit, right on the river. They had twenty-five desserts on the menu, everything from pies to sundaes to cakes. Big Daddy looked at me and said, "Probie, should we do this?" And I said, "Why not?" So Big Daddy told the waitress, "Bring one of each." She said, "Are you serious?" We finished them all.

When I first met Big Daddy, I was still sometimes dating Jackie. It was Sunday morning and we'd been up all night, so I said, "I know where we can get something to eat!" We hopped on my Harley and drove over to Big Daddy's house for breakfast. I had never met his wife, who was also named Ricki, but with an *i*. Ricki answered the door, wearing a pair of big flannel pants and a big sweatshirt with her hair all up in a knot, and she had two kids with her. She looked at me in my leather jacket and acid-washed jeans and Jackie in this half top with high white boots and said, "Oh, no—no, no," and slammed the door. I kept banging on the door—"Big Mama, Big Mama! Open the door, open the door!" Finally, she let us in, and it was the beginning of a wonderful relationship. Big Daddy and Big Mama would become two of my best friends.

That summer, I met Bambi. She was cute and bubbly, no boobs, but a great ass. I was a judge at a Hawaiian Tropic beauty contest she was in. She taught gymnastics. Bambi wanted to teach me about culture, so she rented *The Sound of Music* for us. I dated her for a couple of months, and then, by Christmas, Dani and I were mostly on.

Dani had lost her job at the Relax Plaza because of the incident at the border. Her name had been in the paper when I got busted, so the press had been calling her there. The manager didn't like it and took her aside and told her to find a new job.

I couldn't come over the border into Canada because if I did, I would be basically deporting myself. So I stayed back in Detroit and lifted weights, hung out on my boat and picked up a few more speeding tickets.

As soon as I got out of prison, the club wanted to change my image in the press. Instead of calling me a bum all the time, now they were saying nice things. They set up a lot of interviews. One day, I gave Dani—and a couple of exes who were back in the picture—a call, "Hey I'm going to be on the radio station. Turn to WRIF right now."

Some guy called in and asked, "Hey Bob, are you dating anybody?"

I answered the safest way I could think of. "Yeah, I'm seeing an old girlfriend."

Somebody put him up to it. I mean, why would a guy ask that?

12

MO MELLY

When I first met Sheldon Kennedy in the spring of 1990, it was in the Red Wings locker room. We were introduced and told we were going to be living together, to straighten each other out, if you can believe it. We hit it off. I had just gotten out of jail and he was a rookie fresh out of rehab. We had each other's back. That is what a friend does, and that is how it was with us.

They were also moving another guy in with us. His name was Dave Whinham. Dave was an assistant coach for the Detroit Drive, Mr. I's arena football team. Dave did some strength and conditioning training for the team. He was supposed to be their spy, I guess, but he was upfront about it. He told us the team had asked him to keep an eye on things. We ended up friends.

We moved into this apartment building called the Lafayette Towers in downtown Detroit. It's within walking distance of Greektown. Dave was training us and we started to work out pretty hard. Lots of aerobic training, weights and ice. I felt good. I wanted to get ready for the next season. Of course, I still smoked, and I dipped too—sometimes at the same time, monster pinches of Copenhagen or Skoal.

Nobody had any idea about the baggage Sheldon was carrying. Years later, it came out that he had been sexually abused by his junior hockey coach, Graham James. James went to prison for it for three and a half years. Then Theo Fleury came out with his book and said he was a victim when he'd played for James. Back then, Jimmy D, who didn't know the real story, used to stay on Dave about making sure Sheldon returned Graham James's calls. The Wings considered James part of the trusted circle of family and friends that was supposed to be helping Sheldon stay clean. James, that prick, would call our place fairly regularly.

Dave, Sheldon and I really got along. We had a lot of fun. The food at our place was always good. We would get steaks and grill them up, and go to the store and grab like six flavours of ice cream, with ten toppings, and just go at it. Dave was out a lot and Sheldon and I were really tight. He was like my little brother. I called Sheldon "Mo Melly." One time, we were singing the name game, and I had a Mo Melly moment— "Shelly, Shelly, Mo Melly, banana-fana, bo-belly, fee-fie-fo-Felly. Shelly." I mean, we would laugh all the time. I would wake him up by jumping on his bed at like five in the morning. "Wake up, Mo Melly! Wake up, Mo Melly! Let's go skiing!"

We had Harleys before everyone had Harleys, before they became the in thing, and we'd chop them up too. I remember pulling into practice and guys were like, "What are you guys doing?" We kind of stood out, like, "These guys are bad-asses." But we just liked to ride. We used to like to get on the bikes and cruise up to Alpena, Michigan, a four-hour ride. One time, it was raining like crazy and we were passing semis. We couldn't see because of the big spray off the semis, so we would just guess that no cars were coming—just pull out and pass them. That was the way we lived our lives. We lived hard and played hard, on and off the ice.

Harleys are tough to do wheelies on because they are too heavy. I could get one up once in a while, because my bike was more out front. I had a Nostalgia. I called it "Moo-Moo Cow." It was black with a cowhide strip on the seat. Mo Melly's was real heavy. He was driving a turquoise Fat Boy. I also bought a black and grey Yamaha V-Max, the fastest street-legal bike made. They actually quit making them. If you gunned it and didn't hold on, you would be off the back. It was crazy. Then Mo Melly and I had two WR500 dirt bikes—motocross racers. These weren't little bikes, they were pretty tall. When Mo Melly sat on his, he had to tippy-toe just to reach the ground. We would race around on the street, wheelin', or sometimes we'd throw them in the back of my truck and rip around the trails just north of Flint. Out there, there are mounds of dirt or cliffs up to ten feet high. We'd wear our cowboy boots and jeans and, depending on the weather, a shirt or no shirt. Always helmets and goggles.

We'd fly through the air like a couple of kids, laughing and joking. I mean, those were clean and sober times. Fun times—real fun times. Belly laughs from watching each other wipe out in the mud.

I loved doing that. We rode hard and rode to the point where we couldn't think of anything other than being on the bike. We didn't have to think about all the shit in our lives.

This all had to be hidden because, if management saw us on the bikes, we'd be in trouble. I remember we'd come back and get a call from the team—"Where were you guys?"—because they'd think we were out partying. Mo Melly and I would look at each other, all covered in mud, and just start laughing.

We had all kinds of stuff coming our way—bikes, Sea-Doos, cars. People like to see NHLers using their stuff, and instead of paying us, we'd get the products.

Sheldon got hurt in his second year. He was in the Lafayette parking lot, driving up to where you put your card in to open the gates, and he cut it too sharp against the concrete pole. His left elbow was hanging out the window and it just got nailed. He shattered his forearm from his wrist up to his elbow. Completely exploded the bone, just decimated it. When he got to the hospital, they thought they might have to cut his arm off. The doctors inserted a steel plate with nineteen pins in his forearm, and he had to wear one of those straight-arm casts like the guy in *A Fish Called Wanda*. Mo Melly would go to practice and try to drive my boat with that thing on. The break was so bad he had to go on pain medication.

We were in a game against Chicago on December 1, 1990, and I slid into Eddie Belfour and hit the toe of his skate and chipped a little bone in my left wrist, putting me out for a month. They didn't have to operate because it healed itself.

We'd go out to party a little, and nobody knew. The first time Sheldon ever did coke was with me—during the time I was on the injured list, December 23, 1990. We'd been rooming together for four months. I got some stuff, and it was snowing like crazy. We didn't want to get caught, so we went for a drive. I asked him if he had ever done coke, and he said no.

I said, "Well, do you want to do a bump, Mo Melly?" He was like, "Sure." I was nervous because we both needed to hide our activities from the team, and I was still dealing with the feds and stuff from prison. We had to hide a lot of what we did from people because everybody was watching us. We tried hard to stay under the radar.

One night, Mo Melly went a little berserk at a bar. He had too much to drink and got mad when he was asked to leave, so we went and got him. He was hurting bad the next morning, really down and depressed. He holed up in his room for two days, going into the next night. Finally, Dave said, "I'm going in there." He sat down on the edge of the bed. Sheldon's face was in the pillow—he wasn't saying anything, but he let Dave know he didn't fucking want to talk to anybody. Dave said, "Brother, it's all right, man. These things are going to happen. It's part of the deal." Then Dave put his hand on Sheldon's back, and as soon as he touched him, Sheldon jerked away really violently. At that time, neither one of us knew why, but it made a lot of sense when the James story came out. It took Sheldon a few days to come back.

When one of us was having a tough time, Mo Melly would say, "Bobby, let's get in the friggin' Don Johnson boat and shoot the shit." This one night, we had headed out when a storm came up. Waves were coming over the top of the boat. We couldn't see anything. The bilge pumps were going full blast. I was trying to nose it in and ride it out. It was probably the most scared either of us had ever been in our lives. We were not sure we were going to get out of there. I wasn't saying much, just watching the compass.

I don't think I'd ever put on a life jacket in my life, but this time I grabbed one. So did Sheldon. Then he looked at me and started laughing his ass off. "Hey Baby Huey!! Fuck, if you go in the water, man, you ain't floating!!" Here we were going to die, and he couldn't stop laughing. "Shut up, Mo Melly!" I said. But it was funny.

We had a lot of fun on the water. We weren't always drinking and drugging, it was just good fun. One evening, we took Soupy skinny-dipping, and there was some naked night skiing going on. I had a red-and-white tournament ski boat, Sea Ray Ski Ray with a Mercury engine and tower speakers. It had this million-watt spotlight. One guy would drive and another would try to hold it on the water so the skier could see. But mostly we just skied under the moonlight. One night, Mo Melly was behind, and the next thing you know he was in the middle of this flock of swans—feathers and all this shit flying and gagging him. Nobody got hurt, thank God. But we used to do crazy shit like that.

We'd go fishing too. I'd heard that you could take a quarter-stick of dynamite and a spark plug and wrap them together. If you dropped it under the dock, you'd stun the fish and they'd float to the surface. So we dropped this bomb into the water, and it went *whoomp.* The fish came floating up, but they weren't just stunned, they were dead.

Sheldon and I were both terrible golfers. We'd both shoot about a hundred each. We loved to drive the ball a long way, but we'd drive it for show. We were always competing—who could drive the ball the farthest. Forget about the rules. If we whacked one into the trees, we'd just put another ball down, or tee it up on the fairway on a par-5. It was same as driving a car—how hard, how far and how fast could we hit this ball. We'd make side bets for a hundred bucks, a case of beer or a pack of smokes.

One day, my lawyer, Harold Fried, took Tom Mullen, Mo Melly and me golfing at Franklin Hills Country Club, about a half-hour outside of Detroit. Franklin is a very elite club, with mostly Jewish members. They were all old, rich and retired. Mo Melly and I showed up with our shirts untucked. Harold was swearing and yelling at us to clean up our act. I said, "Hey Hairball, we're not the ones cussing, okay?" Harold was on his cell phone all the time, so every time Harold went to hit, I'd take the battery out of it. This made him go ballistic, which made us laugh. I loved messing with him.

We sure liked our speed. I had the triple-black 'Vette and Mo Melly had a black convertible, tan inside. Then he bought a blue one with a gold roof and a wooden dash. I called it the Pimpmobile. But the car he had that I liked best was his last one—a red 'Vette with white interior.

Lafayette Towers was on Orleans, and Joe Louis Arena (where we practised) was at 600 Civic Center Drive. That's just under two and a half miles, and if you go the speed limit, it takes about eight minutes. Someone told Mo Melly that whether you drive the speed limit from Lafayette Towers to the rink or go as fast as possible, there will only be a minute-and-a-half difference. We were like, "No way." So we timed ourselves for a whole week. First, we drove our usual, like, 110 miles an hour to the rink. Then we drove the speed limit, and you know what? There was a minute-and-a-half difference.

13

LET'S SHOW SOME ENTHUSIASM

Because I only played four games the season before, I really got off on playing in 1990–91. We had some new guys—Sergei Fedorov was one of the youngest guys coming in. He was trying to find his way. Think about what it would be like the other way—going to Russia to live, not knowing the language and suddenly you are a superstar over there. He was a great player, but it had to be so hard to come over here and fit into our society and perform day in and day out. We had a lot of character players, and Sergei was definitely one of them.

Bryan Murray was our new coach. He'd been fired by the Capitals the year before and replaced by his brother, Terry. I got along with Bryan. The team liked to play for him.

At the start of the season on October 4, I got into a scrap with Troy Crowder with New Jersey. I think I hit Claude Lemieux with a hockey stick as payback for something he had done earlier. Claude had a reputation for being a shit disturber. Crowder only had three league fights under his belt. But he came flying off the bench towards me, and I gave him the head-nod.

If you watch the tape of the fight between me and Crowder, you can see we were going around and around. I've got him by the jersey and I'm using my left arm to string him out. We're swinging and pushing and pulling, but not really connecting. Balance is half the battle on the ice. You have to have decent balance to fight. Most guys wanted to have a good grip on you so they could hold on with one hand and throw with the other. I liked to get my jersey off fast, because if there is no jersey, what do you hold onto? Nothing. You are all over the map. Crowder was a big, strong kid. We were very similar in size and height, but he had no experience, so I was thinking it would be over quick. Our sticks were on the ice and I was shuffling one of them between my feet, when all of a sudden, I stepped down on it with my left skate. I took a half-turn on it and kind of slid. I had no balance. I was on one leg while trying to stay up and scrap. You can see my foot kind of cross over in front. That's when he tagged me over the left eye. In those kinds of fights, sometimes you get a good punch in, and he just happened to throw one that cut me. That didn't happen to me very often, so for him, as a rookie in the league, it helped his reputation. Guys started coming after him, and he realized he had done something bigger than protect his teammate. It quickly launched his career. It was a pretty big jump-start.

On October 10, the Calgary Flames were in Detroit. We went to overtime, and the Flames left me alone in front of the net. I picked up a simple rebound and put it in. It felt good, and it gave me a good footing with Murray. He seemed to like my play and made a comment in the room a couple of games later after a scrap I'd had with Jay Miller of the L.A. Kings. He said, "If somebody is going to fight for this team, goddammit, we're going to show a little bit of enthusiasm for them."

That was appreciated, because the fighting was almost expected, you know? There were guys who were capable, but instead of getting in there, they would sit back and expect me to go do something about their problem. I think if a guy's got the balls to stand up to somebody, whether they get the shit kicked out of them or not, if they just stand up, it shows the rest of the players that this guy wants to win bad enough to go out there and get his ass kicked. Yzerman did it.

I was feeling pretty stressed about the whole deportation issue. Our first game in Canada was in Toronto on October 13, and I was refused permission to cross the border to play. Then the Immigration and Naturalization Service sent me a letter ordering me to turn myself in—they wanted to put me back in jail until my appeal went to court. So on October 22, we got a hearing with federal judge Horace Gilmore. I was pretty worried—if the government got its way, I'd either have to go to jail or leave the U.S. forever.

Three days later, the judge gave his decision. The Wings were supportive through all this. Murray thought about sending the whole team to court with me, but I said no thanks. I didn't want to put the guys through all the media questions and stuff. Judge Gilmore ruled that the law the INS was trying to jail me under was unconstitutional, and I could keep working in the States.

When I was sentenced to serve ninety days at the Federal Medical Center in Rochester, Minnesota, the judge had granted me what was called a JRAD—a judicial recommendation against deportation. Basically, it meant I couldn't be deported on the grounds of my drug conviction. By November of 1990, the immigration law was changed, and all JRADs were wiped out. Including mine. My lawyers had to go back to the drawing board. They were able to appeal because the doctors said I was drinking due to ADHD, and they can't stop you from coming into the country when you have a treatable psychiatric disorder. Meanwhile, I was free to play—as long as I didn't leave the country.

The media was full of hype about our game against New Jersey on January 28 because of the last fight between me and Crowder. People were talking about it on the news, on the street and in the papers. I just kind of blew it off. Crowder was cool about it. He didn't start a pissing match—he didn't say two words. He's a cool guy. I planned to fight—because I *wanted* to do it, not because I felt obligated to do it. I wasn't going to fight just for the fucking papers.

Crowder had no shortage of practice opportunities before our next fight. By the time of the game, he had fought maybe fifteen other guys. A lot of guys thought that if they could take him, they'd be ranked up there as well. And Crowds had this trainer who liked to instigate fights. He'd talk to the other trainers before Crowds's games and almost provoke a fight— you know, "My guy is going to go after your guy," and next thing you knew, guys were coming after Crowds.

Most fights that Crowds got into were started because someone was coming after him or he was trying to protect a teammate, so knowing it was going to happen made him nervous. He had a really good captain, Kirk Muller. The night before the game, Muller decided to take the whole team out to let off some steam. So they all had drinks and partied a little. He didn't want Crowds lying in his hotel room the night before thinking about the fight. It was a good distraction.

The first part of the game, Crowder and I were never shifted at the same time. Then, finally, there was a line change and I kind of brushed him. I said, "Well, let's go." He had a hold of my sleeve and jersey and tried to stay close, but I bent forward and my jersey moved up. His hand was around my collar, so my right arm came loose. I was able to pull back and string him out. I got a couple in and he went down.

Later in the period, he went after me. And in the second fight, he threw a couple at my helmet and shoulder pad. My head was out of range, then I got out of my jersey and put a few to his body. He had nothing to grab onto—he was just trying to hold on. I was getting more and more pissed off. We were in pretty close, and he reached back as far as he could and hit me as hard as he could, connecting with my chin. Later, Crowds told me he was thinking, "Oh God, this punch is going to knock him out for sure."

When you look at the tape, you see my head jerk and then

snap back. I remember I was really mad by then. I pulled him forward off the ice. Crowds says it was all slow motion for him. He was just in shock that I wasn't down. He says he thought, "Holy shit! I can't believe I just smacked him with one of my hardest punches, and now he's pulling me up off my skates." Crowds says he was kind of frozen in a combination of disbelief, confusion and fear. I threw at him, he ducked, and I grazed his helmet, but he lost his balance and fell to the ground.

Crowder hit the big ticket after he fought me. Detroit signed him for $400,000 the next year.

14

CEASE THE DAY

Both Dani and Bambi were coming around. Bambi had a friend named Jenna who Sheldon started seeing. The four of us would hang out together. Bambi was still working on trying to make me smoother. She was a nice kid, but it got to be pretty funny. Dani was the opposite. She'd come over from Windsor when I called, and she didn't judge me or try to change me at all. She just accepted me for who I was.

One night, I was out with Dave Whinham, just shooting the shit. Bambi and I had watched *Dead Poets Society* and she had left a note on my headboard the next morning saying, "Cease the day!" I thought it was kind of cute that she thought the line was *cease* instead of *seize*, but Dave busted my balls about it. "Yeah, Bambi's going to show you the road to enlightenment and refinement." And then he said, "I don't know why you are messing around with her when the perfect girl is in Windsor, right across the river."

He had a point.

By Christmas 1990, Dani and I had moved in together.

I'd met Dani's father, Jim. We dropped in to borrow his car—an '86 Monte Carlo, all done up. He was a nice guy, pretty down to earth. He grew up in Windsor, but wasn't much of a hockey fan. Jim always had a lot of chicks around. He's been married or common-law like six times. One of the first things he said to me was, "Hey Bonehead, as long as my daughter is smiling, I'm happy."

We had a lot in common—we were both gearheads and we both liked bikes, so we started hanging out. We had a couple of little feuds in there, like the time he grabbed my balls and damn near ripped them off. What happened was that my brother, Norm, was having some problems with drinking and stuff. When he'd had too much, it was better to leave him alone. One day, he got a little disrespectful toward Dani in front of Jim. Jim jumped up and yelled, "Nobody swears at my daughter!" He gave Norm a shot, and I moved in between them. Jim said, "This is no hockey rink, pal. You want some street stuff?" And that's when he grabbed my balls and yanked them down. He said, "I'm not going to rip them off, 'cause I want grandkids." Then he turned around and forgot about it.

The next morning, we were all at breakfast and Jim said, "Don't worry, boys. That was the first time, and I guarantee it won't be the last."

Jim and I had kind of a love-hate relationship.

We made it to the playoffs against St. Louis, who finished twenty-nine points ahead of us, in April 1991. I was suspended for a game and fined $500 for getting too close to their goalie, Vincent Riendeau, in the final minutes of game two. I knew it was stupid, but I had reached my boiling point. Garth Butcher had been trying to start something and threw one my way. I gave him a little whack with my stick, and Riendeau started yelling at the ref, Bill McCreary, to call it. I skated over to Riendeau and gave him a tap on the cheek, and he made out like he'd been shot. Butcher had an opportunity to go after me then, but he disappeared. Shows you how tough he was. The Blues' GM, Ron Caron, started screaming that I should still be in jail. He was holding one nostril like he was doing cocaine.

Stevie Y had the balls to say something to the papers. He said, "I'm very disappointed, and we consider this a poor decision by the NHL. It should only have been a two-minute penalty, but it was shown on TV and everyone made a big deal of it. It makes me wonder if the people who make the decisions really know what's going on."

Meanwhile, the U.S. government was still after me. The INS wanted me locked up or out of the country, so they appealed Judge Gilmore's decision to let me stay in the States and work. The case went to the Sixth Circuit of the Federal Appeals Court. In August 1991, my lawyers found a rule in the small print of the new Immigration Act that said that, while on appeal, aggravated felons could no longer be locked up unconditionally if they were not a threat to the community. I was free again.

When Troy Crowder signed with Detroit in 1991, I was looking forward to playing with him. But he hurt his back doing deadlift weights in the summer. By October, he was feeling a little bit better, and he started off playing on a line with me and Keith Primeau. We had an average height of about six foot five and a weight of about 240 pounds. We played some exhibitions together, and we got a couple goals and assists. It might have been a lot of fun creating so much space for ourselves. But in the third game of the year, Crowds got hit from behind and he was out. He did three years of therapy and came back, but his back was never the same.

I started the 1991–92 season with two scraps against Stu Grimson. He was with Chicago, and he was a big, tough guy— six foot five, 240 pounds. Grimson was one of those guys who just seemed to improve every time he fought. The more fights we had, the closer the end result would be. His weakness might have been a balance issue. After a combination of him throwing a couple punches and the other guy throwing a couple punches, he would spin himself off his feet, you know? He was a big, strong guy and he could swing hard, but eventually he'd just lose his balance.

But he really improved in endurance, which was where I usually found my edge. To his credit, Grimson was in great shape himself. He knew his job and did it well.

By the end of his career, when Stu was with the Kings and Nashville Predators, I knew it was going to be a tough fight. He was fair, and he could last.

There was this one game, on December 21 in Los Angeles, when we were losing 4–1. Tony Granato came on and whacked me with his stick. I'm thinking, "What the fuck? I will kill you, you little shit."

So Marty McSorley had to save Tony's dumb ass. Later, I heard that Marty told Tony after the game, "Tony, I don't mind fighting for you—whether it's Bob or anybody. But I'm having fun playing and Bob's not bothering anybody. Why do you whack him? Why do you want to wake up the sleeping giant and turn the game into a situation where I am battling one of the toughest guys in the league for nothing? For absolutely nothing?" Marty's point wasn't that he didn't want to fight. It was, "Why do it needlessly?" It should have something to do with the game.

Marty has said that he used to prepare to play against me. He liked to get up for those games. He'd be in the locker room, stretching, and the younger guys would be like, "Okay, stay away from him in warmups tonight," because when he got out there he was focused.

Because people were saying I was one of the tougher guys in the league, I had a lot of young kids coming up trying to prove themselves. They were looking for a spot on the team. I could understand that. I got my start fighting veterans. They were gracious enough to give me a chance, so I wanted to do the same for some of the newer guys. It's part of the game— give others a shot. That didn't mean I fought everybody. The trouble was, I had a lot to lose. When your team is up and you fall, all of a sudden the guys are down.

Paul Kruse was a tough kid out of Calgary. He came after me, and I just looked at him and laughed. There was a pecking order.

He had to fight our young guys—like Darren McCarty—first, and when he was done with them, he could come and see me. He was looking to make a name for himself.

But Tie Domi had been paying his dues. He had fought some tough guys—Jeff Beukeboom out of Edmonton, Tim Hunter from Calgary, Ken Baumgartner from the Islanders and Gino Odjick from Vancouver.

What I didn't like was that Domi had been talking up how he was going to go after me when we met up on February 9, 1992. He had everything to gain from it. What good would it do me to beat a guy six inches shorter? Even if it was close, it would still feel like a win for him. I didn't go into it seriously enough. I was not prepared. I didn't realize how important it was going to be. It turned out that Domi was just a hard guy to fight. The shorter guys often are. He was a lefty too. And to his credit, he was a tough little bastard. He could really take a punch.

He wanted to go right from the faceoff. He must have asked me three times. Finally, he said, "Come on, Bob, Macho Man wants a shot at the title." He was a cocky little shit.

I said, "Aw fuck, let's go."

He grabbed my jersey and swung at air a few times. I connected a few times, but he didn't go down. I got my jersey off and he was still throwing. By this time, most guys were tired, but Domi had some left. I got a little cut on a little piece of skin next to my eye when he wandered through with a left. It didn't hurt but it looked bad. I was getting pissed, so about forty seconds in I tagged him pretty good. The refs came in and stopped it at about fifty seconds. But to give him credit, he was still standing.

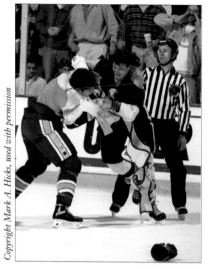

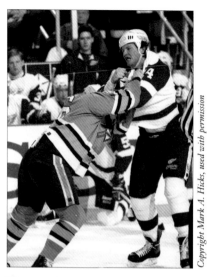

A hell of a fight with a Blues player.

The Ducks visiting Joe Louis Arena on December 14, 1993. Todd Ewen and I scuffled nine seconds in. He stayed close, but I managed to get my right hand free.

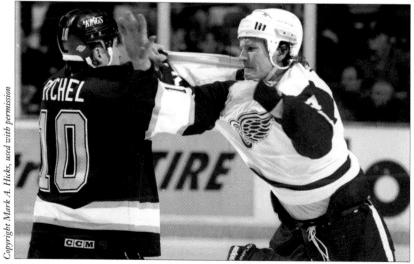

Fighting Warren Rychel of the Los Angeles Kings, October 27, 1993. Looks like I got the edge on Warren in this one.

Skating to the box. I always thought showboating was uncalled for. I personally could not stand it when players tried to entertain after a fight, especially when they went to the penalty box with a hand up in the air or made gestures or smiled. I just thought it was the sign of a young, cocky kid who wasn't going to last long in the league.

I was up against Stu Grimson thirteen times in my career. He was big and strong. I think everybody liked to see those fights.

Marty McSorley was a clean fighter. He never did anything dirty when he and I went at it. We had a mutual respect for one another.

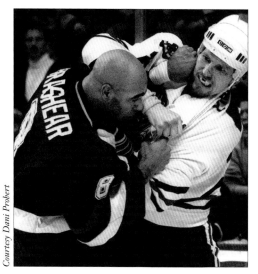

I fought Donald Brashear several times, here when he was a Vancouver Canuck. He was really strong, and would come in tight and hang on.

On March 22, 1996, my new team, the Chicago Blackhawks, was winning 3–0 against the New Jersey Devils. Then they scored twice, so I met up with Reid (Simmer) Simpson at centre ice to see if I could help get things going again. We won the game, 4–2. Simmer became my buddy in Chicago. He got an assist when I scored the last goal ever scored at Maple Leaf Gardens.

Looks like I got clipped. This is not my favourite picture. Lots of times guys get cut and it doesn't hurt, it just looks really bad.

A minute into a game against the Habs on December 15, 1995, Stephane Quintal cross-checked me and a scuffle broke out. I tried to get out there early to get the team going.

Darren Langdon, a tough guy with the New York Rangers, had good size at 6'1", 205 pounds. In this tilt on November 16, 1995, Langer had good stamina. After the game he told a newspaper in New Jersey, "I guess I didn't do too bad—I'm still here."

My wife, Dani, and I met John Candy in 1993, a year before he died, at the opening of a comedy club on Woodward Avenue in Detroit. I liked him.

I met Justin Timberlake while on the set of Mike Myers' movie *The Love Guru*. I had a cameo in the film.

Mark Wahlberg wore my jersey in his movie *Four Brothers*. Actor Rasta Phil (front) put us together, along with Domi, at dinner in Toronto.

Dani and I met Bobby Hull while on a trip to England.

Here I am as an honorary Hanson brother at Joe Louis Arena.

Blonde or brunette, Dani always looks great. This photo was taken at a Blackhawks fundraiser in 1998.

With my Blackhawk road- and roommate Ryan (Bushy) VandenBussche (left) and Mark Bell, another buddy from the Hawks. I was clean in Chicago for six years. Whenever we played in Detroit, I would drag the guys over to look at the progress of my house under construction in Windsor.

Courtesy Dani Probert

Dani has stuck with me through everything for seventeen years. You've got to give her credit.

Courtesy Angela Carson Photography

Courtesy Angela Carson Photography

At my wedding, with Jimmy Devellano, Red Wings owner Mr. Ilitch, Mrs. Ilitch, me, our assistant coach Dave Lewis, and Harold (Hairball) Fried.

Sheldon Kennedy, who I call "Mo Melly," singing my favourite song, "Some Kind of Wonderful," with me and the band at my wedding.

When he was skating off he did this thing with his hands, sort of circling his waist as if he was wearing a championship belt. What it comes down to, I think, is if you're an insecure person, you're a little louder and put on more of a show, and if you're more secure, you take your wins and losses. Maybe Tie was always wondering what people thought of him? For whatever reason, he felt that the belt show was necessary. I don't know who he was doing it for—himself or the crowd—but it was a little too cocky.

I didn't care for that, or for the way Domi acted after. I didn't like the way he was building himself up. And when people start going to the press and mouthing off, well, that's not cool.

Dani's dad, Jim, was all over me getting ready for the rematch. He said, "Domi wants to hit, run and go. He wants to whack you and slide off to the right. He's not going to go head to head. He's going to go off to the right. You've got to keep him in sight." Jim was always looking at the tapes. I think he thought I was Rocky.

Mo Melly was my roommate on the road, and the day of our next fight, December 2, 1992, he and I woke up from our pre-game naps and looked at the front page of the sports section of *The New York Times*. It was crazy. The media was hyping me and Domi like Ali and Frazier. They had our stats—height, weight, reach, number of penalty minutes. I asked Mo Melly, "What do you think?" He said, "I don't know, man. I'm not a fighter, Bob. Just go and do what you got to do, man. You are the one that everybody wants to tackle. You obviously know what you're doing, so just go do it, man." I wasn't scared, just nervous and concerned. The main thing was, I didn't want to get embarrassed. Inside, I guess I cared about being the best.

About thirty-seven seconds in, right at the faceoff, I said, "Let's go, you little fucker."

Domi tried to blow me off. He said, "I'll let you know."

I said, "Right now."

Domi would sometimes fight left and sometimes right. I couldn't really string him out because he was always moving, or else he would be in so tight that I'd be punching down on top of his head, which was so big it was hard to miss. I used to joke that they must use rivets to get his helmet on.

But it was frustrating, because you could never really get in a rhythm, you know? He had a very awkward fighting style, but he pretty much had to because of his height and size and because he didn't have the reach. His style was to kind of spin and throw with the left. He was like a fireplug, because he was short and stocky and he had pretty good balance. He tried to pull you down and throw you off-balance. If you stumbled forward, he would try and throw a punch at you. It obviously worked well enough so that he made a career out of it.

The writers said I threw out forty-seven punches to his twenty-three. I mean, that stat really doesn't mean anything. What counts is what connected. I got a few good ones in. After Domi hit the ice, Stevie Y did the belt thing back to Domi, which was pretty funny. It was a good, clean fight that lasted over a minute. Kris King, a Ranger enforcer, said he got tired just watching. For me, it was just another day at the office. There was no sense yapping about it.

15

REHABILITATED

The end of my immigration case was getting closer. In January 1992, we applied for permission to cross the border and return. The courts ruled that month that I'd paid for my crimes and the INS could not consider the bust at the border in deportation hearings. They also said that you couldn't stop someone from immigrating just because they were an alcoholic.

Harold said he put in more time on my case outside the courtroom than in. He started negotiating with the government the month I was arrested at the border. Harold dealt with a lot of people on the case. Some of the negotiations were done in Washington, some in Detroit. He was sure he could win in court. He always told me he believed he could get me reclassified, and that the main thing was that I had to get my act together to show I deserved to work in the States.

The case cost the taxpayers and me, and would have cost more. At one point, Harold said he was ready to litigate it for the rest of his legal career if he had to. When you fight the United States government, it's not like fighting another law firm that has fifty or a hundred lawyers on staff. You're fighting a multi-billion-dollar organization that has unlimited manpower, unlimited resources and unlimited time.

I think everybody finally realized that enough was enough. Immigration was ready to say, "This guy has been clean for a long time. We believe it's time to move on."

On Monday, December 7, James Montgomery, the director of the INS's Detroit district office, cleared me to travel back and forth across the border, which meant I would be able to play in Toronto two nights later. He said, "Sufficient time has passed and that [I] had demonstrated that [I had] been rehabilitated." I hadn't played in Canada in three and a half years—since the day I was busted. And I liked playing the Leafs. Actually, I liked playing everyone in the Norris Division—St. Louis, Minnesota and Chicago all seemed to tolerate hitters better, and we had a lot of goal scorers, so I could play my game and help the team. The ruling also meant I could see my family and friends a lot more easily. And then there was Tunnel Bar-B-Q in Windsor. Best ribs ever.

The first thing the morning after the decision, Harold Fried picked me up in his black Jaguar and drove me across the border and back. We were kind of quiet on that ride. I was thinking about my family and my career and how Mr. Ilitch believed in me. He was a great guy to work for, whether it was as a Little Caesar's pizza maker or a player. If a guy wanted to help himself and needed his support and guidance, Mr. I would show up.

I think Harold was thinking about the years he'd spent trying to make it happen for me. We were really mellow. On our way back into the States, I was feeling kind of nervous. Harold told me not to worry, he said we had all the right papers, but I kept thinking, "What if they don't? What if they tell me I can't come back?"

Harold stopped the Jag right by the building where I had been busted. We went in, and Harold gave them a document called a Waiver of Excludability as an Immigrant. I felt pretty antsy being in there. But we were cleared through. We got back in the car and headed down the tunnel. When we got to the end, we pulled over. Harold was shaking a little bit, like at the end of a long shift. I gave him a big hug and a pat on the back. It was a pretty special moment. We'd had a lot of little wins through the case, but now it was really over. I could travel back and forth and have a normal life. I felt like this huge weight had been lifted off my shoulders. Things were going great in my life, and I told myself I wasn't going to screw it up.

16

HERE COMES THE BRIDE

I knew Dani wanted to be married some day, but it wasn't something we talked about a lot. I knew she wanted kids. She knew I wanted kids. We just never said it out loud.

In November 1992, after we had been living together about two years, I went looking for a ring. I found a marquis diamond in a basic ring. It was ten grand—about five thousand a carat. I figured that when I gave it to her, she could go and have it sized and have the hardware made differently if she wanted. I took it to the rink every day, because Dani was a snooper—she would find it if I left it at home. She didn't think she was getting a ring, because she had found a receipt for this Louis Vuitton suitcase. As soon as she saw it, she thought for sure that was her big gift that Christmas.

I gave her all her gifts on Christmas Eve, and Dani thought we were done. Then I said, "Oh, hold on. I forgot one," and I got down on one knee and I asked, "Would you marry me, Baby?" Then I got a little choked up.

Dani was crying too hard to answer, but now she says she was just trying to buy some time because she was thinking about it.

After a seventy-two-hour, non-stop party, I woke up on the day of our wedding, July 1, 1993, with cold feet. Dani didn't know anything about this, but a buddy and I were thinking about hopping a plane to Vegas. We'd been talking about how I shouldn't get myself into a trap, so I decided to head to the bank to pick up twenty thou or so. I told Big Daddy, my buddy who owned the Greek restaurant, that I was leaving, so he drove me. This was about ten o'clock in the morning. I told him, "I ain't getting married."

Big Daddy said, "What do you mean, you're not getting married?"

I said, "I'm leaving."

"Where are you going?"

"Vegas."

"C'mon, Bob, you aren't really going to do that. You can't do this to Dani, and you can't do this to all your guests, and you can't do this to yourself right now."

I thought about Dani and how excited we were about the whole wedding. But did I really want to spend forever with this one girl? I always had this worry about settling down and being trapped. Then I started thinking about how Dani had never tried to change me. She just took me for who I was. In fact, our song was Billy Joel's "Just the Way You Are."

I went home with Big Daddy to put on my tux.

Dani's maid of honour, Maureen McCrimmon—the wife of my Wings teammate Brad McCrimmon—is still a good friend of hers today. Dani's sister Jacqueline Wood was our flower girl. She's an actress now on *The Bold and the Beautiful.* Paul Shanbrom, our accountant, and his wife, Dana, both stood up for us. Dani's cousin Stacey and her brother Brad Tayles stood up for us too, and so did her sister Ali Parkinson and my buddy Tom Woodworth. My brother, Norm, was my best man.

Dani was so hot. I'd tried to convince her to pose for *Playboy.* I collected these paintings by the artist Patrick Nagel, who worked for Hugh Hefner. You always used to see his stuff in *Playboy.* I had one that looked so much like Dani, everybody thought I'd commissioned it. She had a really great body and this perfect face. I even had Dani thinking seriously about sending a picture in, but then I started to imagine my buddies and teammates all looking at her, and I changed my mind. Dani and I were looking at our wedding pictures not too long ago and she still looks the same.

The Ritz in Dearborn had a room decorated like a chapel, with white flowers and stuff, it looked really nice. I showed up a little late, about forty-five minutes, but when I stood up there and she walked in, she was so beautiful that I heard this big gasp all over the room.

It turned out to be a pretty hilarious night. I was trying to keep everything under wraps and do what I was supposed to do. When we got back from pictures at the Henry Ford Museum, I headed for the bar in the lobby area and ordered a tall double Jack and Coke. My mother came up to me and said, "What are you drinking?"

I said, "A Coke."

She said, "Oh good, I'm thirsty," grabbed it out of my hand and took a big swig. She doesn't drink alcohol, so she got this terrible look on her face and spit it out all over the bar.

People got pretty loaded. There were a lot of disappearing acts. The wife of my one of my buddies went down on her knees for Dani's cousin Brad, and it almost caused a divorce.

Mo Melly crawled underneath the head table on his hands and knees and did a whipped-cream shoe-check on Soupy. Then Mo Melly and I took over the microphone and sang with the band. I always liked "Some Kind of Wonderful," by Grand Funk Railroad. We jammed that one pretty good. Dino Ciccarelli was a teammate and a buddy, and he taught me to do the two-step, so Dani and I were doing that. Then the whole room did the Hustle, which was cool.

I was a little cooked the whole night because there was a big party going on in a buddy's room. He had mounds of cocaine and booze, so a bunch of us kept wandering in and out. When the reception was over, I joined some guys up in the coke room and Dani spent our wedding night in the bridal suite with her cousin, opening up cards and presents.

Don Cherry and his wife, Rose, were invited to our wedding. They couldn't make it, because Tie Domi was getting married at the same time. Don and Rose sent us a really cool statue of his dog, Blue. We still have it.

About a month after we got married, we were up in the Muskoka area at Paul Coffey's cottage. In Muskoka, people dress to go for a dinner party at somebody's boathouse. Dani was a little worried because everyone was in Ralph Lauren and we pulled up in full leathers. She thought the neighbours might think we were greaseballs. I said, "Who the fuck cares what the neighbours think?" I thought it was fun to shake everything up. Paul loved it. We partied on his boat, then came back to the cottage for a grill. It started to rain. We had John Cougar Mellencamp's "Ain't Even Done with the Night" blasting on the ghetto blaster, and Paul said, "Hey Probie, my deck is looking a little too new."

I agreed, so I rode my Harley, the Moo Moo Cow, up the stairs and did a few donuts on the new wood. Then I burned him a couple of smiley faces. Coff looked at it and said it added character.

Coff was a good guy. He'd been traded to the Wings in January 1993. He always tells the story about his first game with the Wings, on January 30. We were in Vancouver, and there was a little scrum in the corner in front of our bench. Sergio Momesso was roughing Coff up a little bit. Momo was a big guy, and he had 200 penalty minutes for the Canucks that year. Our bench started chirping at him, and Momesso went, "What? You can't hit Coffey?"

Coff says I stood up and crossed my arms and said, "Not anymore."

I remember Coff had two assists that game.

We drove back into Mississauga on my bike because Don Cherry asked me and Dino Ciccarelli to come on his television show, *Don Cherry's Grapevine*. We both showed up. Dani was with me and looked really hot in a tight T-shirt and jeans, with her long, blonde hair kind of tangled up and sexy. Don saw her and pulled her onto the set. She was nervous, but she did great. She was the only wife ever to be on the show.

We didn't go on a honeymoon, but now I wish we had, because we wouldn't have had an incident with Dani's dad, Jim. Jim had this buddy named Dave who worked at Silver's, which is a strip bar on Riverside Drive in Windsor. Dave had a dock behind his place, and he let me keep my boat there. Just after Dani and I got back from our bike trip, Jim and I were up talking and having a few beers when we decided to go out for a late-night cruise. We loaded up the boat and called Dave. He came by and brought a couple of the girls who also worked at Silver's. I said, "Oh yeah, no big deal, hop in." We partied up and down Lake St. Clair all night until the sun was coming up. Then we headed back in.

Jim said, "Listen, guys, before you head back to your dock, we gotta get rid of these chicks. I don't care where you get rid of them, upstream or downstream. Drop them off at the shoreline. Do not bring these chicks back to your dock."

I told him, "Take it easy, Jimbo, no big deal." About a mile out, Dave said, "Who's that on my boat dock?" I said, "Oh shit. It's Dani!" The Formula 1 had this long nose with a cabin, so Jim and the girls hid in there.

I pulled up, and Dani jumped on board. Seeing the craziness in her eyes, Dave just ran. I held up my hands in front of me—"Dani, it's not what you think, take it easy!" She gave me a left hook right across the chin, knocking my good sunglasses right into the lake. I tried to explain. "It was just a ride—it's not what you think! It was no big deal."

Then she ripped open the door to the cabin and found Jim with his arms around the girls. She got even more pissed off. "Dad! I knew you were here, you son of a bitch!" and she went after him with both fists. Marriage was a lot harder than I thought.

On October 15, 1993, while we were playing in Toronto, I was going to the side of the net and Bob Rouse got in the way. He was using his stick to tie me up, so I broke loose, gave him a little poke on the arm—a quick right with my glove—and then, when he turned in, a little whack across the back. He got frustrated and raised his stick and took a two-hander at my helmet. I saw it coming and deflected it with my stick, and then Darren McCarty came in. Rouse and McCarty were going at it along the boards. A five-on-five broke out and both linesmen grabbed me. No big deal, right? Wrong.

I was called to a meeting at the league office. Brian Burke, who's the Leafs GM today, was the NHL's senior vice-president and director of hockey operations. He was Commissioner Gary Bettman's top guy, his number two man. Burke had just been there a month—before that, he had been GM of the Hartford Whalers—and Bettman had been commissioner only eight months.

The whole thing was a joke. There was no hearing, no real discussion. Burke suspended me for four games for trying to stop a guy from taking my head off, and I asked him, "Don't you think that is a little harsh?" He started waving his hand to tell me to shut the fuck up. I said, "Well, if you don't care what I have to say, why am I here? Why don't you just phone me and tell me what I got?"

As far as I could tell, Burke was making it up as he went along. He told me I got two games for the Rouse incident and two games because I was a "repeat offender." I said, "This is bull." Then he told me I'd get five more games tacked onto any suspension if I appeared before him again. I told Cynthia Lambert from the *Detroit News*, "This guy's a disgrace to the league. Four games for what?" Even Bobby Rouse said, "I don't know how Probert feels, but my slash was more vicious."

Because I spoke up, he told the papers, "I want to review the comments of Probert and I may very well take disciplinary action."

Our coach, Scotty Bowman, told Lambert, "I know what I would do if I were Bob Probert. I'd get myself a lawyer. Some guys are going to get forty games if he gets four for that." And Burke threatened Scotty for saying that.

In January 1994, Dani came out of the bathroom with the pee-test strip and told me she was pregnant. I didn't take it too well. I was a little nuts, and threw a frying pan across the sink. I was freaked out at the idea of being a dad. I told her she'd gotten pregnant to make me stay home, to trap me, but the real problem was me. Most things didn't scare me, but this did.

Dani backed off. She never screamed and yelled and gave me shit. She was a strong girl. But I didn't settle down while she was pregnant. Things got wilder.

I loved Vegas. The first time I ever went there was in '92. We stayed at the Golden Nugget and I came away with $35,000.

My worst night was in 1999—I lost $180,000 from chasing my losses, marker after marker. Mo Melly never gambled, but he would sit with me while I played. I always had good luck when he was around. Mo Melly would collect the money. He always told me, "Fuck, Probie. I'm the brains of the operation here."

Dani was worried about the bank account. She used to say I bought the *B* in Bellagio. I started heading to the Windsor Casino to play blackjack. Dani wrote a letter to the casino telling them not to give me credit. They did as she asked, and I wasn't pissed. It was a good idea—she had my back. I hated it when the media targeted her. They could say whatever about me, but she didn't deserve it.

We were out to dinner in Greektown with a bunch of friends one night when she was about four months pregnant. Someone put a couple of shots in front of us. Dani moved hers aside and asked for water instead. As a joke, they brought it in a shot glass. We all tipped back, and the next thing you know Keith Gave, the columnist for the *Detroit Free Press*, was all over it. He said I had been out drinking with my pregnant wife. Fuck. I was twenty-eight years old. I'd done my time and piss tests, and parole. It was a free country. Yet I'm sitting having a beer and Gave writes about it. He seemed obsessed with my drinking. I'd been to meetings with guys like him there. They were on a mission. Between Gave and this asshole with the *Detroit News* named Joe Falls who had a crying fit every time I got into a scrap, I was getting a little sick and tired of it all.

The fight I remember most from the '93–94 season was a scrap on February 4 with Marty McSorley, who was with the Penguins. I was up all night before that fight, out partying. At the end of the first, we were up 2–1, when there was a little shoving and we dropped the gloves.

It was a pretty long fight—somebody clocked it at ninety-three seconds. Two or three different times, the linesmen started to come in and then got out. I think they were a little bit surprised at the fact that we were both looking to keep fighting, but part of that is just who we are. He wasn't going to give an inch, and neither was I. We were both comfortable we could handle the situation.

We were jockeying for position and trying to move each other off-balance. It was a good, clean fight. There was nothing dirty—a lot of mutual respect there. People have watched the tape and noticed that we said something to each other at the end of that fight. You know what it was? My finger was stuck in one of the holes of his helmet. So when the linesmen were separating us, I said, "My finger is stuck." And instead of jerking his head back, Marty put his head down and said to the linesman, "Take his finger out." So the linesman reached over and pulled it out. Then I just kind of acknowledged the fact that he was respectful about the whole thing.

When Marty remembered the fight, he said, "There might be instances where you feel somebody is less than honourable or less than worthy of respect, and in those cases I might not have been as kind or open-minded about the finger."

I was just bagged after that one. It was the most tired I had ever been after a fight. When I came off, Mo Melly patted me on the back and said, "You are a fucking machine to pull that one out of your ass."

Dani was there waiting for me after the game, and as soon

as she saw me, she said, "Hey Baby, anything I can get you? A Coke? A smoke? An oxygen mask, maybe?"

A few weeks before that, after we beat Tampa Bay 6–3, there was an incident in practice. Keith Primeau had been going on about how they missed an assist of his in the Tampa game. Then, while he took some shots, one of the guys who worked at the arena got on the PA system and said, "Hold on a second. We have to add an assist to Primeau on this goal." Primeau got hot and went after Steve Chiasson, but he had the wrong guy. So Chase gave him a face wash. Primeau got hotter, and Bowman said, "Come on, Probie, break that up." But Primeau hadn't had enough yet, so he and I went at it for a few seconds. The whole thing was pretty funny.

17

I'M IN TROUBLE NOW

After the 1993–94 season, my contract with the Red Wings was up, and they had to make me a qualifying offer to keep me on the team. Otherwise, I would become a restricted free agent and listen to offers from other teams—although Detroit had the option of matching any offer I agreed to. Pat Ducharme found a loophole in the offer they had made. He called me up one day—I remember Dani was about seven months pregnant—and said, "Bob, they haven't served you properly."

Under league rules—and this was to protect the player's rights—the team had to make sure the player had the offer in his hand. You couldn't just fax it to an agent or lawyer, because a lot of the players go away in the summer, and if the player doesn't get the offer he might miss out on becoming a free agent. But the Wings overlooked that and just sent a fax to Harold Fried.

On top of that, there was a problem with the amount the Wings had offered. They were supposed to offer me a raise of

10 percent over the previous year. They did—but on top of my base salary. They overlooked some deferred money I received in '93–94. They made a second offer that would have satisfied the terms of the collective bargaining agreement, but it came in after the deadline of midnight on July 1. Pat wrote to the Red Wings, saying their first offer was too little, and their second offer was too late. He told them I was a free agent. The Wings disagreed and took it to the league, who eventually ruled in our favour, making me an unrestricted free agent eight years into my career.

I told Pat I wanted to stay with the Wings and didn't want to become a free agent over a technicality. But they needed to offer me a decent contract.

Jimmy D called me up, almost in tears. Bryan Murray was really worried too. He told Pat that if I became a free agent this way, it meant they had served lots of other guys improperly. Ducharme said, "So what? You're saying that because you do lots of things badly, we are supposed to swallow it?"

My heart wanted to do right by the Wings, but my brain knew I had won the lottery. I always said, "I don't get paid to think, I get paid to react." And my reaction was that it was all business—even when they kept saying they had done this or done that for me. Big Daddy used to say, "Bob, you are entertainment. You are a draw. You helped bring hockey back in Detroit." I was eight years in. I wasn't getting a contract based on my scoring. I wasn't getting a contract based on my assists. I was getting paid based on my reputation. There were a lot of guys who were starting to think twice about roughing it up with me. The Wings knew that I could draw—and would draw in a lot of other places. And I had already heard they were looking to trade me. They'd been bringing in enforcers for a while—Keith Primeau and Jim Cummins, guys like that.

A couple of teams were interested in me. The Rangers and Los Angeles called Ducharme. Toronto was there too. Philadelphia called up Big Daddy, asking, "How do we meet with him?" Then Bob Pulford in Chicago called and asked me to fly in. I did, because next to Detroit, Chicago was my favourite city. And it was still close enough by car for my mom and family and friends to come watch me play. Just a four-hour drive. Their first offer was $1.5 million a year for four years. And then St. Louis offered $2.4 million a year for five years. I said to Pat, "I don't want to go to St. Louis. I want to go to Chi-Town." Pat said, "It's your choice, but you really must like Chicago!"

I came home not knowing what to do. I still wanted to give Detroit a chance. I had Big Daddy and Ducharme with me when we met with Jimmy D, Mr. I and Bryan Murray. I had $1.5 million a year for four years, plus bonuses, on the table from Chicago. I was willing to give up $2 million. "If the Wings make it to a million a year," I told Ducharme, "I owe them. We'll take it."

Mr. Ilitch said, "I have been there for you, I have done everything in the world for you. I'm calling in a chip." And I said, "Okay. What is it?" And he said, "I'm going to offer you $800,000." I looked at Mr. I and said, "Eight hundred versus a million five—that is $700,000. Over four years, that's $2.8 million. That is a very, very expensive chip."

And Mr. I said, "Well, that's what I can do right now, and I would hope that you can accept it."

My time was up in Detroit.

I went to Chicago the first week of July 1994, signed an offer sheet, came home, went to a strip joint, had some drinks and some coke, and got pulled over in Allen Park, Michigan. I didn't have my licence on me. The cop could've taken me to jail, but he knew who I was and gave me a break.

My mother-in-law, Leslie, was in town. I had trouble with her always praying for me and quoting scripture and stuff. I respected Leslie and her beliefs, but I didn't want to hear about it. Leslie wouldn't ever preach at me—Dani wouldn't let her—but the next morning, July 15, as I was lying on the couch hurting from the day before, I looked up and saw her leaning over the balcony, staring at me. Dani was at a doctor's appointment, so I left. Later, Leslie told me the Holy Spirit was telling her to talk to me, but she didn't do it and would always regret that decision.

I went up to the corner deli to get some breakfast. The Russian owner sat down and said, "Come on, Bob, do a shot." I liked Russians, and before you know it, I was going along with Russian tradition—do a shot, another shot, and another shot. We finished a bottle and I decided to head downtown. I jumped back on the Moo Moo Cow. As I came up to the intersection of Orchard Lake Road and Middlebelt in Keego Harbor, the light turned yellow. I was fucked up, and I kind of had to decide whether I was going to turn right or go through the light. At the last minute, I decided to turn, but suddenly changed my mind and went straight. I clipped the front of a Lexus and flew about forty-five feet over the hood. I had this little helmet on—it didn't cover my ears or anything, just the top of my head. It's a novelty item. It's illegal, but I still wear it today because it saved me. The whole intersection was about 36,000 square feet of cement except for one tiny triangle of grass between the road and the sidewalk. That's where I landed. Or, I may have tagged the cement and then flipped onto the grass, because I separated my shoulder and split my elbow open. In any case, I got pretty lucky.

I was lit, so I don't remember much, but I do recall a cop leaning over me and me looking up and saying, "Just charge me with the usual."

They took me to the Pontiac Osteopathic Hospital and handcuffed me to the bed. The doctors put in a catheter, so there was piss in a pan under the bed. A buddy of mine showed up and offered to kick it over so they couldn't test it for alcohol or drugs, but it was too late for that. I don't remember anyone asking me first, but somehow the cops got a look at the results of the blood test. So they knew there was cocaine in my system. The cops released the information to the press. The headlines said, PROBERT ON COKE?

The Wings were super pissed at me. Jimmy D told the press they were putting me on waivers because I was too much trouble. They wanted to save face.

When Dani walked into my room and saw me, she looked like she was in total shock. She was really pale and her eyes looked almost blank. I was very worried about her and the baby. "I'm so sorry, Baby." I said. She walked up to the bed and leaned over and kissed me on the lips. Then she whispered, "You're alive." I wasn't a big crier or anything, but that got me choked up.

Big Daddy walked in behind her. I said, "Big Daddy?"

He said, "Yeah."

I said, "I'm in trouble now."

He said, "Yeah you are."

I think I had something like $14,000 in cash in the side pockets on my bike. The tow truck driver found it and returned it to me, which I thought was really cool. The police were pretty cool too. I knew some of them. One officer who I really liked was there, but I didn't realize it was him, and I told him, "You know what an Uzi looks like?"

And the cop said, "Yeah."

And I said, "Because I'm going to show you mine when I get out of here."

I felt bad about that afterwards and apologized. Big Daddy said, "You know, Bob, there's Good Bob, and every so often there's Bad Bob, and you were Bad Bob that day."

I could make a deal with whatever team I wanted, and I wanted Chicago. They sent two first-class air tickets for me and Ducharme. I was an hour late for the flight, but I got lucky because the plane was delayed an hour. I walked in when they were just about finished boarding. I didn't have my teeth in because my mouth had been banged up, and I had my arm in a sling. It was hard to get into a jacket, so I was just wearing an NHLPA T-shirt.

Bill Wirtz, the owner of the Blackhawks, was chairman of the Board of Governors of the NHL and was having lots of back-and-forth with the players' association at the time. Pat said, "I can't believe you would wear that T-shirt, and not even dress up a little bit to meet the guy who's going to sign your paycheque if we make this deal." I'd heard Mr. Wirtz was a good guy, so I wasn't sweating it. I said, "Don't worry, he'll warm up to me anyway."

When we walked in, Mr. Wirtz, the Hawks' GM Bob Pulford and their lawyer, Gene Gozdecki, were all smoking and having a drink. I bummed a few smokes off them and we got it signed. They weren't freaked out by the accident, but they wanted me out of Detroit right away. They told me the sooner I got to Chicago, the better.

Mr. Wirtz pulled Pat aside and said, "Pat, we're going to get Bob some good teeth." Pat said, "He has good teeth—he likes wearing them like that." Mr. Wirtz thought that was pretty funny. He just seemed so cool. He was old-school. I heard his father was involved with Al Capone and Prohibition and all that. His family owned half the rights to all the liquor sold in Vegas. Every bottle of liquor, they got a piece of that. I liked the old man. A lot of people didn't, but I did.

18

MY KIND OF TOWN

I was hoping for a fresh start in Chicago, and I got one. I really hit it off with Pully. He was just great to me. Darryl Sutter was the coach and he was great too. He was very positive at the press conference. And he'd call Dani up to check in with her. "Is there anything you need? Is there anything we can do?" The club showed her around. They found her a doctor too, because they wanted us to move to Chicago right away. I wish that I had played for Sutter, but as it turned out, that wasn't going to happen.

There was a very large carrot dangling in front of my nose. My contract depended on me staying sober. That meant therapists and blood tests and piss tests and meetings. The urine testing was supposed to be random, but at home they were scheduled. I used to say to Dani, "The piss tester just called. He's on his way." My contract also included a clause that said, "Player agrees not to ride or otherwise use any type of motorcycle at any time . . . including off-season."

I was really good with the rules in the beginning. I managed to stay off my bike for a year. But by the second year, I figured that particular clause was maybe put in there as a joke.

There was another clause that said I had to go to a certain number of Alcoholics Anonymous meetings every week. I'd walk up to the corner of Dickens and Sheffield in Lincoln Park, where they had them almost every night. I was supposed to get signatures to prove I was there, but that didn't last. Being forced to go and get people to take attendance wasn't what AA was supposed to be about.

I signed the contract, but I told Dani, "When I retire, I'm going to crack a Corona and give the finger to the NHL."

I played by the rules in Chicago. I met with the press and jumped through all the hoops. We rented Steve Konroyd's house and sold our house in Michigan and had everything moved that summer because the Hawks wanted Dani to have the baby there.

Chicago was a really neat city. Dani's cousins, Stacey and Brad Tayles, were with us one night when we were driving around, trying to get used to the roads and stuff. We got lost in an area called Cabrini-Green, which was probably the toughest part of town. We were having a great time singing themes to TV shows like *Gilligan's Island* and *The Brady Bunch.* We were circling and circling when we started singing *The Flintstones*, but we got stuck on the words. We pulled up to a light, and next to us there was a car full of gang members. The car had hydraulics and bass speakers, and the guys had do-rags and scars. I rolled down the window, and Dani started to panic. She said, "Bob! I'm going to have this baby right here if you don't roll that window back up!"

"Just a sec," I told her. Then I said to the fellas in the car, "Hey guys, we're singing the *Flintstones* song, but we're stuck. Do you know the first line?"

The guys in the car just looked at me with their mouths kind of open.

I tried again. I started singing. "You know . . . *the Flintstones, they're a da-da-da-da . . . la-la lee.* . . . None of us know the words. Can you help us out?"

Dani grabbed my arm. "Bob, I swear my water is going to break if you don't roll up that window."

Someone on the corner yelled, "Get the fuck outta here, man!"

The light turned green and the car took off.

Stacey, Brad and I chuckled all the way home. Dani thought it was funny too—but not until many years later.

I was ready to have my first kid and start fresh with the Hawks, and then, on September 2, 1994, Bettman suspended me. Technically, he placed me on inactive status indefinitely. He ordered me to "undergo league-supervised treatment of substance abuse." If you think about it, that is really fucked up. The league wasn't my employer. They were a governing body. I was employed by the Hawks, and they didn't order me to go anywhere. For a governing body to just make up rules as they go along, I mean, that's bullshit.

It could have been worse. If I played today, I would have been done right then. The game has totally changed. Now they have the NHL drug program in effect. Once they get hold of you in that program, you're screwed. I guess I was the first one in that program. I don't remember signing anything, but Bettman told me that as soon as our daughter was born that September, I would have to get my ass down to California for rehab. And then they forgot about me.

Bettman, he's an asshole. A frikkin' asshole. I think he's ruined the game of hockey. He's supposed to be impartial. He's supposed to speak for the good of the league, but in my opinion, he's strictly behind the owners. Those 1996 rule changes are a joke. The rules are that an instigator gets ten minutes for a first offence, and a game misconduct for a second offence. The third man into a fight gets two games. If you scrap when the puck drops, that's five games. Five games for going over the boards, and if your sweater comes off, you sit a game. I don't think Bettman realized the consequences of putting in these rules. They target guys who are fortunate enough that they can play the game and fight. When they are on a penalty, it hurts the team. But the rules don't bother guys who get called up strictly to fight. What difference does it make to them to spend time in the box? It took the spontaneity out of the game. It wasn't right.

If a guy takes a cheap shot, you have to be there. I mean, you are a team. You stick up for one another. So you go and give the guy a shot back. Today, if the guy takes a dive, you get the penalty. Now, if you're a 160-pounder and can't back yourself up, you aren't going to last in the league too long.

I was watching a playoff game the other night, and I was like, "Is this really the playoffs?" It looked like frikkin' pond hockey,

6–5. Like, come on. Usually in playoff hockey, everyone steps it up to the next level, to 110 percent. They want to win and they will do whatever it takes to win. This looked like a frikkin' all-star game.

There's not much hitting, and you can't touch a player. If you put a stick on him to slow him down, you get a penalty. Now they call penalties in overtime! That was unheard of, especially in the playoffs. In 2010, Chicago swept San Jose, but in game four, third period, tied 2–2, they called a penalty. A guy shot it into the stands, delay of game. So Chicago has a power play, but they don't score. Then the refs call San Jose on a holding. Okay, maybe it was a hold. Chicago gets a power play—they don't score. Four minutes left in the game, and they called two more penalties against San Jose. Then they called a third penalty against San Jose for a slash. Now, that was terrible. It was definitely a questionable call. Chicago scored with four minutes left. They won the game 3–2. Come on. Third period, a team could be eliminated, it's 2–2 and they call three penalties in a row? Chicago scores to win the series? That's not playoff hockey.

The game is more European now. More skating, less hitting. It's faster, so maybe some fans like to see that. Everyone is in top shape, which is good. You used to have maybe three or four awesome skaters and the other half were maybe average, and then you had a couple of lousy skaters. Now everyone is an awesome skater. I thought I was in the middle, average. I was a bigger guy, so it took me a little longer to get going, but once I got going I did all right. The bigger guys now are so much quicker than I was when I played.

Brogan Victoria was born on September 15, 1994, during training camp. I always called Dani nicknames like Boo-kee, Wood and Dan-Dan. She hated that one. As soon as I saw Brogan, she got one too—Bro-geeta Chiquita Banana.

We couldn't decide which of our parents should be there. Leslie and I hadn't bonded yet, and most girls don't want their mother-in-law in the room when they are having a baby. We both decided the happy medium was to have her father, Jim, there. Today, we both think that was a little weird. Jim stood over her shoulder and did the camerawork, so we have video of her being born. Jim and I were both a little worried, so we paced around. After a while, we got bored of that and started a push-up competition on the floor beside her bed, but Dani told us to knock it off. Brogie was a big baby—ten pounds, six ounces, twenty-four inches long. Through the whole pregnancy, I kept saying, "I only make boys," but it turned out that having a big, healthy girl made me just as proud.

My whole life changed once I held her. Having kids was the best thing I ever did.

Brogan was three weeks old when I was sent to the ASAP Family Treatment Center in Port Hueneme, near Oxnard, California. It was run by Dr. Dave Lewis, who also worked for the NHL owners. The NHL was paying his treatment centre top dollar to have me there. I couldn't leave, because I would have screwed my chances of getting back into the NHL. They had me by the 'nads.

The first part of the season was toast anyway. The collective bargaining agreement between the league and the players had expired. There was a big issue over the salary cap—the owners wanted one, the players didn't. So the owners locked us out on October 1. Bettman was too busy with the negotiations to deal with me, and I understood that. So in January, when the new deal was finalized and they saved half the season by making up a forty-eight-game schedule, I thought, "Okay, they'll let me out and I'll come and play the rest of the games."

Bettman said no to that. Then Sutter wanted me back for the playoffs. I toed the line, and on April 28, 1995, Bettman reinstated me, but released a statement saying I couldn't play that year. He said, "Mr. Probert is not eligible to return to full active status and play in games [until] the 1995–1996 season, provided he complies with the aftercare and maintains sobriety."

I called Port Hueneme "Port Wannabe," but there were some good things about it. Family members were involved in the program. Dani and I did some good work in rehab. I remember being in this big circle, and there had to be about a hundred of us. Each person had to say one word about how they felt. My word was *hopeful*.

Sometimes at rehab they would ask me, "How can a guy make $800,000 and throw it out for booze and drugs?" In other words, "Are you that dumb?" I think decisions are made either intelligently or emotionally, and I had been making them based on emotions. Even if you've got a law degree, it doesn't stop you from making bad emotional decisions. I had to use both my heart and my head, but it wasn't going to be easy.

I left rehab in April, did the big press conference, and we started our lives in Chicago.

At the end of August, I spent three days in jail and paid a fine of $1,395 after pleading guilty for driving impaired and crashing my motorcycle back in July 1994. I got out, and there were some major asshole moves by the papers in Chicago. Rick Telander from the *Sun-Times* had been slamming me in his column. And he decided to get cute. He arranged to meet at a bar. During the interview, he got the waiter to bring out a shot and put it between us. Did he seriously think I was gonna grab it? I mean, c'mon. Then he handed me a rolled-up twenty-dollar bill and said, "Snort away." All class, that guy.

In Detroit, hockey is on the front page. In Chicago, it's way down on the fifth. So if you screw up, it's not always going to make the paper. I'd go to the games and practices and come home—like a typical family man. The pressure was off. I was kind of private, so I didn't like how my life had always been spread out in Detroit papers. Sometimes I wondered what it would have been like if I had been a cop in Windsor, like my dad. Once I had the big money, I wouldn't want to go back, but I don't think I needed a lot of money to be happy. I thought about that a lot, you know?

My teammates in Chicago were incredibly respectful. They went out of their way to try not to make things awkward. It got to the point where we would go to parties and I would say to Dani, "Please have a drink so that my teammates don't feel uncomfortable and can have a cocktail too." They were an awesome group of guys.

At the start of the 1995–96 season, Craig Hartsburg replaced

Darryl Sutter as coach. I liked Hartsy. He'd played in the Soo as a defenceman from 1975 to 1978, and was always pretty supportive. He started me on a line with Jeremy Roenick and Sergei Krivokrasov. The guys on the Hawks took care of each other. Chris Chelios worked with me on fitness, J.R. talked me up, and it was appreciated. Murray Craven went to the net for a hat trick, but slowed down to give me the puck—things like that.

Cheli was one of my new teammates. He was the guy who got me serious about off-ice training. He was super-fit and really cared about nutrition. The first summer after I got out of rehab, he got me to drop everything and go out to California to train with T.R. Goodman at Pro Camp in Santa Monica. T.R. trained a lot of NHLers and sports figures like Gabrielle Reece, the American volleyball player. That first year, I only went for three weeks, but I could see the benefit.

During the season, the Hawks went out to L.A. My old connection was waiting for me after the game, at the bar in the rink. I had been straight for about a year. He handed me an 8-ball of coke and I said, "Oh, thanks buddy." I put it in my racquetball case, and it stayed there for like, six years. And then, in my last year, I had a couple of guys over and said, "Hey, I got this stuff and I've been waiting for a special occasion." Cocaine does not go bad.

Meanwhile, I had piss tests three times a week. I had to stay straight if I wanted to be paid. I didn't know a lot of people that I could get stuff from, and I had my new daughter, so I wasn't inclined to get messed up anyway.

Dani and I wanted to have another baby. Brogan was so easy, and we wanted to give her a buddy. In May 1996, at the end of the first season that I saw ice in Chicago, Dani got pregnant again. We were both really happy about it.

I was home in August when Dani lost the baby. It was tough on both of us.

19

GETTING THE SHOW ON THE ROAD

The young kids were still coming after me—fast and furious. But nothing beats experience. If I grabbed a guy with my arm out, he couldn't really hit me, unless he had a long reach. Another important thing was being able to take a punch. I had to sacrifice a couple to the head and body sometimes to get to the position I needed to be in. But then I could take it from there.

It didn't hurt to tire a guy out anyway. It takes a lot of effort to swing. Guys get tired real quick. A thirty-second fight is a long fight, even if a guy comes out of the gate real strong. Once you have done it for a while, you learn to defend yourself in a manner that, even though it looks like you are getting hit, you can brush it off. It's a combination of throwing your head back and cushioning the punches. When you get in a fight, things are so crazy that younger guys don't know what is going on. But after you gain a lot of experience, you can see the punches coming and you know how to dodge them.

The most fights I had in a season was twenty-three. That was in 1987–88. There were eighty games in a season, so that was roughly one every four games. And that's like a high season. My average was probably around twenty, and then one year, including playoffs, I had maybe twenty-eight fights.

The jersey tie-down rule was implemented in 1997, but the NHL general managers had met in the summer of 1996 to discuss it. It's called the Rob Ray rule, after the Buffalo Sabres enforcer who wore oversized jerseys so they'd come off easy. The rule said that the uniform of every player had to have a strip to hook your jersey to your pants and it had to be fastened. If not, you were gone. Once the rule came in, I got the goalie-cut jerseys—they have bigger sleeves. With one of those on, you could pull your arm out pretty easy, even if a guy had a hold of it. So if you fought and your tie-down was not secure and you got out of your jersey, you got penalized. If you got your arm out of your jersey, that was okay. Today, they've started clamping down on the size of the jersey and all that shit.

I never sliced up my tie-down so it could be broken. But there might have been occasions where I didn't do up the snap-on button, just the Velcro. Then, if you gave the jersey an extra tug, it would pull off. A lot of guys did that.

In 1995–96, I played in all but four games and scored 19 goals. The Blackhawks had a pretty good year all around. Cheli had 72 points and won the Norris Trophy as best defenceman. We went 40–28–14 and finished second in our division—sixth overall. We met Colorado in the second round, and they beat us in six games, but four of them went into overtime. They went on to win the Cup. But in '96–97 we hit a rough stretch, and by January 23, we were 8–15–3 at home. Hartsy thought we were too comfortable, so he pulled the couches out of the dressing room and put bikes in front of the TV. Then he disconnected the cable. Tim Sassone from the Arlington Heights *Daily Herald* wrote about it:

> "They're getting rid of the country club, I guess," said Chris Chelios.
>
> "The TV still works, but now we only get three channels," Tony Amonte said.
>
> Nobody seemed to know what happened to the couches.
>
> "They must be in Pully's entertainment room," said one player.
>
> "It looks like my house now," said James Black. "No furniture."

I fought Troy Crowder for the last time on January 22, 1997. By this time, he was with Vancouver. Their goalie, Kirk McLean, went behind the net to play the puck, I gave him a bump and Troy jumped over the boards and dropped the gloves. Things started well—we grabbed each other by the arm and started throwing. We fought around the hash marks, along the boards and all the way around the other corner. He started hanging on, and when he slipped down on top of me, the refs came in. Troy's jersey had kind of rolled up and he was lying there on top of me with a bare gut. He got up, and I gave him a couple of belly slaps and said, "It's good to have you back, Crowds."

He was kind of laughing, and the linesmen were looking at each other like, "Did we hear that right?"

We played Vancouver again on March 10, and I fought Donald Brashear for the first time in a long time. I did all right. The linesmen didn't let us get anywhere. The first time we met up was in December 1993, when I was with the Wings and he was a rookie with Montreal. Brashear was careful about trying not to get hurt, and he was just so strong that he could control you. He would pull you in with his arms instead of stringing you out and then throw quick little hook punches at you. It was a defensive style of fighting. Nobody ever really got hurt, because he was in so in tight. You would think the commentators would figure out the difference between a real fight and one that's not, but they go, "Oh my God! They threw forty, forty-five punches there." Well, you can barely break open a popcorn bag with some of the punches guys throw because they're quick, little rabbit-style punches.

Brashear would never really lose big or win that big. He'd just hold on. If you know how to hold on, then you will do all right, but nobody wants to see that. They want to see a really good fight. That was Brashear's big knock before he made it to the NHL, because that's what he used to do all the time—just hold on. Every time I fought Brashear, I'd think, "I'm going to get fucking big and strong this summer so I can come back next year and break free of that cocksucker and kick the snot out of him!"

This was the first year of Bettman's rules, and sometimes it was frikkin' impossible to play the game. Some of the refs were taking things to extremes, and it was fucking up our chances to get into the playoffs. It was getting ridiculous—clean checks were getting called. Little retaliation shoves were called. I don't mean in the first period—they were called when the game was on the line. On April 3, Bill McCreary called a bullshit interference penalty that changed the outcome of the game. One of our defencemen, Michal Sykora, took a clean check on Mike Grier against the boards. We were tied 2–2 against Edmonton and they scored on the power play. Buchberger tripped me, and I pushed back and the ref called me. I felt like I was playing with my skates tied together.

We played the Flames, and then a couple of nights later we played them again with a chance to clinch a playoff spot. One of their tough guys, Glen Featherstone, had blindsided Cheli. He cross-checked him in the back. It wasn't a really bad thing. It just caught Cheli in a really good spot. He'd taken harder hits than that. Hartsy told the media that one of their best scorers, Theo Fleury, might have to watch his back, because I might come after him. It was all in good fun. We lined up in the circle and Theo looked across. "C'mon, Probie, if you are going to do it, let's go!" he said.

I laughed, "You would too, wouldn't you? You little fucker."

I was in maybe the best shape of my life, but on November 10, 1997, I fought against a lefthander with the Flames, Mike Peluso. He had the most penalty minutes one year (1991–92) with 408. And I got hurt pretty bad. Everyone thought it was from my fight with Sandy McCarthy earlier in the game, but it wasn't—it was from the fight with Peluso. He was a big guy— my size, maybe taller. He threw a few lefts, which I blocked, but then he fell backward and took me with him. I landed on my shoulder, and that's when I got hurt.

The next night, in Toronto, I had a scrap with Kris King, who had been roughing up Cheli. We went down and came up and he came down on top of me. We kept going, but not much happened. I played three games after that, but I knew something was wrong because it hurt like hell. I was waiting to see if it would get better. And then, finally, I was doing this test with a rubber band and I couldn't even pull the thing apart. I decided to play that night anyway. It was November 16, and we were up against Detroit. During the first period, I couldn't move my arm, so I left the bench.

The trainers told me to have an MRI and to get 'scoped. As the doctor was looking at it, he said, "Oh yeah. It's torn right off the bone here." He had to go in and sew it all back up. It was tough, because I'd only played seven games. I was put on the injured reserve list on November 19 and didn't come back till April. It sucked even more because I'd got off to a great start. In the first game, in Phoenix, I played almost twenty minutes and had a goal and an assist. A few nights later, in San Jose, I was on the ice for fifteen minutes and had three shots on goal. Then, in the third game, some little fucker from the

Tampa Bay Lightning came in and hit me knee on knee and tore my cartilage. It was during a scrum around the net. The doctors had to look at it, and on October 16, *zip*—another arthroscopic surgery. So that put me out for three weeks, and then I got into the fight against Peluso and tore my left rotator cuff. Here I thought I was on pace to do real well, and then my shoulder blew out and I missed another fifty-three games.

The only good thing about my injury was that I could play with the kids. Tierney Rose had been born in July of '97. Dani was induced, so we got to pick the date, and I picked my number, 24.

The timing of the rotator-cuff injury was brutal because I was in a contract year. I was due to become a free agent on July 1, 1998. Before the season started, I had written Pat Ducharme and told him I'd decided to handle all of my own matters pertaining to the NHL. I told him I appreciated everything he had done for me and my family and wanted to remain friends. I'd paid him a couple hundred thousand for the last contract, and he'd done all right off all the other legal matters that the Wings and I had paid him for. So he was good with it. Big Daddy gave me a hand instead.

The Hawks offered me a two-year extension at a million per year, and I turned that down. I thought I was worth more. The clean living and workouts and everything were extending my career. Except for my shoulder, I was feeling good. In '95–96, including the playoffs, I played 88 games and had 42 points and 260 penalty minutes. In 1996–97 I had another 88 games, 26 points and 367 penalty minutes. And I had been really lucky with injuries. In those two years, I only missed three games, because of sprained knee in January 1996. My aim was to play 1,000 games in the NHL. That was something that meant a lot to me. I had 648 under my belt. If I stayed healthy, I could do it in four more seasons.

In January, I signed a fourteen-page contract extension with the Blackhawks for four years, backdated to October 1, 1997, for $6.5 million. It felt pretty good knowing the team had that much confidence in me. The offer came with a four-page addendum that included performance bonuses. I would get an extra $100,000 if I achieved three out of four conditioning points, and $50,000 for achieving two of them: my mVO_2 (myocardial oxygen consumption) had to be at least 63, I couldn't weigh over 227 pounds, my body fat had to be 14 percent or lower, and I had to do at least 600 watts on the bike. There was a goal-scoring incentive: a 25-goal season meant $75,000. And I'd get another $75,000 if I played 73 or more games in a regular season. The addendum also outlined all the things I could not do, like drink, drug and ride my Harley.

I came back against Detroit on April 4, 1998, just as the Hawks were about to miss the playoffs. In our last seven games, we went 0–6–1. On the fifteenth, we were in Toronto to play the

Leafs—another team that was having a tough time—and I fought with Tie Domi. Tie had sucker-punched one of our big defencemen, Cam Russell.

The reason Domi went after Russell was that Russell had put him down in a fair fight a couple of months earlier. But this night, Domi didn't wait to square off. He started taking shots to Cam's head before Cam even got his gloves off. He pulled Cam's jersey over his eyes and kept punching while Cam was off-balance and had lost his helmet. Domi shoved him backward to the ice, where Cam hit the back of his head and was taken off on a stretcher. It was ugly.

Domi had worked on this move where he would turn away so you were almost facing his back. I grabbed at his jersey and tagged the side of his big head. Once he started getting hit, he went down fast. The linesmen came over and Domi kept yapping.

There was another guy on my team who could have stepped in, but he didn't. I was starting to notice a change in the game. People were out for themselves now.

20

BOB DYLAN'S GYM

In the spring of 1998, Chicago traded for Ryan VandenBussche. He became a good buddy of mine. He was not a huge guy, but he was tough. He'd already spent five years in the American Hockey League in the Leaf and Ranger systems. Even after the trade to Chicago, he spent a year and a half with our farm team in Indianapolis before he finally caught on in 1999. We shared the same type of role. He was a right winger and I was a left winger. We played a lot of hockey together on the same line and eventually became roommates for three years. When you are roommates with somebody, you really get to know them. I wasn't drinking or doing anything illegal at the time, and we saw some good times. We would sit up late and have a lot of discussions about life in general.

The summer of 1998 was the fourth I spent out in California to train. And I worked harder than ever that year. Tough guys like Georges Laraque and Donald Brashear had started getting bigger, and there were more like them coming in. I was like, "Holy shit, I have to get into shape." Dani came with me to California for eight weeks, and it was one of the best summers of my life. We shipped my bike out there and we had this phenomenal house on the Strand, which is this cool neighbourhood in Marina Del Rey.

We'd get up at 5 A.M. and make it to the gym by six, work out for two hours and then go over to the Firehouse Restaurant, which used to be a real firehouse. We'd order up a healthy breakfast—ostrich–buffalo–egg white–broccoli scramble with sweet potatoes. Then back to the house to play with the kids. I'd chill out on the floor or take them to the beach. At 5 P.M., We'd head back for our second workout of the day, either running the stairs in Santa Monica or boxing at Bob Dylan's gym with a coach named David Paul. We'd do plyometrics in the parking lot. Plyos are a certain kind of movement that helps the muscle become explosive. We'd do squat jumps and floor ladders and box hops for foot speed, a lot of push-ups. It was ballistic training, and it's really good for hockey. I drank lots of protein shakes and was in bed by eleven. I even quit smoking. I was in the best shape of my life.

I met Doug Gilmour in the summer of 1998. He had signed with Chicago, and he and his wife, Amy, bought a house right around the corner from us. We really had a lot of fun together. We'd drive to the rink together and hang out and have lunch. There was one thing the four of us were on a mission to do—to go to this really hoity-toity five-star restaurant around the cor-

ner from our house. Charlie Trotter's on Armitage Avenue—
it's world-famous. We finally got in, and it was so stuffy we
hated it from the minute we sat down. All four of us smoked,
so we had to keep going out to the patio. We hated sitting for
hours, and we hated the tiny servings.

Every time the waiter came by, we had to ask for another
bread basket. It cost over eight hundred dollars for the four of
us, and we were still starving. When we left, I headed straight
for the Greek place up on Lincoln Avenue for some gyros.

Amy and Dani were airtight. When guys went out with their
wives, nobody talked hockey. What happens in the dressing
room should stay in the dressing room. Why rip on a guy after
a game?

But some guys shared a little too much with their wives. So
you had to be careful, because the girls liked to share things.
One girl was going with a buddy, and when he dumped her,
she picked up with another buddy. This girl told Dani that the
new guy sucked in bed because he had a small dick. And then
he signed a multimillion-dollar contract, and all of a sudden
he's good in bed and he's got a big dick. Funny what money
does, right?

Dani used to catch wind of things that pissed her off in the
wives' room. One day, she walked in and one of the girls was
talking about the "goon" factor. Bitching about how she didn't
want her kids fighting in hockey and saying it didn't belong in
the game, and Dani got into it with her. "You are talking about
my man! If you wanna call him an enforcer, that is fine, but if
you call him a goon, you don't know him and you don't know
hockey! Tell you what—he can be the puck-hog superstar and

your husband can watch over his ass!" Sometimes, the girls got a little excited.

Dougie changed cars like I changed my shorts. He'd only keep them for a couple of months and then he'd find something better. The guy had some awesome cars, and he was really cool about letting me drive them, even his Ferrari. One time, he said I could take the Maserati for a drive, pick up Dani, whatever. I told him I had to pick up Brogan from preschool. We got there, and I put her in the jump seat, but I couldn't figure out where to put her tricycle without hurting the paint job. Finally, her teacher came out and threw it in her van.

It was Dani's birthday, and I wanted to get her a car, so Dougie sold me his new Beemer, a 540i. He gave me the best deal ever. It meant a lot. Cheli and his wife, Tracee, were generous with us too. He let us stay in his house in Bloomfield Hills, Michigan, while they spent the summer at their Malibu place. He let us use it three years in a row—no rent, no nothing. Just a good guy. One time, we were at a bar with Cheli and some asshole started going off at me. There was always one jag-off who wanted to get in my face. I was still clean, and I told him, "Ah, that's okay, buddy."

He kept lipping off, calling me out, stuff like that, and Cheli picked up a plastic mustard bottle and walked up to the guy and squirted it all over his face and T-shirt, then came back to our table and sat down. He looked at me, shook his head and said, "You can't hit people anymore. That's just the way it is in our society. So I figured, do the next best thing."

Pully was the Blackhawks' vice-president, but he was also the GM for about twenty years. Pully was a great guy. We had a lot in common. We both liked muscle cars—two-door, American cars from the late '60s with big engines and lots of horsepower. We both liked them stock or original, not tinkered with—but a little quicker than the one that came off the line behind it. My cars were always street legal, beefed up a bit in the engine. I put cheater slicks—back tires with enough tread to drive on the street, but just barely—on my black-and-white Chevelle. You could squeal the front tires in first and second gear on that car. I took it to Grand Bend Speedway one weekend to have it clocked, and it was impressive. Pully loved that. He was the guy I would consider to be like a father to me. He wasn't a pushover, but he treated me with respect. I think it is fair to say I loved him.

In July of '97, Bob Murray took over as GM, and we didn't make the playoffs that spring, so he fired our coach. I had never called a coach about getting fired, but I called up Hartsy. I told him I was sorry to see him go. He was a good guy. After they fired Hartsy, they hired Dirk Graham to coach. That was a mess. He'd never coached in the NHL before. He was a six-year captain of the Hawks and a good player. His last year as a player was 1994–95. He'd played under Mike Keenan and Darryl Sutter, and I don't think there are two tougher coaches than those guys. The story was that when he played, he and Jeremy Roenick had blown out their knees heading into the 1995 playoffs. But Dirk played through it, and that made J.R. suck it up and play too.

Dirk went from being a nice, quiet leader to a pretty vocal coach. He was very hard on guys, mostly for the right reasons, but you'd think an ex-player would have more connection to the guys. Instead, he used to embarrass players. He'd make fun of guys who were hurt. As a coach, Dirk was a bag-skater. He treated us like kindergarten kids.

We lost the game the night before the 1998 Christmas party. So when we all brought our families down to the rink for the family skate, Dirk kept us on the ice for a couple of hours and bag-skated us so hard a couple of guys had to go on IV drips for dehydration. The families sat in the hall and waited for us the whole time. Punish us, sure, but not our wives and kids.

He was finished after an ugly practice in February. Mr. Wirtz had traded J.R. for Alex Zhamnov. But Alex had a bad back. Dirk didn't think he was getting anything out of him, so he started riding him about his injury. Then he had a major blow-up with one of our best guys, Tony Amonte. We lost ten out of twelve games, and Dirk was gone.

We had Doug Gilmour on the team that year, but he missed ten games with injuries and was struggling. Paul Coffey was injured for almost the whole season. We went through forty-seven different players that year—a real revolving door. Management felt we were in a transition year and that there was a decision to be made about whether we were going to go young or keep going with veterans. Eventually, they decided to go young. Bob Murray said he wanted to get rid of all of us, but the guy he singled out was Cheli. He traded him to Detroit on March 23.

I ran into Cheli when he was on his way to catch a plane, and he said, "Don't be surprised if you see me in 24." I didn't think anything of it, because I thought he was joking. Nobody had worn my number in Detroit since I'd left, and if a guy wanted it, I was pretty sure he would call and discuss it. Cheli wore 7 with Chicago, but he couldn't wear it in Detroit, because it had belonged to Ted Lindsay and had been retired. But the next thing I knew, there was Cheli in a Red Wings sweater with 24 on the back. I guess he had a right to, because he had worn 24 when he won the Stanley Cup with Montreal. What the hell, I am glad it was Cheli and not some European.

When Bob Murray fired Dirk, he said he'd never hire an inexperienced coach again. So he turned around and made Lorne Molleken, one of our assistants, the head coach. Lorney had coached a few years in junior and a few more in the American league, but he was new to the NHL. He had never even played in the NHL.

We opened the next season in San Jose and got our asses kicked, 7–1. A lot of the tough guys were not in the lineup. Then, about a month later, we were back in San Jose. There was a pre-game skate, and afterward, we had a little meeting on the ice. We were all circled around the coach, discussing things we were going to do, and Lorney said to Chad Kilger, "Kilger, I want you to grab so-and-so. Probert, the first thing I want you to do is grab Brantt Myhres and kick the fuck out of him. Then Bushy [Ryan VandenBussche], you grab Grant Marshall and kick the fuck out of him. Then Brownie and Allison, you guys grab whoever the hell you want to grab and kick the piss out of them too." I had never heard anything like that before at a pre-game skate.

I said, "What do you think, Bush?"

He said, "Well, Probes, Marshall is kind of my buddy. We grew up together."

I said, "Don't worry, Bushy, I've got him."

But that was the first time I'd ever had a coach actually send me out or tell me to go fight somebody. I always knew my job and didn't need anyone telling me what to do. Sometimes, if we were losing the game, the coach might send me out and say, "Hey Probie, take left wing, or pull off the left winger." And if the guy I was lined up against happened to be a tough guy on the other team, I knew what I had to do. It's kind of like, they put you out there for a reason, but they don't say it. Once the guy would see me skating out there, he knew what was going to happen. Maybe some were afraid, but some looked at it as an opportunity—"Well, here's my big chance." In one of my first preseason games with Chicago, there was one guy, Dennis Bonvie of the Oilers, who said, "Hey Probie, let's go. You were my idol growing up, but I'm here to fight you." And I was like, "Yeah, whatever." Dennis was interviewed after I retired, and he said, "Well, I got beat by one of the best." So he seemed kind of happy just to be able to fight me.

I got that all the time. I was lined up against one guy who played for Colorado, Scott Parker. A big, strong kid. Six-five, 240 pounds. Same thing—on January 12, 1999, he was lined up out there and he said, "Probie, you were my idol growing up, but the coach sent me out here for a reason."

I said, "Hey buddy, you really don't want to do this right now."

He said, "Bob, you are either going to make me or break me."

I waited until the third period, when we were down 4–1, and

then I kind of cross-checked him—"Okay, kid, let's go." It was kind of funny. He took his time—fists up, that kind of thing. I waited for him to come in, and after about twenty seconds, he finally grabbed on. I got a good hold and whacked him a couple of times in the temple. His helmet came off and I clocked him pretty hard. He went down on one knee, and his face blew up like a balloon. The linesmen came in, and I looked at him and said, "Well, I guess I broke ya."

The officials got hold of us, and Parker was kind of out of it. He would not let go of the neck of my jersey. The linesmen were yelling at him, "You're choking him! Let go! Let go!" Parker was using his free arm to keep swinging at them—and me—while the ref was trying to loosen his grip, just pounding on his arm. About forty-five seconds later, I was still bent over with a linesman on my back, and I was using two hands to hold the neck of my jersey away from my throat. That jersey was stretched out about two feet.

Parker's teammate Adam Deadmarsh came in and grabbed him from behind, but he was still hanging on. I remember Parker just saying, "No no no no." Over and over again. Jeff Odgers came up and was trying to talk Parker into letting go. He said, "Hey Parks, what's up, man? What are you doing?" It actually got pretty strange.

Parker was supposed to be an up-and-coming tough guy, the next heavyweight champion of the league. The next day, Big Daddy got a call from Scotty Bowman, who was coaching the Red Wings. Scotty said, "Did you see what your friend did?" Big Daddy said, "Yeah, I saw it." And Bowman said, "That could have been the hardest punch I've ever seen thrown in hockey."

When Bushy was with the New York Rangers in 1997–98, he met up with Stu Grimson, who was then with Anaheim. The first time they fought, Bushy took a few serious blows to the head. He knew he would have to fight Grimson again eventually, but he wasn't looking forward to it. The next time they hooked up was in November 1999, when Bushy was with Chicago. He lined up beside the Grim Reaper, who was a big man, and tagged him with a good one right in the nose. Stu dropped pretty quick. Then, after the period was done, Bushy was in the dressing room and Dave Manson told him, "Bushy, you know Stu is going to want to fight you again, and I suggest you don't, because he is pretty fucking mad." Bushy said, "Yeah okay, whatever."

Sure enough, the second period started and Bushy was lined up beside him again. Stu didn't say a word, but as soon as the puck dropped, he dropped his gloves and stick and stepped back and said, "Let's go." Bush was like, "Oh fuck, here we go." Stu was so pissed that Bushy says he was frothing at the mouth. Bushy dropped his gloves and went at it pretty good, throwing haymaker rights, but Stu broke his nose the fourth punch in. Bushy dropped to his knees, then got right back in, swinging for his life and falling on top of Stu. There was blood squirting out everywhere. It was a pretty nasty scrap.

Bushy was in a similar situation with Colorado's Wade Belak during the first period of a game on January 6, 2000. Bushy got some shots in, but it opened his nose again. We were in the room between periods, and I said, "Bushy, don't worry. I will take care of Beelee." Bushy said, "Fuck off, Probie, I'll do it."

But when I got out there again, I went after him.

On February 21, there was a lot of back and forth on the ice between Brashear, who was with Vancouver, and McSorley, who was with Boston. They had a fight in the first two minutes, and then later, Brashear fell on their goalie, Byron Dafoe. The way Marty told it, Brashear was in front of the net and Dafoe barely bumped him. Brashear got up with the big smile, sticking his tongue out, all of that. Marty went up and tried to fight Brashear again, but he wouldn't go. He said, "I don't have to fight." A little while later, Brashear skated past Boston's bench, flexing his muscles and showboating. He was just driving Boston's coach, Pat Burns, crazy. McSorley left it alone because Boston was losing and they were trying to get back into the game.

Then, with forty seconds left and Vancouver winning 5–2, Marc Crawford put Brashear on the ice. So Boston pulled their closest defenseman and said to McSorley, "Get out there, get out there, he is out there!" McSorley was put in a position, but he was running out of time. He was yelling at Brashear, "Get back here! Turn around and fight." Brashear was right near his bench, and there were guys with one leg over because the buzzer was going to go any minute. So McSorley went to whack him. But Marty said he unintentionally hit Brashear in the side of the face.

I could see what Marty was thinking. "Why am I having to chase a tough guy around at the end of a game? He challenged our bench, he hurt our goaltender for the rest of the year, and Brashear knows why I was put back on the ice, but he's running away." A lot of times, a tough guy will give another guy a whack because it's dirty to jump on someone from behind.

Marty couldn't fight after the buzzer—that would mean an automatic ten-game suspension. Marty was an honest fighter. He battled hard and didn't take too many cheap shots, but he just lost it at Brashear and snapped. It's too bad, but it happens. I'd been in similar situations, trying to get a guy's attention. It's a fast game. Brashear went down, his helmet came off and he was out cold. Then it all just snowballed.

Marty was charged by the cops with assault with a weapon, which I thought was total bullshit. What happens on the ice should stay on the ice. He went to court in B.C., was found guilty and was granted a conditional discharge.

The league suspended him for twenty-three games, and I thought that was too harsh too. Fifteen games, maybe. Then Bettman changed the suspension to a year. He told the press, "It is difficult to imagine a more irresponsible and dangerous act on the ice than the one that was involved in this case." Marty had a history with Bettman. In 1994, he had been on the Players' Association's negotiating committee, and Gary and Marty exchanged some serious fuck yous back and forth across the table.

Now Bettman was basically saying, "We're going to crack down on the game. Look at us crack down on the game." But it was about perception. The reality is that the coaches and GMs wanted tough guys on the ice, but at the same time, the league felt that it needed to be politically correct. So they made these inconsistent decisions. The rules are different for everybody. Chris Simon two-hands Ryan Hollweg, and he's suspended fifteen games as well as the postseason. Other guys almost cross-check somebody's head off, and they don't even get a penalty. Take a guy like Chris Pronger—did you see the elbow on Dean McAmmond in 2007? Pronger got one game, because "he just plays hard." Come on! Be consistent. The league is going to protect its stars and protect its game. The disciplinary situation is not set up for unbiased, open-minded discipline. It is about control and controlling the league's message. So they can take a tough guy and just throw the book at him because the media says, "This is a tough guy."

I fought Georges Laraque twice when he was with the Oilers. The first time was November 14, 1999, and the second was December 21, 2001. He didn't hit me—thank God. We threw a couple of punches, but none really connected. We were in pretty close. I got my sweater off, but the refs broke it up. I was a second-half fighter. The longer the fight went on, the better. Laraque had my respect, but it wasn't the most entertaining scrap.

The second time we met up, we kept our distance for thirty-five seconds before I went for his sweater with my left hand, and the same thing happened as before. We stayed in close and threw a few, but no punches got loose. Laraque was strong.

One of the highlights of the 1998–99 season for me was on February 13—the last game played at Maple Leaf Gardens. We were up 5–2 in the third, and at 11:05 I got the puck. Danny Markov played the puck instead of the body, and I put it in on Curtis Joseph. The Leafs really tried to score after that, but didn't. Jocelyn Thibault was in net for us, and he stopped thirteen shots that period. With about four minutes to go, I started to get kind of excited, because it looked like I might have the last goal ever scored at Maple Leaf Gardens. But when the clock got down to 3:06, the asshole refs gave Todd White a bullshit penalty for high-sticking. I thought, "Oh, they don't want me to be the guy who scores the last one."

Reid Simpson had a great game that night. He had two goals and an assist and was named first star. He was chirping about the penalty being bullshit, and Domi came back at him. They both went off for unsportsmanlike conduct. There were a couple of shots on the power play, but Thibault kicked the first one out, and when Jason Smith took a high shot over the blue line with one minute left, Thibault caught it in his glove. Finally, with fifteen seconds to play, Mike Johnson took a shot on Thibault's right side, but he stopped it with his pad. That was it, the game was over, and I was the last guy to score at Maple Leaf Gardens. It was a big thrill for me. One of the top ten best things in my career.

I'd been having a hard time putting the puck in the net that season. I only had two goals and eight assists going into that game, so I was pretty pumped.

I liked to collect things—motorcycles, cars and parts, paintings, watches (one of the nicest I had was a Blancpain that Dani got me at Lester Lambert on East Oak Street in Chicago), coins, police and fireman memorabilia, military stuff, postcards, licence plates with my number on them, a rare Harley-Davidson tool chest, pop bottles, Bic lighters. All kinds of stuff. Dani said we needed a bigger house—not for us, but for all the crap I collected. I wanted to keep some of my hockey souvenirs for my kids. So I framed the last puck to go in at Maple Leaf Gardens and hung it up on the wall.

Steve Chiasson was a buddy. When he died in a single-car crash on May 3, 1999, I felt really bad about it. You play with so many players over the years, and it's tough to stay in touch because people get traded. I heard the story about what happened. Chase was with the Hurricanes when they lost in the playoffs to Boston, and after the last game they went over to a teammate's place for a few beers. His buddies said, "Let us call you a cab."

He said, "All right, no problem." Then he went into the garage and had a cigarette while he was waiting for the cab. Everyone else went back into the house. And Steve jumped into his truck and left before the cab got there. He went off the road, hit a fence and died. What a shame. He got a buzz on and said, "Ah shit, I can make it home." It was just a short distance on a back road.

And you know what's weird? His wife actually woke up around the same time as he got in the accident. Then she heard the sirens, and she knew.

For me, the brutal thing was that Jimmy D made comments to the press after Steve's funeral. They interviewed him, and he said that the organization always knew they were going to have problems with Steve someday. He said the Wings had tried to help him with his alcoholism, and it's too bad that in the end it had to cost him his life, or something like that. I mean, why bring that shit up? He's dead, okay? Basically, they're calling him an alcoholic and saying that is why he died, which is not true. He had a few beers with the guys—period. I hope that at my funeral, people who helped me don't go yapping about my problems. Shut up, you know? That's why I am writing my own book—to tell it my way before someone else screws it up.

21

A ONE-WAY TICKET

At the beginning of the 1999–2000 season, Bob Murray was worried about his job. He wanted to change my contract. Murray really broke up a good group of guys—a pretty good nucleus of players. He had already tried to put Dave Manson, Doug Zmolek and me on waivers in March. I had two years, worth $3.5 million, left on my contract. Then Murray sent me a letter in August, giving me three choices. I could take a pay cut to $1 million for one year, with an option for a second year at a million, which the team could buy its way out of for $200,000. Or, I could sign a new three-year deal for $400,000 a season. Or, because I was on a one-way deal, I could get paid my current contract, but I'd be sent down to the minors. And then the dumbass told the press I was nothing but a fourth-liner. He was bluffing.

I called up Manson and Zmolek, and they said, "Tell him where to go. You've got a one-way ticket." I felt the same way. So I told Murray to go right ahead and send me down. I said,

"I don't care if I have to ride the bus in the East Coast league the whole year. At the end of the year, I'll buy the bus."

Murray was gone by Christmas, and so was Lorne Molleken. Pully was back behind the bench on December 2. Our record up to then was 5–15–4. I was moved to the first line with Dougie Gilmour and Tony Amonte. By January, we were back on a good streak, 8–4–2. What goes around, comes around, as they say.

Dani was pregnant again. This time with twins. The ultrasound told me that one of them was a boy. With two kids already and two more on the way, we needed a bigger house. We figured I would probably retire in three years, when my contract was up. We thought about staying in Chicago or moving back to Detroit, but without a work visa I might have problems going back and forth across the border. And the property we could buy in Windsor was a lot cheaper than what was available in West Bloomfield, Michigan.

We went looking and found exactly what we were looking for. An older house on a quiet street that backed onto Lake St. Clair, which is basically the Detroit River. I could look across at the States. We tried to save the old house, but it just didn't work, so we tore it down and broke ground for a new home in August of 2000. It would take three years to finish our Forever House.

The twins were induced two weeks early, on May 2, 2000. Dani named all our girls. She liked cool names—names that not everybody had. She named our new daughter Declyn. I got to name my boy—Jack, after Papa Jack, my dad's father. Like all our babies, they were a good size. Jack was seven pounds, twelve ounces, and Declyn was seven pounds, four ounces. I picked them up, one in each arm, and I cried like a baby.

My role with the team shifted as the years went on. By 2000–01, I was playing on the fourth line, but that was cool. I was still having fun. There were a lot of laughs in the dressing room. I liked to do my duck call, which I thought sounded like a dolphin. You flatten out your lips, and then put your fist in front and blow. The guys all called it my turkey call. It drove them nuts, but it kept things loose. I liked working with guys who were cheerful, not always bitching and complaining. You could be upset, but everyone hated watching a guy sit around feeling sorry for himself.

I knew I had to play two roles—the family guy who loved his wife and kids, and a tough guy on the ice. I didn't need some coach playing head games with me. In the past I'd heard it all. "You're a has-been, what are you smiling about? There's nothing to smile about! We've got to win some games!" I could be happy at practice, talking and laughing with everybody, and then in the game that night, I knew what I had to do.

In April 2001, I woke up really sick. I rarely got flu or even a cold, but I was coughing and stuffed up and had a brutal fever. I soaked in a hot tub and could barely drag my ass out of it. I played the next night, and a couple days later I was even sicker. I saw a doctor who said I had a sinus infection, and I went to bed for a week.

We missed the playoffs for the fourth year in a row, so the next month, on May 3, Brian Sutter was brought in as head coach. He made it clear that conditioning was his number one concern. I hoped the change meant I would get more ice, because Sutter liked physical play. My problem was I couldn't shake this flu. I stopped at the bookstore and picked up a copy of *Harrison's Manual of Medicine* and started looking for my symptoms. Only one disease matched them all: HIV. "Oh fuck!" I thought. "I'm thirty-six years old and I'm dying of AIDS!"

I got at least three blood tests in the next three months, and I made Dani get them too. She was my biggest worry. I didn't mind being condemned to death as much as I didn't want her to die. Each of our tests came back negative. But I was sure I had HIV. Maybe the tests were bogus. I was losing weight like crazy, and every ingrown hair looked like an HIV zoster to me. Dani got a cold sore on her lip and I freaked out.

She came home with the results of her fourth or fifth blood test and said, "Will you look at this? I'm fine!"

I said, "They are not telling you everything."

She said, "You're right, it's a conspiracy." And then, just like that scene in *Moonstruck* with Cher, she smacked me across the face and said, "Snap out of it!" Dani arranged for me to go to the Mayo Clinic and then to the Brigham and Women's Hospital in Massachusetts on August 1, 2001, for more tests. They gave me a brain MRI ($2,464), Lyme disease test ($119), spinal cord MRI ($1,870), a private room

($9,800), urine and blood tests for antibodies, thyroid test and anything else you can think of. Altogether, the bill came to $19,337. I was sent home with a prescription for Klonopin to treat anxiety, Celexa for depression and Percocet for pain. It turned out I didn't have AIDS, I had Epstein-Barr, which is like an adult mononucleosis.

At the start of the 2001–02 season, Sutter put me on for the first 28 games. I thought things were going okay. I understood he was looking for new talent, so I sat out a few while he tried out Jim Campbell. I called him Soupy too, although he wasn't related to Colin. I wasn't scoring, so I worked at making my presence known to the other teams, and even though I played in only one of the last eleven games of the schedule, I ended up with 176 penalty minutes in 61 games.

There was a lot of speculation that I might not be back, and I was nervous. But I wanted one more year. I was at 935 games. Sixty-five more to 1,000 and then I'd be done.

Off the ice, I had been doing really well. For six years, I hadn't ordered anything stronger than an O'Doul's. But about a month before my last full season ended, I was out for dinner with a buddy. I told him, "Aw fuck, they want to rip up my contract." Then I ordered a Bailey's and coffee.

My buddy said, "Well fuck, whatever. I'm not going to babysit you."

Within a couple of weeks, the Bailey's turned into triple vodka-and-waters that I'd down real quick or put in a water bottle. I had it all figured out. The piss testers would call me a few hours ahead to say they were on the way. Piss is a certain temperature when it comes out—96 degrees Fahrenheit. It'll stay that way for four minutes. I always stored clean piss. When the tester knocked on the door, I wouldn't answer it right away. I'd grab the clean piss and put it in the microwave for exactly 12.5 seconds. I'd take it out, test the temperature and pour it into a little tube with a stopper. Then I'd stick it inside my pants beside my dick and go and answer the door.

The tester's job was to see me pissing into this bottle. He'd follow me into the bathroom. When he got to the threshold, I'd say, "Fuck off! Having you standing here in my bathroom as I'm pissing is enough. I'm going to take my dick out right now"—I'd turn my back on the guy and pull out the tube— "and I'm going to piss into it." Before I filled the bottle, I'd squirt the contents of the tube into the toilet for a second to make it sound like I was pissing. When the bottle was full, I would hand it to the guy and finish my real piss into the toilet. The guy would look at the temperature strip on the bottle and say, "Okay, it's good." I had it down to a science.

I didn't tell Dani any of this until years later, and she got kind of mad. She said, "Damn it, Bob, what frigging thermometer did you use? The meat thermometer? The latte thermometer?"

During one of our road trips, I went out for dinner with a bunch of guys on the team. A teammate and I both knew we weren't playing the next day, so we sat at the bar afterward. Later, we jumped into a cab with a bunch of people we'd just met. One of them was a cop. He was a huge partier. He made

Having Tierney (left), Declyn, Jack and Brogan was the best thing I ever did.

Dani and me with Tierney. She's my little hockey player.

On one of our awesome holidays at Dolphin Cay Atlantis in the Bahamas.

Dani and me, just before the trip we took to Paul Coffey's cottage right after we were married.

June 2010, in my garage.
Believe it or not, I know where
everything is.

Our troops in Afghanistan are our
country's real heroes. The guys
let me try out a lot of things, from
flying the transport plane to riding
on a tank.

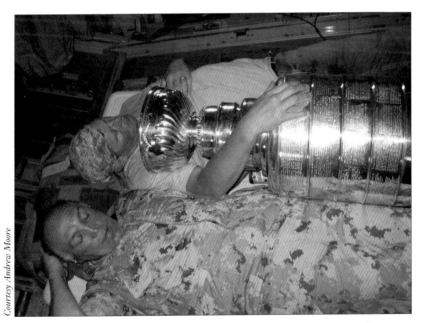

Sleeping with the Stanley Cup, next to Tiger Williams, on the plane
into Kandahar. Neither of us ever got to take the Cup home, but at least
we got to spend time on the road with it.

Riding a camel in the Persian Gulf, one of the grossest experiences of my life.

With the family, getting ready to go tubing on Lake St. Clair.

Waterskiing at Keego Harbor. We got up every morning at 6 A.M. to get out there while the water was like glass.

On July 5, 2010, while boating with his family, Bob Probert suffered a heart attack and died. His wife, Dani, asked some of his good friends and teammates to be his pallbearers. His casket was transported on a motorcycle sidecar. Clockwise, from front left: Tony Amonte, Mark LaForest, Ryan VandenBussche, Sheldon Kennedy, Dave Hutchison (in sunglasses), Doug Gilmour, Gerard Gallant, Joey Kocur.

Courtesy Kirstie McLellan Day

Courtesy Kirstie McLellan Day

Bob's final ride.

More than a thousand people attended Bob's funeral at Windsor Christian Fellowship on July 9, 2010. Steve Yzerman gave a touching eulogy and afterwards was surrounded by the press.

Dani Probert, August 2010.

Bob Probert, June 5, 1965–July 5, 2010.

a pit stop to pick up a bunch of blow, and then we headed downtown.

We made it back to the hotel by 7 A.M., which just gave us time to catch the seven-thirty bus for practice. Denis Savard was running it. My buddy wasn't used to partying like I was. He stepped out on the ice, did a crossover, tripped and landed on his face. His nose and lip got all bloodied up. Savard said to him, "What the hell is wrong with you?" I thought for sure Savard was going to figure it out, so I said to my buddy, "Yeah, for fuck's sake, buddy, get control of yourself."

On the bus back to the hotel, my buddy was quiet for a while, then he turned to me and said, "Probie, you can be out all night and perform the next day. You are an animal. Just an animal."

22

DEAR DISEASE

On May 2, 2002, I went to Vegas for the weekend and didn't come back for the twins' second birthday, and that's when Dani realized I had relapsed. It was the end of the season and the guys were going to Vegas. I thought it would be a good idea. We did it every year. I called Dani and got a hall pass.

We checked in at the Bellagio. They upgraded us to this huge three-bedroom suite. First thing we did was hit the blackjack tables. With blackjack, you can usually grind it out and recoup some of your losses. So I would pull back when I was losing and then start building it up again until I was winning again, pressing my bets to make more money. Whenever I won a couple of hands, I liked to double my bet.

It's a fast game. I learned how to play very quickly. I liked totalling the numbers. But I hated playing next to boneheads. You have to follow basic strategy, because in blackjack there are certain things you should do to improve your chances.

I didn't like when people walked up in the middle of the

shoe, either. The shoe is this plastic box with an open top that you stick up to eight decks of cards into. The dealer uses it to deal. When the dealer puts fresh shuffled decks in the shoe, he's starting the shoe. But when some dumbass jumps into it, especially when you are on a run, it's rude because it changes the cards. I didn't mind losing money when everybody was playing the right way, but it bugged me when someone else screwed it up for me.

One time, while I was still clean, the team was staying at the MGM Grand and we had a table all to ourselves. Chelios was with me. I was on a roll. When I wanted a small card, I'd say, "Tickle me." If I wanted a face card, I'd yell, "Paint me!" or "Monkey!" The cards were listening—it was great! I think I was up fifty grand when Reggie Jackson stepped up to the table and started playing stupid. He stopped on a face card and a five of diamonds when the dealer was showing a ten.

I said, "What are you doing? You were supposed to hit that one."

Reggie said, "Don't you know who I am?"

And I said, "Yeah, I know who you are. I don't care. We were doing good here. You'll have to leave."

Reggie knew something was up, so he just took off.

But the night I got there with the team in 2002, I was doing all right at the tables, just kind of breaking even. I wasn't crazy like in the old days, throwing down huge bets. I was thinking I had to watch it—retirement was just around the corner. I was also flying under the radar with the alcohol. The whole time I had been in Chicago, I had been sober, and except for the one buddy, none of my teammates knew I was kind of slipping back. The waitress came by about ten times, and I had about twenty O'Doul's before I finally knocked back a Jack Daniel's.

Some of the single guys decided to go hit a titty bar, so I went along. I moved around. I'd go up to the bar, down another Jack, then come back to the table to drink a regular Coke. I was getting buzzed. I scoped the room to see who might have some shit.

There was this cute dancer, she came over and danced. I asked her if she had any party favours. It turned out she was a slinger, so she could help me out. She got me a couple of 8-balls and we got a room. Cocaine makes you hornier than a three-peckered billy goat.

I got home the day after the twins' birthday. I was feeling low. I tried to keep my head down, make a little joke. I slept for a couple of days, then came out and things got back to normal.

I knew I was wrong, but I figured what was done was done, I couldn't take it back, so let's start again, you know?

I went to California that summer and worked out like a fiend. I was lucky, because I didn't have any injuries. I was able to lift really heavy. I started taking in a lot of protein, and my muscles got thick and big, which made me gain weight. But I was cut—it wasn't flab.

I came into camp at 240 pounds. Brian Sutter, who I didn't really care for at all, was pissed. I did really well in exhibition, but Sutter had pegged me not to play. It was that simple. For whatever reason, I wasn't playing for the Chicago Blackhawks. Apparently, he objected when, thanks to Pully, I signed on June 28 for $600,000 for the year, plus bonuses of $50,000 as long as I played fifty games. Sutter had just begged Theo Fleury to sign for four million a year.

When Theo came in, I thought, "What an asshole. Why won't he get his shit together for four million?" I had gotten clean for what I thought was huge money—a million and a half a year for four years. Granted, I missed the first year and they didn't pay me that whole year, so I lost a million and a half dollars. But they were piss-testing me. I had to stay straight to get paid. I always had it in the back of my mind that when it was all over I could do what I wanted.

I thought about saying, "Come on, Theo, wake up, man. Go make your friggin' money." I didn't know until his book came out that he had been molested as a young kid by the same coach who molested Sheldon. I felt really bad for him.

Even though I was drinking a little, I kept in shape and tried to help out in the dressing room. I was convinced that if I could get into a regular-season game, I could show Sutter what I could do. But I didn't play any games. Not one. I was feeling bitter about it. I was like, "That Sutter. That fucking cocksucker. When I get on the ice, I'm going to play hard." November rolled around, and I still wasn't playing, and I had no idea why. Then, suddenly, we traded for Chris Simon from the Washington Capitals. I liked Chris—we were buddies. We trained together in the summers. But with him in the picture, I knew I was gone. If Pully had been behind the bench, I think I would have played in those games. A thousand career games would have been a nice accomplishment.

But I can't blame Sutter for the fact I didn't make that milestone. Without suspensions and rehabs, which were because of my own drinking and drugging, I would have reached it easily.

November 13, 2002, was D-Day for me. The Hawks no longer needed my services. I called Dani. I was totally fucking upset. She said she felt terrible for me, but her grandmother had died that day and she needed me to come home to help her take the kids to the funeral. It was awful timing. The mandatory piss testing was over, so I had free rein. I decided to have a few drinks before I headed home, and I ended up not making it. She packed up all the kids, got in the car and drove up to Toronto without me. She told me she cried her eyes out at her grandmother's funeral, but a lot of those tears were for me.

The Blackhawks put me on their radio broadcast team, but I didn't want to be part of the radio group, not when I looked at the ice and knew I could be out there. That was the hardest part. Even when a regular, well-adjusted guy retires, he will tell you it's the toughest thing he has ever done. It brings you down, man. My whole life had been built around hockey. From the age of sixteen I knew not to quit and that I had to be the tough guy. I kept thinking, "Why be sober? They're saying they'll pay me the rest of my contract, but I have to sit in this radio room, this fucking closet across the hall from the dressing room, and watch the boys go in to do their jobs?" It hurt. I didn't know how to deal with it. My whole life, all my dreams and aspirations revolved around hockey. And now I could only talk about hockey? That ripped me up. I lost my identity. I lost everything.

What was I going to do for the rest of my life? I had reached most of my goals. What was left? And in the back of my mind I couldn't shake the thought that the doctors weren't telling me everything. I had this feeling something was seriously wrong. I never thought I would live very long anyway. I was thirty-seven. I figured I might have three years left.

The Percocet the doctors had given me wasn't doing the job, so I got a prescription for Vicodin. A month later, things got pretty bad. I went back to drinking and partying and wasn't hiding it anymore. Like they used to say in AA, the progression continues where you left off. Then I got into some legal problems again. The only time I'm ever in trouble is when I'm drinking or doing drugs.

I spent Christmas passed out on the couch. Then the league stepped in. Dan Cronin, who co-ordinated their drug program, along with Dr. Brian Shaw, who represents the Players' Association, and Dr. Lewis were calling me daily. They kept asking me what was wrong. Then they started talking to me about going to rehab again.

Who wants to go to rehab? Every time I went, I felt forced. I honestly didn't want to go for me. I liked partying, but I knew it was a problem for Dani and the kids. Dani was pretty angry with me. She was pissed off that I had relapsed, and really worried about where it was headed. She had a lot on her plate. She was handling four kids and we were two years into building this house on Lake St. Clair. She didn't ask me to go to rehab, but I knew I had to.

The next seven years were filled with ups and downs. There were a lot of times I really let my family down. When I look back on it, I'm not proud of it. In fact, I can't even believe I did some of those things. I've hurt so many people in my past that I try now not to hurt anybody, especially Dani and the kids, but, well, shit. You might as well hear it from me.

I went back to rehab in February 2003. They'd lined up the Caron Foundation in Wernersville, Pennsylvania. A lot of celebrities go there. It's like twenty-five grand a month. I did see some famous faces. One crazy chick wore sunglasses and a big hat all the time. She was pretending she didn't want us to recognize her, but it just made everybody look.

Dani sucked it up during spring break for the kids. One of the therapists recommended she come out with them. So she did. It was about a five-hour drive. She visited for a couple of days. It was nice. We did some family work.

At Caron, they had us write a letter to alcoholism.

What is an alcoholic? You know, you talk to all these therapists and people that are in AA, and they say, "Once an alcoholic, always an alcoholic." Sometimes I feel like I've never been an alcoholic. It's weird. It's almost like I've outgrown it. Now, I can drink one or two beers and that's it. I don't want any more. I had two yesterday, and before that it was probably two months since I had a beer. I think as you get older, you can't be bothered with it. At Caron, they really pushed the disease thing. Is it a disease? I'm not sure. Is smoking a disease? C'mon.

Anyway, they had me write a letter about how I felt.

Dear Disease,

You have taken away my freedom to make healthy
choices. You have taken away my valuable time from
my wonderful wife Dani and my four kids. You have
taken away my self-respect and dignity. You have
turned me into someone I am not. You have hurt me
financially. You have controlled my thoughts and my
feelings. You took me away from things I used to do
to have fun. You took away my ability to keep prom-
ises by running my will. At times you took me away
from people that truly love me. You took away from
me our twins' second birthday. You took away from
me Christmas '02. You took a lot from me, but that is
about to (STOP) change.

Yours Truly,
Big Bob

I got out of rehab and we moved back to Canada. I had
this Suzuki Hayabusa, this really cool bike that I rode from
Chicago to Windsor. Dani and the kids were in the big Denali
behind me. This thing would do, out of the box, almost two
hundred miles an hour. I went through traffic from Chicago
to Jackson, Michigan, like I was in a video game. I was doing
150 to 170. I rode hard, but not like a maniac. I was in control.
I'd slow down to let Dani and the kids catch up, and then take
off again. When we were just outside of West Bloomfield, I
turned my head to see if they were behind me, and my sunglasses flew off.

It was a rush, a natural high. I was completely straight. When you are on a machine like that, you want to have full control of your faculties. Ever since the accident on Moo Moo Cow, when I was all messed up, I didn't ride when I was off the wall.

By September 2003, only part of the house in Windsor was finished. We had an apartment over the six-car garage, and Dani and the kids were camped out there. I would come and go. She was in survival mode, trying to make sure that we had enough money to pay for the house and take care of the kids. She was worried about me blowing it all.

Dani's mother, Leslie, came to visit. She's an early riser. Every morning, she would sit in a chair with her Bible and reading glasses and her tea. Leslie was deep into the religion thing. As long as we stayed away from the subject, we got along fine. Leslie had converted to become a Christian later in life, and it had turned her life around. Dani was close to her dad's aunt and her grandmother. She was raised Catholic, like they were. Dani went to Windsor Christian Fellowship Church once in a while. It was very evangelical. But we weren't raising the kids that way. Dani and I didn't want to be pushed, and we didn't want the kids pushed. We wanted them to decide for themselves.

One morning, I was just getting in and there was Leslie. I passed out on the couch, and a few minutes later she started shaking my arm.

She said "Bob, Bob, I've got to talk with you."

I opened my eyes and said, "Yeah?"

She said, "You're a walking dead man. You know this, don't you?"

I thought, "Okay, here we go again."

She said, "I'm going to leave you with a choice today. Either you're going to continue serving the devil, or you're going to make a decision today to serve the Lord, and you're going to live."

I said, "Yeah, yeah," and got up and went into the kitchen for some juice. I felt like shit. I looked for Dani, but she was out with the kids at school.

She came up to me again and said, "Well, have you made a decision, Bob?"

I said, "I'm just going to go into the garage for a cigarette. When I come up, I'll let you know, okay?"

Dani got back, and I looked at her. She was still so hot. I went up and put my arms around her. She gave me a shove— "Yeah, yeah, Big Boy, go take a shower."

I started to feel amped up and nervous. I couldn't sit down. Was she going to leave me? A couple of guy friends who hung around us would try to console her, and I hated it. A couple of times at parties, I'd gone a little nuts when guys spent too much time with her. I'd said something to her about it, but she got mad. "Are you nuts? I don't have time to shave my legs for you, let alone some other guy."

I went for another smoke and gnawed on my fingers. Leslie came up to me again and said, "Well, Bob, have you made a decision?"

Something inside me just broke. I didn't want to lose Dani and the kids. The kids had a little wooden table-and-chair set in the kitchen. I sat down on one of the chairs and dropped my head in my hands and started bawling. I said, "Yeah, I have."

Leslie said, "Can I pray with you and Danielle, your wife, here?"

And she asked me if I wanted to accept Jesus Christ as my Lord and Saviour. I said, "Yeah."

We moved into the main part of the house on December 23. Dani wanted to pull off Christmas dinner, so she rented some tables and chairs and put together a big turkey dinner. Dani and Leslie and Dan went grocery shopping on Christmas Eve, and I set up a big surprise. They drove up and saw a wooden ramp on the front steps, and something shining in the front window. I'd bought a 1990 Harley-Davidson Fat Boy—first edition, gun-metal grey, with yellow stripes around the valve cover. It had 146 miles on it. It had taken me a year to find it, and it was mint.

The Fat Boy was modelled after a World War II American B-29 bomber. They got the name from the two atomic bombs that were dropped on Japan, Fat Man and Little Boy. It was a beauty.

Leslie looked speechless. Dani walked in and said, "I'm not going to dust that thing just because it's inside the house. It's not in the job description."

23

YOU DON'T HAVE TO TELL JIM

I liked sex. Dani always called me a horny bastard. She would know if I was messing around. It would always come out, or I'd feel a need to get honest. The minute I screwed around, or went and got loaded, I didn't run back home and tell her, but it always came out eventually. This is why I think that the whole Tiger Woods and Sandra Bullock stories are bullshit. Dani says people know who they are married to, and she's the first to say she knows who she married.

Windsor's a small town. Things got out. I'd call her up to test the temperature. On the phone, there was never a problem. She'd say, "Hi Baby, you comin' home? Oh good, can't wait!" Then I'd walk in the door and *bam!* "What the fuck is this? Look at this phone bill! Who the hell were you calling?"

After I retired, it became almost a game. I was never sober when I hit on chicks—I was loaded, usually on booze and cocaine. One night in January, I was heading out and Dani said, "That's it! I'm going with you."

I said, "I'm going to Silver's," which was a peeler place.

She said, "Fine."

I got loaded and hit on the female bartender. I think I gave her one of those weird handshakes with the middle finger with the long slide of the hand down her arm. Smooth, right?

Ten years earlier, Dani would have been pissed, but now she just laughed. She gave me the smoke-show index finger, and clicked her tongue. "You still got it, Baby! You are hot!" I was too loaded to feel embarrassed.

On the ride home, she was quiet. Then she said, "So what do you want, Bob? Do you want me to jump into this world with you to see what you're getting from this? What do I need to do for you here? Am I not good enough?"

I got a little nervous. I said, "What do you mean?"

She said, "Is that what it's going to take to make you happy, Bob? Some kind of threesome?"

That shocked the shit out of me. Dani and I, we're soulmates. Dani had been through the worst with me. She stuck it out and stood by me. She was my lifeline to normalcy. I didn't say anything, but I spent the next couple of days thinking about it. Was I hurting her that bad that she thought I wouldn't stop partying because there was something wrong with her?

I called up Dan Cronin and told him I wanted to go into treatment again. This time, I went to the Renaissance Institute of Palm Beach in Florida. I definitely tried while I was in there. It was my favourite rehab of them all. I think I was starting to get somewhere—until I made it to the halfway house.

Dani and the kids were back in Windsor when I started the after-care plan in Delray Beach, Florida. I moved into an apartment with a couple of guys who were in treatment with me. Part of the plan was to get an everyday job. So I applied at this beach club. I was doing the cabana boy thing—I painted cabanas and brought people their drinks. We were supposed to find a job that was humbling, but it turned out to be a lot of fun. The people there were great and really friendly. They were on holiday, right? But a bar was not the best place to work when I was in recovery.

On June 4, 2004, I ran into some trouble after my shift was done for the night. The club was full of wealthy couples, and I started talking to this guy and this girl. He was a real-estate agent. She was divorced and had money. They asked me to sit down and offered me a shot. I said, "No thanks." They asked me a few more times, and finally, I said okay. Anyway, the topic came up about some coke. I said, "Well, I know a place where you can go." So instead of heading back to the halfway house, I ended up driving her Lexus because she was too buzzed to get behind the wheel. I went into this one area that would be considered a bad neighbourhood. It's west of the ocean, next to some railroad tracks over the Dixie Highway. It's the real deal, very rough.

I pulled over in front of a gas station convenience store. The couple got out and were talking to these black guys, but these guys only had little crack balls for ten or twenty bucks. They sell it on the street corners, with the stuff right in their pockets. An argument started when one of the guys made a rude comment to the girl. I jumped out of the truck and said, "What the fuck?"

I think the street guys thought we might be cops. They said, "What do you want, white boy?"

I said, "What are you giving me lip for? I just want to buy a little coke. What's your problem?"

They kept giving me the gears, and I said, "Fuck you, I just want to get high."

Meanwhile, an undercover truck had pulled up next to us. And I heard this voice behind me. "What are you doing here?"

The problem was that the police patrolled these areas heavily, and when they saw a white Lexus, it seemed out of place.

I wasn't trying to hide anything. I was just standing there. I didn't have any drugs on me, but I was starting to feel a little worried because I didn't need the cops involved.

Another cop said, "Why are you in this neighbourhood?"

I said, "What the fuck? I'm not doing anything."

He said, "Are you selling?"

I said, "Fuck off. I don't know what you are talking about. I just got off work."

He said, "Well, you are down here scoring some coke then."

I said, "Fuck, I just want to get high. I'm not doing anything wrong here."

He said, "Get on the ground."

I said, "I didn't fucking do anything."

He pulled out this Taser and said, "I told you to get on the ground. Now!" And then he shot me with a Taser. It comes out on a string and it sticks in you. I didn't feel anything, because I had a little buzz on—I must have been anaesthetized. But I went down on one knee. I was starting to get up, when a different cop came over and got me with a stun gun. It was like *z-zz-z-z-z-tt*. When it stopped, I was thinking, "Geez, I'm glad that's over." And then he hit me with it again—*grn-g-gagagaga!* There was no need to zap me three times. I was already going down with the second shot. By this time, there were like six cops on me. I was thinking, "You don't have to jump me. You don't have to Taser me. Why are they calling for backup like crazy? I don't have any drugs on me." Then one of the cops picked up my six-hundred-dollar sunglasses, tried them on and put them in his pocket.

My hands were cuffed behind my back, and the cop who had stolen my sunglasses had his knee on the back of my neck. I turned my head and looked at him and said, "You were probably the fat kid in the school who everybody picked on, and that's why you became a cop."

They took me in and charged me with resisting arrest and assaulting a cop—same old bullshit, right? They have to charge you with assault. It's a stock charge in case I went to court and said, "These guys beat on me. They put the cuffs on so tight there were scabs on my wrists. I didn't have feeling in my left hand for about six weeks." They needed to have an excuse. Ninety-nine per cent of the time, they drop the case.

I was feeling bad because the only reason I went to rehab in the first place was for the family. I didn't want to let Dani and the kids down. I was worried it might get in the papers, and I hated embarrassing them. It did get into the news that I had tried to flood the toilet at the jail, but that's not what happened. When they Tasered me the third time, I shit my pants. So when they booked me and put me in a cell, I tried to wash out my shorts and the bowl overflowed.

Dani's dad, Jim, had this buddy named Art who lived in Florida. They had been friends since they were kids. Art looked a little like Peter Frampton. He was kind of like an uncle to Dani. I knew him just to say "Hey, how you doing?" When we tore down the old house that was on our property, Art bought all the old stuff—the brick, the windows, the cupboards, the hardwood, the bathroom hardware and all the heating and cooling—to use to build a place on Lake Erie.

Jim called Art. He said, "Art, Bob's in jail in West Palm Beach. Can you go help him out?"

Art got there, and the desk sergeant said, "You can't visit him, you are not family."

Art's a very personable guy. He talked to the guy for a few minutes, and then the desk sergeant leaned over and said, "Listen, I'm from Detroit. We all love Probert in Detroit, so go on in."

They came and got me from the cells and said, "You have a visitor." I knew it wasn't Dani. She was doing the tough-love thing and wouldn't even take my calls. I hadn't called the rehab centre or the halfway house, so I came walking out and looked around. I went right past Art, thinking, "I don't know anybody here." He called out to me, "Bob, come back here. It's Art—Jim Wood's friend."

Then I recognized him. It was good to see a friendly face. He said to me, "Geez, Bob, your face is raw! You have complete round circles on your cheeks and your nose has red marks. You look like a rodeo clown!" I told him I had been face down on the asphalt when I made the fat-kid remark.

Art and I talked for a while. I told him the whole story and that I didn't want to have this problem in my life—this thing with drugs. When I took them, I liked the feeling so much. It was like when I was a kid and on a merry-go-round. And I'd spin and get dizzy. It was such a fun, exciting buzz. It made me feel more comfortable inside my own skin.

He said, "Bob, you do me a favour. If you have this thing in you, that you want to get high, you don't have to do it in public. You have enough money that you can get someone to bring it to you at home. You can stay out of the public eye to get your buzz."

Then I asked him if he could help hook me up so I could do that.

Art said, "First of all, I am a Canadian. I've got a place down here. I don't want nothing to do with that. And anyway, if I got coke for you, my friend Jim Wood would kill me."

I said, "Well, you don't have to tell Jim."

He said, "I tell Jim things. He is my friend."

Art gave me his number and told me that if I wanted to come over for a visit and hang out at the beach, or go for a walk and talk, I could call him.

Then I called my buddy who had a condo there and he bailed me out.

The whole thing blew up. I saw it on TV, in the newspaper, everywhere.

I think it took about six months to clear up. Back and forth, back and forth. They don't like to drop the charges right away. They like to play with you, leave you dangling.

The case didn't go to trial until Thursday, February 15, 2005. "I didn't do anything," I testified. "I didn't touch anyone. There was no reason to Taser me. The cop even stole my sunglasses. They charged me with three felonies and a misdemeanour for doing nothing! Come on."

After a two-day trial, the nine jurors took only forty-five minutes to find me not guilty on all charges. It was unanimous.

The prosecutor was a young frikkin' asshole. He was totally pissed. He threw his fucking file down on the table and said, "Yeah, great. Well, Mr. Probert, immigration will be waiting for you downstairs." They weren't. I thought he was just being a dick because he lost.

24

YOU CAN'T STAY HERE

I came home from the Florida incident before the trial. Dani had our funds locked up so I couldn't get any money, and I kept it together until the fall of 2004. Then, in September, I met some people in Windsor who liked to party. I had been totally clean, but I started going for beers with this one guy and one thing led to another. Dani used to say it was brutal. She hated that, everywhere I went, I was offered booze or drugs or pills. I told her it was up to me whether to use or not, but she hated how we couldn't get away from it in Windsor.

I was going through a dark period, partying all the time. I didn't know what was going on in my life. There was a lot of boredom. Most people have no idea what it's like. How it's in your brain, how it's in your body, how all you can think about is getting high. Because when you're high, you are free to have all the fun you want, and you just don't fucking care.

Dani's dad, Jim, belonged to a bike club, and I liked to ride with them. Some of my buddies I went to school with in

Windsor liked Harleys too, and we started getting together. A couple of the guys were associated with the Hells Angels and they got caught up in a big coke bust in Windsor. They were in court in March of 2005 and I went to watch. The next thing you know, my picture was on the front page.

On July 1, 2005, a couple of my new friends were hanging out with me in my garage. I had just turned forty. I loved it out there. It was my sanctuary. I had three engines, a couple of chassis, all my tools, including my big Harley tool box, tires, a couple of my motorcycles, including the Moo Moo, which had been fixed, some chairs, ashtrays and a table. But I could tell when people moved my stuff. We were drinking, and somebody gave me a bag of mushrooms.

We were pretty buzzed and only had one bottle of whisky left. Canadian Club. We didn't have any mix. So we were sipping that straight out of the bottle and taking mushrooms by the handful—getting really fucked up. And then I just kind of blacked out and only remember parts of it. Meanwhile, Dani and the kids were home.

One of my friends and I started wrestling around in the garage. And we ended up falling on Dani's little two-seater Porsche and punching holes in the wall. We got kind of stupid. Dani heard the noise and came out. She said something to me, and I followed her into the house. We have this block of knives that sits on the counter. I grabbed a handful of them and threw them on the floor. It wasn't like a knife-throwing act or anything. I just went for the closest thing. But I was shouting at her too, and she got a little freaked out with that. She called the police and her dad.

When Jim got there, Dani was scared, and that really pissed him off. He walked into the kitchen, and I was still there, kind of talking gibberish. Jim says I was slurring and saying that I was fed up with this person or that person taking advantage of me. His main concern was that I might get out of control and he wouldn't be able to restrain me. So he didn't even try to calm me down. He said he could see I hadn't meant to harm anyone. I was just out of it.

Seven cop cars came. We have cameras all around our house, so I watched the whole thing later. The tapes showed that I was walking backwards down the driveway and trying to talk to one of the officers. I said, "Come here, I want to talk to you." The police had written in their reports that I took a stance like a boxer and approached them in a menacing manner. But the tape showed they were actually the aggressors. They put black gloves on at roadway before I came out. Then they went right at me, grabbing me and throwing me against my garage so hard my head bounced off the door. Then they maced me. I was rubbing my eyes when they jumped me, cuffed me and took me in.

They took me over to Belle River, where I spent the night. In the morning, they transferred me to Windsor. Usually, they keep you there for two or three days and then transfer you to the county jail. But I never made it to the county—I got out. A buddy found a judge in London on a Sunday. The judge signed my release, and my buddy paid my bond, which was a thousand bucks. I was out in two days.

The cops filed their report, charging me with breach of peace, resisting arrest and assaulting a police officer. They said that was why they had to subdue me. Meanwhile, I gave the tape to my lawyer, Pat Ducharme. And a week before my trial came up, Pat called the assistant Crown. His name was Tim Kavanaugh. Ducharme didn't usually show this kind of evidence before court—so he could have the element of surprise on his side—but he respected Kavanaugh, so he invited him to his office to look at the tape. When he saw it, the prosecutor was pretty concerned and said he was going to show it to the police. Then, an hour before the trial, he said, "I'm not going to proceed with this. I'm going to withdraw the charge."

I thought it was a bullshit charge, but I didn't know for sure it would be dismissed until that day, so I was supposed to show up in court at 10 A.M. While he waited, Ducharme was getting pretty antsy. The prosecutor called the case and the judge asked, "Is Mr. Probert going to be joining us?" Ducharme said, "Your Honour, we knew in advance that the prosecutor was going to withdraw the charge, and every time Mr. Probert shows up here, there is a media circus. So if you don't mind, I'm here on his behalf. I'm his designated counsel. Could we just do it without him here?" And the judge said, "Oh yeah, that's fine."

I called Pat at eleven-thirty and asked what happened. He said, "You must have been pretty confident we were going to win—you didn't even show up. I wasn't sure he was going to withdraw the charge until this morning."

I should have sued the assholes, because they still give me a hard time today. But the tape clearly showed that the charges were bullshit.

Before that whole case went to court and was thrown out, I

was on probation. I wasn't supposed to drink or go anywhere liquor was served. But I was still hanging out with the same guys. On August 19, I was with a friend. We were in downtown Windsor, and all of a sudden, he disappeared on me. I went to his house and started pounding on his apartment door. I was supposed to be staying with him, but he wasn't answering the door. Dani and I were on a little break after the mushroom incident. She worried about what the kids might be seeing and told me to get my shit together. I knew she was right, but I wasn't there yet.

I went and grabbed a sub, came back and pounded on his door again. Still no answer. I sat on the curb out front, eating my sub. When I finished, I just kind of leaned back on the sidewalk, waiting for him. And I frikkin' passed out. I was awakened by the cops. There was a station right across the street from my buddy's apartment. One of these cops happened to be a female and she kept coming at me with frikkin' questions. You know, just stupid things like, "Okay, we need an address. Where do you want to go, Bob?"

I said, "Why do you need an address? I'm staying at my friend's right here and he's not home. I'm waiting for him."

She said, "We need to send you somewhere where we know you're going to be safe."

I said, "Well, I can't go home. That's why I'm waiting for my buddy."

She said, "That's not good enough, Bob. Where would you like to go, because you can't stay here."

And all I said was, "What the fuck?"

That was enough. She said, "Okay, cuff him."

I had been at the Windsor Blues Festival earlier in the day and somebody had handed me a packet in a five-dollar bill. You know, "Hey Bob, here's something to help you out." It was folded up nice and neat and tucked into my wallet—twenty dollars' worth of coke. I'd forgotten it was there.

But this cop decided she was going to go through every little piece of paper in my wallet. There was no need for that. They go through your wallet if they're trying to figure out who you are. She was calling me Bob the whole time. She knew who I was. And the cops had my home address because they had just paid me a visit there a month before. She looked through every piece of paper and found the folded five-dollar bill. She unfolded it.

That twenty dollars' worth of coke cost me twenty grand. Paying Ducharme to defend me, again, cost me $14,000, and I got fined and put into a rehabilitation diversion program for the rest. It went on my criminal record, so I can't go back to Detroit because it's on my record—drugs. Now when I go, I need a waiver. They let me in to do charity things—I pay my sixty bucks and I get over there for a day or two.

Twenty dollars' worth of shit, and I'm still paying for it.

I was still partying a bit, and it was tough on Dani and the kids. She'd call up Jim when she needed help, and he'd come over to give me shit. "Hey asshole, why is she upset? What did you do now? You're off base again. Get rid of the demons, straighten out."

That July, Brogan was eleven, and Tierney's ninth birthday was coming up. I had rolled in with some biker friends to change my clothes, then jumped on my Harley with the two couples and we took off for a ride. Brogan gave Jim a call. She said, "Papa, Daddy's changed his clothes in front of two strange women."

Jim said, "What? Put your mother on the phone!"

Dani got on and Jim said, "What's going on, Dani?"

Dani said, "Oh, he's got a couple of low-lifes from Windsor over. Hey Dad, can you help me out? I've got a major birthday party for Tierney tomorrow. The windstorm has left the back yard in a mess."

Jim came over and cut the grass. He left it all in the driveway, piles of it. I'd just got a brand new Ford Expedition—the Eddie Bauer edition, worth $60,000. He opened up every door of my frikkin' truck and filled it up with grass. Then he closed the doors, rolled up the windows and let it sit for three days in ninety-five-degree weather. Next, he cleaned up the yard, picking up every bit of shrapnel and shit from the construction, and dumped it into my 502-horsepower 1970 Chevelle convertible, black with white stripes.

I never said a word to him about it, because I knew he was right. I acted like a total jerk and deserved even worse.

But whenever I get into that truck, I can still smell that fucking grass.

25

BROGAN'S LETTER

I had cut down on the boozing and drugging, and then, early in the fall of 2006, something just kind of hit and I decided to almost stop altogether. The kids were getting a little older, and they weren't stupid, right? When they were young, I could kind of get away with things, but not anymore.

Brogan was twelve years old and was looking forward to her second cross-country meet. I promised her I'd be there, and I wasn't, and she wrote a letter.

Today was my second track meet. I came in eighteenth out of 100. I did Awesome!! My mom and [the key word here is "and"] my dad both promised me they would be there, but guess who didn't show up. Him!! It was one of the meanest days of my life. It was like my heart was there, but then someone was ripping it apart. I actually thought he might actually show up, but he never did. Now he has officially lost my trust. He really hurt my feelings. It killed me. I don't think I will be able to speak to him for at least two weeks. I don't think I should bother asking him to come to my next meet at all. He'll say, "Yeah, I promise," but then he won't show up.

I couldn't get that letter out of my mind. I always wanted to be a hero to my kids.

Paul Coffey and I were booked for a banquet in Halifax on September 2, 2007. Gordie Howe was at this one. So were Sparky Anderson and Gerry Cheevers. These guys were legends.

That afternoon before the banquet, Coff and I had a bowl of clam chowder, then we decided to check out the landscape at the banquet hall. We went over there, and we were both blown away because it was set up for 1,500 people. There were tables everywhere. I was a little bit intimidated. Coff knew what he was going to say that night. He was going to talk about the sport, and championships, and what it takes to play in the league and all that sort of stuff. But I had no idea what to say.

I said, "Coff, can you come up with something for me?"

He said, "Just jot down a few ideas, Probie, and you'll be fine."

But I couldn't really think of anything. We were sitting at the dinner and I was getting more and more nervous.

I said, "Come on, Coff! Coff, you got to help me!"

He grabbed a piece of paper and wrote down a starting line or two—"It's great to be in Halifax. It's an honour to be at a head table with Gordie Howe . . ."—then he wrote, in big letters, FAMILY.

He said, "Bob, it's all you talk about anyway."

So I went up there and went through the opening lines, thanking people in Halifax, and I went through a few of my fights. I talked about my troubles and how it was a battle every day to stay sober. And then I talked about my family. I talked about Dani and the kids, and the joy that they bring me every day.

I told them about Brogan, how proud I was of her and how she was a great public speaker and how nervous I was, but if she could do it, I could do it. I told them about Tierney—how it was her first year of hockey, and I thought she had a future because she's really competitive and has good height. I told them how smart she is and how she takes care of everybody, like her mom does. I talked about the twins—how Jack was like me because he couldn't stay still for two minutes. I told them I was teaching him the longest word in the dictionary, *pneumonoultramicroscopicsilicovolcanokoniosis*, which is a disease you get from breathing volcanic ash. I told them about Declyn, who's so tough. Even when she was just a little baby, she would grab her teddy and bonk Jack on the head with it.

And then I talked about Dani. I told them she had been there for the whole time. She wasn't someone who came in at the end, she was there for it all—the Chicago move, the move back, the stuff that was a little rocky. She was there. And I told them that I knew that I was work, but that my family was everything to me, and I didn't want to let them down. It got pretty emotional. Coff said he had to look for something under the table a few times.

The last time I was in the States legally was on January 2, 2007, when they retired Steve Yzerman's jersey. That was awesome. They called me six weeks in advance, trying to set it up for me to come over, but I could never really commit to doing anything over in the States because what if I didn't get across the border?

Mr. I was a big part of clearing it with immigration so that I could be there for Stevie, but I didn't really believe U.S. customs would let me through. I was at the point where I said to Dani, "I'm just going to try it."

We were supposed to be in Detroit at 7 P.M., so we left the house a couple of hours early. We decided to take the Ambassador Bridge, which was only fifteen minutes from our house. I was still sure we were going to get there and get turned around. We were sitting in the lineup in our car, nervous as crap, and I said to Dani, "Okay, worst-case scenario? We're going back home. We can deal with that." Joey Kocur kept calling me on my cell. "Probie, where are you? Probie, where are you? How many cars in front of you? How many cars?"

The guards asked us to get out and took us into this little holding area. I had to get fingerprinted, fill out some forms and pay sixty dollars for a waiver. It seemed to take forever, but we finally did get across. We had seven minutes until game time. I turned to Dani and said, "We can do this." We flew the wrong way down one-way streets, through lights and stop signs, alleys and back streets, and made it with two minutes to spare. I pulled up and slammed the Expedition into park while it was still moving. Then we jumped out and ran. Security was helping me through—"Come on, Probie! Let's go! Let's go!" I saw Stevie. He was happy to have me there, and surprised I had made it. You had to see his face. It was awesome. It was the real deal. And then I said hi to his hot wife, Lisa. I loved Lisa Yzerman. She was funny and cute and always good to me. Lisa was one of the cool wives. I think Dani was happy to see Stevie. When she first met him, she used to have a crush on him, and I would tease her big-time, calling her out on it in front of him to see how many shades of red she could invent.

Somebody threw my jersey at me. I was supposed to go out with Joey, but because they didn't know if I was coming, they changed the lineup, and instead I went out with Vladi Konstantinov. He had been paralyzed in a limo accident after a party celebrating Detroit's 1997 Stanley Cup win. His driver hit a tree on Woodward Avenue in Birmingham, Michigan.

As always, the Detroit fans were good to us. It was amazing. But I was shocked at how they felt. I could see Dani right behind the penalty box in Big Daddy's seats. There were tears streaming down her face. I gave a little wave.

Stevie made his speech, and the crowd went crazy. I was really happy for him. He meant a lot to the club and deserved all the praise. I was really proud to be part of Stevie's night.

26

A TACTICAL LANDING

I went to Afghanistan with General Rick Hillier in 2007 and 2008. The middle of May 2007 was the first time they took the Stanley Cup to the war zone. Everybody met at the military hangar in Ottawa. General Hillier was having a small cigar outside the plane, and I joined him for a smoke. I recognized him right away. I said, "You're the general!"

He said, "Yes, Bob, I am. We're going to do this together, and the troops are going to be real appreciative of you coming over. I know it will be quite an experience for you. I'm confident when I say that."

He was right. It was an awesome experience, especially meeting the soldiers. When they invited me back for a second trip, I called up Trees and said, "Trees, you gotta go."

He said, "What do you mean?"

I said, "You've got to go."

I called him a couple of days later and said, "Trees, are you going? You've got to go. It's unbelievable. You gotta go."

He finally agreed, and in 2008 we did a lot of same things we did on the first trip. We spent ten days in the Persian Gulf, where a military caravan picked us up and brought us to this camp. We were still in the free world, but everybody in the barracks was kind of quiet because it's a jumping-off point into Afghanistan. Chris Nilan—the former Bruins and Canadiens tough guy—and Trees and I went down to a beach to ride on a camel. Those things are really gross. They snort and burp and belch. The stench was really bad.

Then we headed to the war zone. I told Trees, "If the military tells you to do something, just do it. If they say don't do something, don't do it."

The first thing you get on the transport plane to Kandahar is a helmet and a flak jacket. Once you are into an area that is a threat, everybody puts on their gear and you don't take it off very much until you leave.

The cargo plane has nets for seats, just like in the movies. They let me fly it, which was so cool. Then we made a tactical landing, which is a quick descent, almost like a nosedive. In a civilian landing, you kind of glide in, nice and easy at a very shallow angle. It makes it smooth and comfortable for the passengers. But for planes landing in Kandahar, that would be too risky. You don't want that long, slow, shallow approach because the enemy can see you coming, figure your flight path and shoot at you from miles out.

A tactical descent in a fighter plane sounds cool, but when you are in an aircraft the size of a 747 cruising along at 20,000 feet, and then you drop to 1,500 feet—twisting left, then right . . . left, then right—well, you just want to puke. It's a pretty hairy experience. The Giant Drop is nothing in comparison—it just gives you a few seconds of what we experienced. And we did it based on a very real threat, not just for fun.

We headed out to this gathering place called Canada House to play ball hockey. It was hot there—about 120 degrees Fahrenheit. At the first game, there were probably a thousand soldiers watching. And not all Canadians—there were Brits, lots of Americans, even a few Afghans. It was pretty fast-paced. A couple of soldiers were testing me in the corners, which was fun. We just had a great time. We went to a barbecue for all the Canadian troops and civilians on Kandahar airfield. That night, the commander gave the order that everybody got two beers. The soldiers liked that.

Nobody was ready to go to bed. So we sat out with a couple of Cokes and talked until 1 A.M. At about midnight, I looked around and there were three or four hundred people sitting out there. A lot of the guys were smoking cigars, just relaxing, talking. Some had laptops. A young soldier came up to me and the general. "Hey sir, would you and Probie mind saying hi to my fiancée and my mom back in Canada?" He handed us the laptop so we could see their faces on the camera, and they could see us. We were joking around—"What's a good-looking woman like you doing with this guy right here?"

It was a pretty incredible, pretty surreal sort of atmosphere. I felt proud to be Canadian, proud to be in Afghanistan, proud to sit there with the toughest guys in our country. Canada House pumps in satellite radio—maybe a Calgary station one day, maybe Q107 in Toronto the next. And there are two big-screen TVs, one with CTV and one with CBC.

One of my favourite things was when Trees and I would sit and smoke cigarettes outside on the patio, listening to Canadian music and talking to the Canadian soldiers who walked by. We met snipers and gunners, all kinds of military. They all had really interesting things to say. And they asked a lot of questions. Did you ever fight this guy? Did you ever fight that guy? Who was the toughest guy I ever fought against? (I'm sure there was someone tougher, but I really never met him.) What were the most fights you got into in a game? (Thirty-one times, I had two fights in a game, and I once got into three in a single game—January 10, 2002, against Jody Shelley.) Did you really have three hundred fights in the NHL? (I had 238.) How many penalty minutes did you get? (Three thousand, three hundred.) Who was your favourite player? (Bobby Orr—no ifs, ands or buts about it.) Did you ever play against Gretzky? (Many times.) Who was the best scorer? (Lemieux. I'm a big fan of the guy. One time, I heard he said if he ever died and could come back as another hockey player, he would come back as Bob Probert. It was maybe the biggest compliment I ever got.) Who had the hardest shot? (Al Iafrate.) Who had the hardest punch? (Sandy McCarthy.) Were you scared of anybody ever? (No.) Did you ever plan for a fight? (Only once—the rematch with Domi.) Who did you fight the most? (Stu Grimson, thirteen times.) Was Tie Domi dirty? (He turned it around by the end.) What's Tie Domi like? (I'd tell them, "Ask Trees, he was Tie's roommate.")

General Hillier took a couple of us out to some of the general patrol bases where our soldiers were. Two-thirds of our troops are deployed outside of Kandahar airfield, in Taliban country. When you are riding in a car or truck through Kandahar City, you get a better impression of what the mood is. When you fly over it by helicopter, which is relatively safe, you don't learn what the people are thinking.

We jumped into this Jeep—two special forces guys in the front, and the general and me in the back. The driver turned around and said to the general, "Sir, if we get hit by the Taliban on the way, you and I go out to the right." And I was sitting behind the passenger seat, so he told me, "Mr. Probert, if we get hit, you go out to the left-hand side. And you see this weapon right here between us in the seats? It's called an M72 rocket launcher. Mr. Probert, if we get hit and you go out the vehicle, your job is to take that rocket launcher with you, because we are going to need it." I took a look at it. It was about three feet long and about four inches in diameter. We drove for about an hour and a half, through the city and the sprawling landscape of people and culture and vehicles. I was taking it all in, but my hand never left that rocket launcher. If we got hit by the Taliban in that vehicle and I got out, that rocket launcher was going with me. It's weird—I was almost was hoping for something to happen.

We had basically been incommunicado with anybody back in North America, except for the media side. We were out one night in the Persian Gulf on our way back, and Brian Williams, the sportscaster, got out his cell phone and we started phoning people. We phoned a bunch of the families, and then I called Dani and the kids. Hearing their voices kind of choked me up. She and the kids were safe. I had to go all the way to fucking Afghanistan before I finally understood, that is what it's all about.

The soldiers were the toughest guys alive. They had a purpose, you know? In rehab, they always tell you life is just beginning, tomorrow is your future, the possibilities are unlimited. For me, life was kind of upside down. Most guys start to get really successful when they are in their forties. All the hard work finally pays off and they get their promotions and do pretty well. It was the opposite for me—my career was over. I had to figure out what to do next, or I was going to get in trouble again.

Back home, I'd been hurting. My knees and lower back were killing me. So I'd been screwing around with pain pills. I started playing hockey with the NHL alumni and I was taking Percocet, but you really gain a tolerance for it. So I switched to OxyContin. It didn't make me stoned or drunk or stupid. In fact, when I took it, I didn't even want to drink. It just made me happy. You're hyper and you can do stuff. You can talk a lot more. You're in a good mood. I used to think, "Why can't they make something like this that is over the counter? Why can't I feel this way all the time?"

When I did coke, back in the day, I would do two lines. Everyone else would do these three-inch lines. Mine were six inches long. I called them monsters. Pills were the same. I'd say to a buddy, "C'mon, let's do a monster."

I had tools for the Oxy—my own little kit. I'd use these small foot scrapers that I found at the drug store. I called them grinders. I'd dip a pill into a capful of Coke to dissolve the coating, scrape it clean, knock the remainder off with a card and then make the line.

My life became about the hunt for these pills. I was consumed with where I could find more. Before I went to Afghanistan, I was doing twenty a day.

On the road, wherever I was, I'd find a doctor. Most places, they would recognize me. They knew I had pain, and because I had prescription bottles with my name already on them, I'd say, "I just have to take a few more because I injured myself," or "I fell and I need some more." Every city. You would be amazed how many doctors give you this stuff. I could only get about sixty OxyContin a month in Windsor, but when I went on the road to places like Vancouver or Calgary, I could stop in at each clinic and get twenty more.

When I got home from Afghanistan, I got a prescription for Suboxone. It helps you quit.

I'm not sure why I always beat myself up when things went really good for me. Just a couple of months ago we got a phone call that I was going to be inducted into the Essex Sports Hall of Fame. I was really excited about having that kind of legacy for the kids. Dani said, "Just because you are getting good news, and this is great, do not screw this up! Don't embarrass us any more." The old me would have headed out and wrapped my car around a pole, but this time, I took the family out for dinner.

In the spring of 2009, I signed up to figure skate on the TV show *Battle of the Blades* on CBC. My partner, Kristina Lenko, who is a professional ice dancer, and I skated for a charity called Wounded Warriors. We made $25,000 for them. They give stuff like clothes and books and CDs to soldiers who are in the hospital. I worked really hard with Kristina in Windsor that summer. She was a really sweet kid, and we had a lot of fun on the ice, even though we were voted off the first episode. I worked for four weeks on figure skates. Then we got there in the fall, ready to go, and Tie, who was one of the competitors, couldn't work on the figure skates. So we all had to switch to hockey skates. I was bummed out, but that's Tie.

I saw Trees in Sarnia a couple of weeks ago at an NHL alumni baseball game. I gave him a buddy hug and we talked for a while. I always liked bringing up his fight with Sean Burke back in 1989. Trees' dad always told him to watch out for his little brother. His brother, Bob, played in the NHL for five games with the Los Angeles Kings in 1983–84. In the NHL, the guys on your team are your brothers. If they get into trouble, it's the same type of thinking—you go help out. In 1989, Trees was in his second game with the Leafs at Maple Leaf Gardens. They were playing the Devils and losing 5–2. Then Lou Franceschetti—who they called Little Francis Guido—just hammered somebody with a shoulder at the other blue line. Helmet, sticks, gloves, everything went flying. The Devils just jumped on him, and then they jumped on Dan Daoust when he came in to help Louie out. Finally, it was, like, five on five and Sean Burke was at the other end in goal. He had his mask off, and he yelled, "Come on down and fight!" then took off his mask. So Trees had to go, right?

Trees says he always felt like it was the longest fight ever. He said, "You know what, Bobby? Fighting is hard. After the game, I couldn't lift my hands above my head, I couldn't wash my hair, I couldn't breathe. I mean, I didn't have a smoke for three hours."

We remembered travelling to the east coast when we were in the American league. He remembered a lobster place we went to. We each grabbed a bowl of clam chowder and got a couple of huge lobsters. Ever since I was a kid I had had this fish allergy, but I wasn't sure that shellfish counted. I'd never had lobster before, and he was teaching me how to open them. He cracked one, and the juice hit me in the eye, so I got him back with one, and we went back and forth. We got on the bus afterward, and Trees said, "Bobby, why are you all red?" My neck and ears were itching, my throat tightened and my face was kind of swollen up.

I said, "Oh, I think maybe I'm allergic to lobster."

Trees said, "Are you kidding me?!"

I said, "Yeah, I think I'm allergic to crustaceans."

"Oh my God, you big dummy. Why did you eat it?"

I told him, "Oh, because I wanted to."

Trees was a really good buddy, so I told him the doctor had given me Oxys, and he said, "Oh my God, Probie, you have to be careful with that shit."

I said, "I know, I know," and told him I was quitting.

I've really cut back on the pills. I asked Dani to help me with that. She doles them out for me. I'm doing pretty good.

I gave Trees a big kiss goodbye, which was funny because when we used to play, I'd always skate up to him and ask, "If I was a girl, would you do me?" And he'd say, "Yeah, Bob, I would, you pig."

I told him I would see him at the next game in a couple of weeks.

I still had this flu. I was really having trouble kicking it, so I asked him for Rolaids. I was docking the boat the other day, wading in and out of the water, trying to drag it into the lane, and I thought I was going to puke.

Dani has been on me every day to go to the doctor. "We need you around," she keeps saying.

I'm a little nervous about going. I guess it's because my dad died early, but I hate getting checkups and shit. What if there's something serious in there? And the doctor tells me, "You can't eat this, you can't eat that, you are limited in what you can do." That would be a slow death. I wouldn't wish that on anyone.

July 1, 2010, was our seventeenth anniversary. Dani and I decided to order pizza and hang out with the kids and the dogs, Carly and Simon. I always wanted a golden retriever or a chocolate lab—a nice, big dog. A good guard dog for when I went on the road. But the kids are allergic, so we got the Yorkies. The dogs are cute, but kinda gay.

We all loaded into the boat to go tubing and picnicking at

Peche Island, which is this hundred-acre park on the Detroit River between Windsor and Detroit. It used to be a provincial park, but now it's part of Windsor.

The water on the north side is American, so it's patrolled by Detroit police helicopters and boats. The water on the south is Canadian, so it's patrolled by Windsor police boats. When I couldn't come back into Canada during the summer of 1990, Sheldon Kennedy and Dave Whinham would do the "Dani drop." They would pick her up at the marina and bring her to Peche Island, where I'd pick her up in the boat and we'd hang out for the day.

The kids were on the tube all the way to the island. The water was smooth as glass and the weather was beautiful. We threw down the blankets on the beach and set up the food and Cokes. We watched the dogs swim from the beach. I tried to teach them to fetch, but they're Yorkies—you know.

Two young guys on WaveRunners blasted into the no-wake zone just off the sand. It pissed me off because our boat was moored on the beach and the waves made it rock loose. I stood on the shore, yelling at them, "Hey, slow down! It's a no-wake zone!" I pointed to the sign, and they gave me the finger.

I came back and sat down beside Dani and said, "Frikkin' punks."

She looked at me and said, "Hello, pot, this is the kettle calling . . ."

There were Canada geese on the island, and the dogs took off down the nature trails after them. The kids ran behind, leaving Dani and me by ourselves. It was spooky quiet. There was no one else around, just the gulls circling over our pizza crusts. Dani laid her head on my shoulder. I smooched her on the lips. She said, "Seventeen years, Baby. We beat the odds."

I said, "A lot of bets were lost."

About 7 P.M., I stood up and did my duck call. The dogs and the kids came running. I scooped up the little female dog, Carly, and started singing a song I made up.

> *I love to play with you out in the sun, Carly*
> *My poopy fou-fou-boo-kee-too-kee.*

The girls and Dani joined in and we were all laughing like crazy. Jack untied the boat and helped me push it back into the water, while Dani and the girls picked up the garbage and folded the towels. Declyn did one last cannonball off the back platform. I fired up the boat and we headed home.

I hated taking the boat home on the Canadian side. You had to go slow because of the no-wake zone. I wanted to make it home before dark, so I didn't want to putt along to get out of there. I decided to take the boat around the island. It put us in American waters, which I knew was a bit of a risk. If I got caught, I could get thrown in jail because of all my immigration issues. But there's no speed limit, so it was lot more fun. I pulled back the throttle and opened her up.

What a perfect day.

EPILOGUE

On July 5, 2010, at 2 P.M., Bob Probert was boating on Lake St. Clair with his wife, Dani, two of his children, Tierney and Jack, and his in-laws, Dan and Leslie Parkinson, when he collapsed. His death was confirmed at 5 P.M. by Ontario Provincial Police spokeswoman Shawna Coulter. The coroner's report concluded he died of natural causes. Bob had an 80-percent blockage of the left coronary artery. He had severe cardiac disease. His heart was enlarged and had been under strain for a long time.

The funeral service was held on July 9 at Windsor Christian Fellowship church.

On July 22, Dani chose the largest urn the funeral home had—an XXL. It was still too small. Bob was larger than life.

TIMELINE

1965

June 5—Born in Windsor, Ontario.

1981

Problems with alcohol begin.

1981–82

Plays midget AAA with Windsor Club 240 (55 GP, 60 G, 40 A, 100 Pts, 40 PIM).

1982

May 29—Drafted by the Brantford Alexanders in the seventh round of the Ontario Hockey League midget draft.

August 28—Probert's father, Al, dies one week before Bob leaves for training camp with Brantford.

1982–83

Plays major junior with Brantford (51 GP, 12 G, 16 A, 28 Pts,

133 PIM regular season; 8 GP, 2 G, 2 A, 4 Pts, 23 PIM playoffs). Brantford finishes fourth in Emms Division (70 GP, 34 W, 33 L, 3 T). In OHL playoffs, Brantford defeats London in first round, 6 points to 0, loses to Sault Ste. Marie in second round, 8 points to 2.

1983

June 8—Selected by the Detroit Red Wings in the third round, forty-sixth overall, of the National Hockey League Entry Draft. In the fifth round, eighty-eighth overall, the Wings select Joey Kocur. Probert and Kocur will later be known as the "Bruise Brothers."

1983–84

Plays with Brantford (65 GP, 35 G, 28 A, 63 Pts, 189 PIM regular season; 6 GP, 0 G, 3 A, 3 Pts, 16 PIM playoffs). Brantford finishes second in Emms Division (70 GP, 39 W, 28 L, 3 T) and earns bye to OHL quarterfinals. Sault Ste. Marie defeats Brantford, 8 points to 4.

1984–85

Brantford Alexanders move to Hamilton, are renamed Steelhawks. Probert begins season with Hamilton (4 GP, 0 G, 1 A, 1 Pt, 21 PIM), then is traded to Sault Ste. Marie Greyhounds (44 GP, 20 G, 52 A, 72 Pts, 172 PIM). Greyhounds win OHL championship, and are eliminated by Prince Albert Raiders in the semifinal of the Memorial Cup tournament.

1985–86

Is one of the Detroit Red Wings' last cuts at training camp. Begins season with Adirondack Red Wings of the American Hockey League. Splits season between AHL and Detroit (32 GP, 12 G, 15 A, 27 Pts, 152 PIM in regular season with Adirondack; 10 GP, 2 G, 3 A, 5 Pts, 68 PIM in Calder Cup playoffs; 44 GP, 8 G, 13 A, 21 Pts, 186 PIM with Detroit).

1985

November 6—Makes NHL debut with Detroit Red Wings in a game against St. Louis Blues.

December 15—Records first NHL point—an assist on a goal by Eddie Johnstone—in a 6–4 road loss against Chicago Blackhawks.

December 21—Scores first NHL goal in a 6–3 home loss against Chicago Blackhawks.

1986

January 17—Is suspended for four games by NHL for head-butting Bob McGill during a fight in a game in Toronto on January 13.

April 4—Is arrested for impaired driving in Windsor.

May 21—Wins Calder Cup championship as a member of Adirondack Red Wings.

July 2—Is charged with assaulting a police officer in Windsor. In October is placed on probation for two years.

July 22—Is treated for alcoholism at Hazelden rehabilitation centre in Center City, Minnesota, and Abbott-Northwestern Hospital in Minneapolis.

December 19—Is arrested for impaired driving in Windsor. Is suspended indefinitely by Detroit Red Wings, and misses two games. In January, pleads guilty, is fined $1,100 and has driver's licence suspended.

1986–87

Plays part of season with Adirondack (7 GP, 1 G, 4 A, 5 Pts, 15 PIM). Appears in 63 regular-season games with Detroit (13 G, 11 A,

24 Pts, 221 PIM). In playoffs, appears in all 16 games (3 G, 4 A, 7 Pts, 63 PIM).

1987
February 11—Checks into Brentwood Recovery Centre in Windsor, Ontario, for treatment of alcohol addiction. Is discharged for rules violations about a month later.

March 5—Scores a goal on a penalty shot during a game against Minnesota North Stars at Joe Louis Arena.

1987–88
Probert has best season of his career. Appears in 74 regular-season games. His 29 goals and 33 assists for 62 points are all career highs. Leads league in penalties in minutes with 398. In playoffs, appears in 16 games (8 G, 13 A, 21 Pts, 51 PIM) and breaks Red Wings team record for points in one playoff season set by Gordie Howe in 1955. Continues to hold record until 1995 (Sergei Fedorov, 7–17–24 in 17 GP). Plays on a line with Steve Yzerman and Gerard (Spuddy) Gallant.

1988
February 9—Plays for Clarence Campbell Conference team at NHL All-Star Game in St. Louis. Assists on a goal by Wayne Gretzky.

May 10—On the eve of game five of the Campbell Conference final, six Red Wings players, including Probert, Petr Klima and John Chabot, are accused of breaking curfew at Goose Loonies in Edmonton. Oilers win and advance to Stanley Cup final. Jacques Demers issues a public apology.

September 20—Is demoted to Adirondack for missing team flight from Chicago to Detroit. Three days later, after reporting late, is suspended by Detroit.

October 3—Undergoes treatment for alcoholism at Betty Ford Clinic in Rancho Mirage, California. Leaves before program is complete.

November 27—Plays his first game of the 1988–89 season.

December 15—Is suspended for three games by NHL for hitting Maple Leafs goalie Allan Bester with gloved hand while still holding his stick during game in Toronto on December 10.

1988–89
Plays 25 regular-season games for Detroit (4 G, 2 A, 6 Pts, 106 PIM). Does not appear in playoffs.

1989
January 2—Chicago immigration judge Anthony Petrone orders Probert deported.

January 25—Is benched for home game against Buffalo Sabres after arriving late at Joe Louis Arena. Is later suspended indefinitely by Red Wings. Plays his next game on February 25.

March 2—Is arrested on the U.S. side of the Windsor–Detroit Tunnel for attempting to smuggle cocaine across the border. U.S. Customs find 14 grams of cocaine on Probert's person.

March 4—Is suspended indefinitely by the NHL for the March 2 arrest.

July 18—Pleads guilty to charge of importing cocaine.

October 17—Is sentenced to ninety days in prison and fined $2,000 for smuggling cocaine into the U.S. Serves sentence at the Federal Medical Center in Rochester, Minnesota, then serves three months in a halfway house.

1990

March 7—Is granted a ninety-day work permit, enabling him to practise with Red Wings. Is unable to leave the U.S., an act that would be considered "self-deportation" and would prevent him from returning.

March 9—Is reinstated by NHL.

March 22—Returns to the Red Wings lineup. Appears in four regular-season games, scoring three goals and spending 21 minutes in the penalty box.

October 25—Judge Horace Gilmore of the U.S. District Court in Detroit rules that a law under which the U.S. Immigration and Naturalization Service is trying to jail Probert is unconstitutional. The ruling means Probert remains free until his deportation case is finished.

December 1—Collides with Blackhawks goalie Ed Belfour in the late minutes of a game against Chicago at Joe Louis Arena. Suffers a slight fracture of left forearm and misses 12 games.

1990–91

Appears in 55 regular-season games for Detroit (16 G, 23 A, 39 Pts, 315 PIM). In playoffs, appears in 6 games (1 G, 2 A, 3 Pts, 50 PIM).

1991

February 27—Coach Bryan Murray names Probert as an alternate captain of the Wings during Gerard Gallant's injury. "I think he is well respected in the room," says Murray. "We may not say it much, but we recognize what he does to help this hockey club."

April 9—Is suspended for one game and fined $500 for striking St. Louis Blues goaltender Vincent Riendeau in playoff game on April 6.

1991–92
Plays in 63 games (20 G, 24 A, 44 Pts, 276 PIM) in regular season, 11 in playoffs (1 G, 6 A, 7 Pts, 28 PIM).

1992
January 29—U.S. Sixth Circuit Court of Appeals in Cincinnati rules in Probert's favour that the judge who sentenced him in 1989 issued a judicial recommendation against deportation.

March 6—Is suspended for three games by the NHL for swinging his stick at Garth Butcher in a game against St. Louis on February 29.

November 25—Scores 100th goal of his NHL career in 11–6 home victory over St. Louis.

December 7—Is cleared by the INS to cross the Canada–U.S. border freely.

1992–93
Plays in 80 games (14 G, 29 A, 43 Pts, 292 PIM) in regular season, 7 in playoffs (0 G, 3 A, 3 Pts, 10 PIM).

1993
October 18—Is suspended by the NHL for four games after stick-swinging incident with Bob Rouse of Toronto during game on October 15.

1993–94

Elects to play out option. Plays 66 games (7 G, 10 A, 17 Pts, 275 PIM) in regular season, 7 in playoffs (1 G, 1 A, 2 Pts, 8 PIM).

1994

July 14—Is arrested and ticketed in Allen Park, Michigan, for failing to carry his driver's licence after being seen driving erratically.

July 15—Suffers minor injuries after he is thrown from his motorcycle in a collision with a car in Keego Harbor, Michigan. Is found to have a blood-alcohol level approximately triple the legal limit. Cocaine is also found in his system.

July 20—Is waived by Detroit Red Wings.

July 23—Signs as a free agent with Chicago Blackhawks.

July 25—Is charged with drunk driving in connection with July 15 motorcycle crash.

September 2—Is placed on indefinite inactive status by NHL and ordered to undergo league-supervised treatment for drug abuse. Misses entire 1994–95 season.

1995

April 28—NHL reinstates Probert, but he is not cleared to play until 1995–96 season.

1995–96

Plays 78 games with Chicago in the regular season (19 G, 21 A, 40 Pts, 237 PIM), 10 in the playoffs (0 G, 2 A, 2 Pts, 23 PIM).

1996–97

Plays 82 games in the regular season (9 G, 14 A, 23 Pts, 326 PIM), 6 in the playoffs (2 G, 1 A, 3 Pts, 41 PIM).

1997

October 9—Suffers torn cartilage in right knee during game against Tampa Bay Lightning. Undergoes arthroscopic surgery and misses 14 games.

November 10—In his first game back from knee injury, damages rotator cuff in game against Calgary Flames. Aggravates the injury while fighting Darren McCarty of the Red Wings on November 16. Undergoes surgery and misses 53 more games.

1997–98

Injuries limit Probert to 14 regular-season games (2 G, 1 A, 3 Pts, 48 PIM). Blackhawks miss playoffs.

1998

January 22—Signs a three-year contract extension with Blackhawks.

April 4—Returns to Chicago lineup for game against Detroit.

1998–99

Plays in 78 regular-season games (7 G, 14 A, 21 Pts, 206 PIM). Blackhawks miss playoffs.

1999

February 13—Goal at 11:05 of the third period is the last to be scored at Maple Leaf Gardens. In attendance is 90-year-old Harold "Mush" March, who scored the first goal at the Gardens, also for the Chicago Blackhawks, on November 12, 1931.

October 6—Suspended for four games by league for attacking Sharks goalie Steve Shields from the bench during the Hawks' 7–1 opening-night defeat in San Jose.

1999–2000
Plays in 69 regular-season games (4 G, 11 A, 15 Pts, 114 PIM). Blackhawks miss playoffs for third straight year.

2000
March 11—Becomes sixth player in NHL history to spend 3,000 minutes in the penalty box.

2000–01
Appears in 79 regular-season games (7 G, 12 A, 19 Pts, 103 PIM). Blackhawks miss playoffs for fourth straight year.

2001
July 17—Re-signs with Chicago Blackhawks.

2001–02
Plays in 61 games during regular season (1 G, 3 A, 4 Pts, 176 PIM) and two in playoffs (no points or penalties). Is a healthy scratch for 15 of the team's last 20 regular-season games.

2002
June 28—Re-signs with Chicago Blackhawks.

October 8—Is placed on injured reserve list.

November 15—After clearing NHL waivers, unofficially retires. Joins Blackhawks radio broadcasting team.

2003

February—Checks into NHL substance-abuse program under the supervision of Dr. Dave Lewis and Dr. Brian Shaw.

Summer—Announces retirement.

2004

June 4—Arrested in Delray Beach, Florida, after having to be subdued by police with a Taser and a stun gun.

2005

February 17—After a two-day trial in West Palm Beach, Florida, is acquitted of battery on a police officer, resisting an officer with violence, threatening an officer and disorderly conduct.

July 1—Is arrested for breach of peace, resisting arrest and assaulting a police officer at his home in Lakeshore, Ontario.

August 19—Is arrested at a bar in Windsor for violating a bail condition that he not frequent an establishment that serves liquor. Is released after paying a fine.

November 4—Charges filed against Probert on July 1 are dropped.

2007

January 2—Participates in ceremonies at Joe Louis Arena to mark the retirement of Steve Yzerman's number 19.

May—Visits Canadian troops in Afghanistan, as part of a group of ex-NHLers that includes Dave (Tiger) Williams, Ron Tugnutt, Réjean Houle and Yvon Lambert. The Stanley Cup is brought along.

November—*The Hockey News* conducts a poll of 30 current "enforcers," one from each NHL team. Probert is voted the greatest enforcer of all time, earning 23 of the 30 votes.

2007–10

Makes frequent appearances in charity games organized by the NHL Alumni.

2008

March—Makes a return visit to Afghanistan, this time with Mark LaForest, Chris Nilan, Mike Gartner and Mark Napier.

June—Mike Myers' film *The Love Guru* is released. Probert has a bit part.

October—Appears in Canadian comedy series *Rent-a-Goalie*.

2009

Participates in CBC television series *Battle of the Blades*, skating with Kristina Lenko. The pair are the first eliminated, but his appearance nets a $25,000 donation to Wounded Warriors.

February 22—Is honoured by Chicago Blackhawks with a Bob Probert Heritage Night.

May 22—Drops puck for ceremonial faceoff before game three of the 2009 Western Conference final between Detroit and Chicago.

2010
January 19—Acts as a judge in the Showdown Breakaway Challenge at the Canadian Hockey League Top Prospects Skills Competition in Windsor.

July 5—While boating on Lake St. Clair, near his home, develops severe chest pains and collapses to his death.

July 9—Funeral services held at Windsor Christian Fellowship church.

CAREER STATS

BOB PROBERT

Left Wing

Born: June 5, 1965—Windsor, Ontario

Died: July 5, 2010—On Lake St. Clair, near Windsor, Ontario

Height: 6.03—Weight: 225

Shot: Left

REGULAR SEASON

Season	Team	League	GP	G	A	Pts	PIM
1981–82	Windsor Club 240	OMHA	55	60	40	100	40
1982–83	Brantford Alexanders	OHL	51	12	16	28	133
1983–84	Brantford Alexanders	OHL	65	35	38	73	189
1984–85	Hamilton Steelhawks	OHL	4	0	1	1	21
1984–85	Sault Ste. Marie Greyhounds	OHL	44	20	52	72	172
1984–85	Soo Greyhounds (Memorial Cup)	—	—	—	—	—	—
1985–86	Adirondack Red Wings	AHL	32	12	15	27	152
1985–86	Detroit Red Wings	NHL	44	8	13	21	186
1986–87	Adirondack Red Wings	AHL	7	1	4	5	15
1986–87	Detroit Red Wings	NHL	63	13	11	24	221
1987–88	Detroit Red Wings	NHL	74	29	33	62	398
1988–89	Detroit Red Wings	NHL	25	4	2	6	106
1989–90	Detroit Red Wings	NHL	4	3	0	3	21
1990–91	Detroit Red Wings	NHL	55	16	23	39	315
1991–92	Detroit Red Wings	NHL	63	20	24	44	276
1992–93	Detroit Red Wings	NHL	80	14	29	43	292
1993–94	Detroit Red Wings	NHL	66	7	10	17	275
1994–95	Chicago Blackhawks	NHL	DID NOT PLAY—SUSPENDED				
1995–96	Chicago Blackhawks	NHL	78	19	21	40	237
1996–97	Chicago Blackhawks	NHL	82	9	14	23	326
1997–98	Chicago Blackhawks	NHL	14	2	1	3	48
1998–99	Chicago Blackhawks	NHL	78	7	14	21	206
1999–00	Chicago Blackhawks	NHL	69	4	11	15	114
2000–01	Chicago Blackhawks	NHL	79	7	12	19	103
2001–02	Chicago Blackhawks	NHL	61	1	3	4	176
NHL TOTALS			**935**	**163**	**221**	**384**	**3300**

PLAYOFFS

Season	Team	League	GP	G	A	Pts	PIM
1981–82	Windsor Club 240	OMHA	—	—	—	—	—
1982–83	Brantford Alexanders	OHL	8	2	2	4	23
1983–84	Brantford Alexanders	OHL	6	0	3	3	16
1984–85	Hamilton Steelhawks	OHL	—	—	—	—	—
1984–85	Sault Ste. Marie Greyhounds	OHL	15	6	11	17	60
1984–85	Soo Greyhounds (Memorial Cup)		4	1	2	3	34
1985–86	Adirondack Red Wings	AHL	10	2	3	5	68
1985–86	Detroit Red Wings	NHL	—	—	—	—	—
1986–87	Adirondack Red Wings	AHL	—	—	—	—	—
1986–87	Detroit Red Wings	NHL	16	3	4	7	63
1987–88	Detroit Red Wings	NHL	16	8	13	21	51
1988–89	Detroit Red Wings	NHL	—	—	—	—	—
1989–90	Detroit Red Wings	NHL	—	—	—	—	—
1990–91	Detroit Red Wings	NHL	6	1	2	3	50
1991–92	Detroit Red Wings	NHL	11	1	6	7	28
1992–93	Detroit Red Wings	NHL	7	0	3	3	10
1993–94	Detroit Red Wings	NHL	7	1	1	2	8
1994–95	Chicago Blackhawks	NHL	DID NOT PLAY—SUSPENDED				
1995–96	Chicago Blackhawks	NHL	10	0	2	2	23
1996–97	Chicago Blackhawks	NHL	6	2	1	3	41
1997–98	Chicago Blackhawks	NHL	—	—	—	—	—
1998–99	Chicago Blackhawks	NHL	—	—	—	—	—
1999–00	Chicago Blackhawks	NHL	—	—	—	—	—
2000–01	Chicago Blackhawks	NHL	—	—	—	—	—
2001–02	Chicago Blackhawks	NHL	2	0	0	0	0
	NHL TOTALS		**81**	**16**	**32**	**48**	**274**

CAREER MILESTONES

* Selected by Brantford Alexanders in the seventh round (#95 overall) of 1982 OHL Midget Draft.
* Selected by Detroit Red Wings in the third round (#46 overall) in 1983 NHL Entry Draft.
* Named to Emms Division team in Ontario Hockey League All-Star Game, 1983–84. Did not play.
* Traded by Hamilton Steelhawks with Shawn Tyers to Sault Ste. Marie Greyhounds for Alex Haidy, John English and sixth-round selection in 1985 Midget Draft, November 1984.
* Won Ontario Hockey League championship with Sault Ste. Marie Greyhounds, 1984–85.
* Made NHL debut November 6, 1985, vs. St. Louis.
* First NHL point at 8:57 of 2nd period, December 15, 1985, at Chicago (Detroit 4 at Chicago 6).
* First NHL goal at 12:57 of 3rd period, December 21, 1985, vs. Chicago (Chicago 6 at Detroit 3).
* Played for Campbell Conference team in NHL All-Star Game, 1988. Wore #24, assisted on goal by Wayne Gretzky at 18:46 of 1st period.
* Led NHL in GP (82), 1996–97.
* Led NHL in PIM (398), 1987–88.
* Ranked in top ten in PIM in 1990–91 (315—3rd), 1992–93 (292—8th), 1993–94 (275—7th), 1996–97 (326—2nd) and 1998–99 (206—9th).
* Ranked in top ten in shooting percentage in 1987–88 (23.0—9th) and 1995–96 (19.6—10th).
* Ranked in top ten in playoff scoring in 1987–88 (21 Pts—7th).
* Ranked in top ten in playoff power-play goals in 1987–88 (5—2nd).
* Ranked fifth all-time in career PIM (3,300).

* Set Detroit club record for points in a playoff season (8–13–21 in 16 GP), 1987–88. Record stood until 1995.
* Signed as a free agent by Chicago, July 23, 1994.
* Missed majority of 1997–98 season after injuring rotator cuff in game vs. Detroit, November 16, 1997.
* Chicago's nominee for Bill Masterton Memorial Trophy, 2000–01.
* Retired November 16, 2002.

FIGHTS

1985–86

DATE	OPPOSING TEAM	OPPOSING PLAYER
November 11, 1985	Vancouver Canucks	Criag Coxe
November 16, 1985	Minnesota North Stars	Bob Rouse
December 14, 1985	Philadelphia Flyers	Dave Richter
December 14, 1985	Philadelphia Flyers	Rick Tocchet
December 17, 1985	Minnesota North Stars	Tim Coulis
December 23, 1985	New York Rangers	Larry Melnyk
December 31, 1985	New York Islanders	Clark Gillies
January 5, 1986	Toronto Maple Leafs	Gary Nylund
January 10, 1986	Chicago Blackhawks	Al Secord
January 13, 1986	Toronto Maple Leafs	Bob McGill
January 25, 1986	Boston Bruins	Brian Curran
January 25, 1986	Boston Bruins	Gord Kluzak
January 28, 1986	Washington Capitals	Rod Langway
January 31, 1986	St. Louis Blues	Lee Norwood
February 8, 1986	Montreal Canadiens	Chris Nilan
February 18, 1986	St. Louis Blues	Kent Carlson
March 6, 1986	New Jersey Devils	Ken Daneyko

1986–87

DATE	OPPOSING TEAM	OPPOSING PLAYER
October 11, 1986	Chicago Blackhawks	Curt Fraser
October 30, 1986	Minnesota North Stars	Willi Plett
November 21, 1986	Washington Capitals	Scott Stevens
November 26, 1986	Toronto Maple Leafs	Bob McGill
December 27, 1986	Toronto Maple Leafs	Wendel Clark
December 31, 1986	Calgary Flames	Tim Hunter

January 11, 1987	Chicago Blackhawks	Gary Nylund
January 15, 1987	Toronto Maple Leafs	Kevin Maguire
January 17, 1987	Quebec Nordiques	Richard Zemlak
January 24, 1987	St. Louis Blues	Todd Ewen
January 24, 1987	St. Louis Blues	Todd Ewen
March 5, 1987	Minnesota North Stars	Willi Plett
March 7, 1987	St. Louis Blues	Todd Ewen
March 10, 1987	Vancouver Canucks	Michel Petit
March 19, 1987	New York Islanders	Brian Curran
March 28, 1987	Philadelphia Flyers	Craig Berube
April 1, 1987	Philadelphia Flyers	Craig Berube
April 1, 1987	Philadelphia Flyers	Craig Berube
April 12, 1987	Chicago Blackhawks	Curt Fraser
Playoffs:		
April 23, 1997	Toronto Maple Leafs	Al Iafrate
May 1, 1987	Toronto Maple Leafs	Chris Kotsopoulos
May 5, 1987	Edmonton Oilers	Kevin McClelland

1987–88

DATE	OPPOSING TEAM	OPPOSING PLAYER
October 16, 1987	Toronto Maple Leafs	Chris Kotsopoulos
October 17, 1987	Toronto Maple Leafs	Wendel Clark
October 17, 1987	Toronto Maple Leafs	Dave Semenko
November 19, 1987	Vancouver Canucks	Craig Coxe
November 19, 1987	Vancouver Canucks	Daryl Stanley
November 28, 1987	Boston Bruins	Jay Miller
December 4, 1987	Chicago Blackhawks	Curt Fraser
December 14, 1987	New York Rangers	Mark Tinordi
December 23, 1987	Buffalo Sabres	Kevin Maguire
January 3, 1988	Winnipeg Jets	Paul MacLean
January 13, 1988	New York Rangers	Michel Petit

DATE	OPPOSING TEAM	OPPOSING PLAYER
January 23, 1988	Calgary Flames	Joel Otto
January 24, 1988	Hartford Whalers	Neil Sheehy
January 29, 1988	Toronto Maple Leafs	Dave Semenko
February 5, 1988	Calgary Flames	Jim Peplinski
February 13, 1988	St. Louis Blues	Tim Bothwell
February 15, 1988	Los Angeles Kings	Ken Baumgartner
February 23, 1988	Philadelphia Flyers	Scott Mellanby
February 23, 1988	Philadelphia Flyers	Dave Brown
March 6, 1988	Chicago Blackhawks	Glen Cochrane
March 19, 1988	Los Angeles Kings	Denis Larocque
March 19, 1988	Los Angeles Kings	Dean Kennedy
March 22, 1988	Edmonton Oilers	Marty McSorley
March 29, 1988	Washington Capitals	Yvon Corriveau
Playoffs:		
April 9, 1988	Toronto Maple Leafs	Brian Curran
April 9, 1988	Toronto Maple Leafs	Brian Curran

1988–89

DATE	OPPOSING TEAM	OPPOSING PLAYER
December 9, 1988	Toronto Maple Leafs	Ed Olczyk
December 9, 1988	Toronto Maple Leafs	John Kordic
December 10, 1988	Toronto Maple Leafs	Brian Curran
December 22, 1988	St. Louis Blues	Greg Paslawski
December 23, 1988	Chicago Blackhawks	Dave Manson
December 23, 1988	Chicago Blackhawks	Bob McGill
January 15, 1989	Philadelphia Flyers	Jeff Chychrun
January 15, 1989	Philadelphia Flyers	Jeff Chychrun

1989–90

DATE	OPPOSING TEAM	OPPOSING PLAYER
March 24, 1990	Chicago Blackhawks	Bob McGill
March 25, 1990	Chicago Blackhawks	Dave Manson
March 25, 1990	Chicago Blackhawks	Wayne Van Dorp

1990–91

DATE	OPPOSING TEAM	OPPOSING PLAYER
October 4, 1990	New Jersey Devils	Allan Stewart
October 4, 1990	New Jersey Devils	Troy Crowder
October 23, 1990	Vancouver Canucks	Ronnie Stern
October 27, 1990	Minnesota North Stars	Shane Churla
November 27, 1990	Los Angeles Kings	Jay Miller
November 27, 1990	Los Angeles Kings	John McIntyre
November 29, 1990	Chicago Blackhawks	Bob McGill
December 31, 1990	Chicago Blackhawks	Stu Grimson
January 9, 1991	Edmonton Oilers	Jeff Beukeboom
January 9, 1991	Edmonton Oilers	Dave Brown
January 28, 1991	New Jersey Devils	Troy Crowder
January 28, 1991	New Jersey Devils	Troy Crowder
February 4, 1991	Los Angeles Kings	Bob Halkidis
February 13, 1991	Hartford Whalers	Grant Jennings
February 16, 1991	Minnesota North Stars	Neil Wilkinson
March 10, 1991	St. Louis Blues	Darin Kimble
March 22, 1991	Toronto Maple Leafs	Kevin Maguire

1991–92

DATE	OPPOSING TEAM	OPPOSING PLAYER
October 3, 1991	Chicago Blackhawks	Stu Grimson
October 3, 1991	Chicago Blackhawks	Stu Grimson
October 10, 1991	Montreal Canadiens	Mario Roberge
October 23, 1991	Winnipeg Jets	Shawn Cronin
October 23, 1991	Winnipeg Jets	Shawn Cronin
October 25, 1991	Toronto Maple Leafs	Craig Berube
November 2, 1991	Boston Bruins	Stephane Quintal
November 5, 1991	Minnesota North Stars	Shane Churla
November 14, 1991	San Jose Sharks	Link Gaetz
November 19, 1991	Chicago Blackhawks	Stu Grimson
December 21, 1991	Los Angeles Kings	Jeff Chychrun
December 21, 1991	Los Angeles Kings	Marty McSorley
January 3, 1992	Toronto Maple Leafs	Bob Halkidis
January 25, 1992	New Jersey Devils	Scott Stevens
February 9, 1992	New York Rangers	Tie Domi
March 20, 1992	New York Rangers	Jay Wells
March 22, 1992	Philadelphia Flyers	Terry Carkner
March 24, 1992	Pittsburgh Penguins	Troy Loney
April 12, 1992	Chicago Blackhawks	Stu Grimson

1992–93

DATE	OPPOSING TEAM	OPPOSING PLAYER
October 8, 1992	Los Angeles Kings	Mary McSorley
November 13, 1992	Pittsburgh Penguins	Jay Caufield
November 25, 1992	St. Louis Blues	Kelly Chase
November 25, 1992	St. Louis Blues	Stephane Quintal
December 2, 1992	New York Rangers	Tie Domi

December 9, 1992	Toronto Maple Leafs	Wendel Clark
December 9, 1992	Toronto Maple Leafs	Wendel Clark
January 2, 1993	Quebec Nordiques	Tim Hunter
January 13, 1993	Tampa Bay Lightning	Mike Hartman
January 23, 1993	St. Louis Blues	Dave Lowry
January 26, 1993	Calgary Flames	Craig Berube
January 26, 1993	Calgary Flames	Craig Berube
February 3, 1993	Chicago Blackhawks	Cam Russell
February 14, 1993	Chicago Blackhawks	Stu Grimson
March 18, 1993	Minnesota North Stars	Shane Churla

1993–94

DATE	OPPOSING TEAM	OPPOSING PLAYER
October 8, 1993	Anaheim Ducks	Stu Grimson
October 13, 1993	St. Louis Blues	Basil McRae
October 27, 1993	Los Angeles Kings	Warren Rychel
October 30, 1993	Quebec Nordiques	Tony Twist
December 6, 1993	Winnipeg Jets	Tie Domi
December 11, 1993	San Jose Sharks	Jeff Odgers
December 14, 1993	Anaheim Ducks	Todd Ewen
December 17, 1993	New York Rangers	Joey Kocur
December 18, 1993	Montreal Canadiens	Lyle Odelein
December 18, 1993	Montreal Canadiens	Donald Brashear
January 6, 1994	San Jose Sharks	Jeff Odgers
January 6, 1994	San Jose Sharks	Jeff Odgers
January 25, 1994	Chicago Blackhawks	Cam Russell
January 25, 1994	Chicago Blackhawks	Greg Smyth
January 27, 1994	Chicago Blackhawks	Greg Smyth
February 2, 1994	Tampa Bay Lightning	Rudy Poeschek
February 4, 1994	Pittsburgh Penguins	Marty McSorley

DATE	OPPOSING TEAM	OPPOSING PLAYER
February 11, 1994	Philadelphia Flyers	Jim Cummins
February 15, 1994	Toronto Maple Leafs	Ken Baumgartner
April 2, 1994	Calgary Flames	Sandy McCarthy

1995–96

DATE	OPPOSING TEAM	OPPOSING PLAYER
October 12, 1995	Pittsburgh Penguins	Chris Tamer
October 21, 1995	St. Louis Blues	Denis Chasse
October 26, 1995	Toronto Maple Leafs	Rob Zettler
November 9, 1995	Vancouver Canucks	Alek Stojanov
November 14, 1995	Winnipeg Jets	Kris King
November 16, 1995	New York Rangers	Darren Langdon
November 28, 1995	Edmonton Oilers	Bryan Marchment
December 2, 1995	Winnipeg Jets	Jim McKenzie
December 15, 1995	Montreal Canadiens	Stephane Quintal
December 23, 1995	Dallas Stars	Bill Huard
January 17, 1996	Washington Capitals	Kevin Kaminski
January 24, 1996	Toronto Maple Leafs	Tie Domi
February 4, 1996	Anaheim Ducks	Todd Ewen
February 8, 1996	St. Louis Blues	Tony Twist
March 17, 1996	New York Islanders	Bob Halkidis
March 22, 1996	New Jersey Devils	Reid Simpson
April 3, 1996	Toronto Maple Leafs	Tie Domi
April 5, 1996	Dallas Stars	Bill Huard
April 7, 1996	Detroit Red Wings	Stu Grimson
April 11, 1996	Toronto Maple Leafs	Tie Domi
Playoffs:		
May 8, 1996	Colorado Avalanche	Chris Simon

1996–97

DATE	OPPOSING TEAM	OPPOSING PLAYER
October 13, 1996	Dallas Stars	Patrick Cote
October 13, 1996	Dallas Stars	Todd Harvey
October 20, 1996	Los Angeles Kings	Matt Johnson
October 24, 1996	St. Louis Blues	Tony Twist
November 7, 1996	New Jersey Devils	Lyle Odelein
November 19, 1996	Edmonton Oilers	Kelly Buchberger
December 12, 1996	Detroit Red Wings	Brendan Shanahan
December 12, 1996	Detroit Red Wings	Darren McCarty
December 13, 1996	St. Louis Blues	Tony Twist
December 23, 1996	Boston Bruins	Jeff Odgers
January 5, 1997	Detroit Red Wings	Joey Kocur
January 22, 1997	Vancouver Canucks	Troy Crowder
January 24, 1997	Toronto Maple Leafs	Tie Domi
January 27, 1997	New York Rangers	Jeff Beukeboom
January 27, 1997	New York Rangers	Darren Langdon
February 13, 1997	San Jose Sharks	Todd Ewen
March 10, 1997	Vancouver Canucks	Donald Brashear
Playoffs:		
April 16, 1997	Colorado Avalanche	Adam Foote

1997–98

DATE	OPPOSING TEAM	OPPOSING PLAYER
November 10, 1997	Calgary Flames	Sandy McCarthy
November 10, 1997	Calgary Flames	Mike Peluso
November 11, 1997	Toronto Maple Leafs	Kris King
April 15, 1998	Toronto Maple Leafs	Tie Domi

1998–99

DATE	OPPOSING TEAM	OPPOSING PLAYER
October 10, 1998	New Jersey Devils	Sasha Lakovic
October 13, 1998	Dallas Stars	Brent Severyn
October 19, 1998	Montreal Canadiens	Dave Morissette
October 22, 1998	San Jose Sharks	Owen Nolan
October 24, 1998	Nashville Predators	Patrick Cote
November 4, 1998	Florida Panthers	Peter Worrell
November 4, 1998	Florida Panthers	Paul Laus
November 12, 1998	Toronto Maple Leafs	Tie Domi
November 17, 1998	Nashville Predators	Patrick Cote
November 21, 1998	Los Angeles Kings	Mark Visheau
December 3, 1998	Anaheim Ducks	Stu Grimson
January 12, 1999	Colorado Avalanche	Scott Parker
February 17, 1999	Vancouver Canucks	Donald Brashear
March 7, 1999	Vancouver Canucks	Donald Brashear
March 20, 1999	Colorado Avalanche	Jeff Odgers
March 21, 1999	Colorado Avalanche	Chris Dingman
March 21, 1999	Colorado Avalanche	Jeff Odgers
March 25, 1999	Boston Bruins	Ken Belanger
April 5, 1999	Vancouver Canucks	Donald Brashear
April 15, 1999	Nashville Predators	Patrick Cote

1999–2000

DATE	OPPOSING TEAM	OPPOSING PLAYER
October 21, 1999	Anaheim Ducks	Stu Grimson
November 12, 1999	New York Islanders	Eric Cairns
November 14, 1999	Edmonton Oilers	Georges Laraque
December 23, 1999	Dallas Stars	Grant Marshall
January 6, 2000	Calgary Flames	Wade Belak

January 9, 2000	Colorado Avalanche	Chris Dingman
January 12, 2000	Vancouver Canucks	Donald Brashear
February 3, 2000	Calgary Flames	Wade Belak
February 18, 2000	Washington Capitals	Jim McKenzie
April 7, 2000	St. Louis Blues	Kelly Chase

2000–01

DATE	OPPOSING TEAM	OPPOSING PLAYER
October 21, 2000	St. Louis Blues	Reed Low
November 14, 2000	Vancouver Canucks	Donald Brashear
November 17, 2000	Edmonton Oilers	Patrick Cote
December 3, 2000	Columbus Blue Jackets	Lyle Odelein
December 3, 2000	Columbus Blue Jackets	Jamie Pushor
December 7, 2000	Minnesota Wild	Steve McKenna
December 10, 2000	St. Louis Blues	Reid Simpson
February 18, 2001	Los Angeles Kings	Stu Grimson
March 10, 2001	Los Angeles Kings	Stu Grimson

2001–02

DATE	OPPOSING TEAM	OPPOSING PLAYER
October 4, 2001	Vancouver Canucks	Donald Brashear
October 6, 2001	Calgary Flames	Bob Boughner
October 11, 2001	Phoenix Coyotes	Todd Simpson
October 28, 2001	Boston Bruins	Andrei Nazarov
October 30, 2001	Los Angeles Kings	Ken Belanger
November 2, 2001	Anaheim Ducks	Kevin Sawyer
November 21, 2001	Nashville Predators	Stu Grimson
December 14, 2001	Atlanta Thrashers	Darcy Hordichuk

Fights

DATE	OPPOSING TEAM	OPPOSING PLAYER
December 21, 2001	Edmonton Oilers	Georges Laraque
January 4, 2002	Tampa Bay Lightning	Gordie Dwyer
January 10, 2002	Columbus Blue Jackets	Jody Shelley
January 10, 2002	Columbus Blue Jackets	Jody Shelley
January 10, 2002	Columbus Blue Jackets	Jody Shelley
January 12, 2002	Columbus Blue Jackets	Jody Shelley
January 16, 2002	Florida Panthers	Paul Laus
February 13, 2002	Florida Panthers	Peter Worrell
February 13, 2002	Florida Panthers	Brad Norton

INDEX